Remembering Us

WHEN MEMORIES FADE, LOVE REMAINS

HONEYMOON ALJABRI

HONEYMOON PUBLISHING HOUSE

Copyright ©2024 Honeymoon Publishing house Printed in the United States of America
.

Honeymoon
Publishing House

Disclaimer:

All characters, events, and situations depicted in this book, "Remembering Us: When Memories Fade, Love Remains," are purely fictional. Any resemblance to actual persons, living or dead, or to real-life events or locales, is entirely coincidental.

The author asserts that the content of this book is a work of fiction and should be interpreted as such. While inspired by elements of real-life experiences and emotions, the narrative and characters are products of the author's imagination.

Readers are reminded that the portrayal of events and individuals within these pages is entirely fictional and does not reflect the lives, actions, or beliefs of any specific person, living or deceased.

No part of this publication may be reproduced, stored in a retrieval system, or transmitted in any form or by any means, electronic, mechanical, photocopying, recording, or otherwise, without the prior permission of the author and/or publisher except as permitted by U.S. copyright law.

All rights reserved.

Acknowledgement

As I reflect on the journey of crafting "Remembering Us: When Memories Fade, Love Remains," I am profoundly grateful for the inspiration and support that have guided me along the way.

Two years ago, I made the transformative move to Redmond, Washington, where I found myself captivated by the city's charm and the serene beauty of Lake Sammamish. It was amidst these picturesque surroundings that the seeds of this novel were planted, nurtured by the warmth of love and the inspiration drawn from the embrace of the lake.

To my dear friends, your unwavering presence during moments of uncertainty and doubt provided the anchor I needed to persevere. I extend my heartfelt gratitude to Joi, my editor, whose dedication and meticulous attention to detail have shaped this novel into a heartfelt narrative, resonating with depth and meaning.

Throughout the writing process, I embarked on a journey of understanding and empathy, confronting the profound pain inflicted by the relentless adversary, Alzheimer's disease. To all those bravely battling this soul-thieving affliction, you are the true superheroes, and your resilience inspires me endlessly.

To my beloved family, your boundless love and unwavering support have been my rock. My dearest Mother, I love you so much Da Zuu, you are my rock. To my amazing auntie, although you have gone too soon, your love will always be my angel , RIP Baby Jeuri, I will always love you. To my sisters, who bring balance to my life, and my brothers, who have played an instrumental role in shaping the person I am today, I am eternally grateful. My nephews and nieces, you are the jewels of my heart, filling my life with pride and joy.

To my cherished cousins, who have been my steadfast companions through life's twists and turns, your friendship is a priceless gift that I treasure deeply. And to my brothers from other mothers, AbdulKarim Faraji and Stephen Owoko, your unwavering friendship and support have been a source of strength and solace.

Finally, to all my friends who have chosen to walk alongside me on this journey, your belief in me fuels my passion and commitment. Your support has been a beacon of light, illuminating the path to realizing this dream.

With deepest gratitude,

Honeymoon Naima Mohammed Aljabri

Angels Living – Room #026

In the heart of Redmond's vibrant midtown, nestled among the bustling streets and serene surroundings, stands Angel Living, an assisted living facility that exudes warmth and comfort. The building, with its welcoming exterior adorned with tasteful landscaping, boasts an inviting entrance, providing a sense of tranquility to all who enter.

Angel Living, situated strategically in Redmond midtown, is designed to be both elegant and practical. The architecture combines modern aesthetics with homely touches, creating an environment that is not only functional but also aesthetically pleasing. The exterior features large windows that allow natural light to filter in, casting a soft glow across the communal spaces.

Room 026, the abode of Mr. and Mrs. Yang, is a cozy sanctuary within Angel Living. The room is thoughtfully furnished with tasteful decor that strikes a balance between comfort and functionality. Soft hues and gentle lighting create a soothing atmosphere, providing a backdrop for the dance of memories and emotions that unfold within.

As Mr. and Mrs. Yang navigate the labyrinth of dementia, their room becomes a haven a place where the threads of their shared history intertwine. Family photographs adorn the walls, capturing moments frozen in time, reminders of a lifetime of love. A plush sitting area near the window invites reflection, offering a glimpse into the outside world and allowing residents to reconnect with the present.

The facility's central location in Redmond midtown ensures easy access to local amenities, fostering a sense of community and engagement. Angel Living, with its well-appointed common areas and compassionate staff, strives to provide not only a place of residence but a supportive environment where residents like Mr. and Mrs. Yang can find solace in their shared journey.

Within the walls of Room 026 at Angel Living, the love between Mr. and Mrs. Yang becomes a poignant narrative a dance of memories and emotions that transcends the challenges of dementia, making their journey through life's labyrinth a testament to the enduring power of love and connection.

Each morning, a gentle East African caregiver named Amina knock on their door, her smile a testament to her genuine affection for the couple. As the door swung open, Mrs. Yang would often stand by the bedside, her gaze fixed on her husband Bill, who sometimes resisted the call to start the day. With a soft touch and her irresistible charm, the caregiver coaxed him into action, honoring the dignity of a man whose mind was slowly slipping away.

The routine was familiar, carefully scripted by years of devotion. The caregiver had studied the notes Mrs. Yang had provided, instructions on how to dress Bill, an expression of love encapsulated in practical details written by his wife. Amina would grasp his hand, a gesture that conveyed more warmth than words ever could and lead him through the process of getting ready for the day.

Mrs. Yang would always help to get Bill ready, gently straightened her husband's tie or brushed a speck of lint from his coat, the room transformed into a sanctuary of love and tenderness. Amina observed them, her heart swelling at the sight of a connection that transcended time and circumstance. A photograph hung on the wall, frozen in a moment of youthful radiance.

A tall man with striking blue eyes and ginger hair stood beside a radiant lady in a flowing white wedding dress, a long veil cascading behind her. Amina's curiosity prompted her to ask about the photograph's origin, inviting a flood of cherished memories.

With a wistful smile, Mr. Bill allowed his thoughts to wander back to a day etched vividly in his mind, though so much else had faded. October 25, 1960, a day of promise and devotion. As he spoke, his words were a bridge connecting the present with a past filled with the scent of flowers and the taste of red velvet cake. The memory was a beacon in the fog of his fading mind, and his eyes found his wife's gaze, their shared history unbroken.

Bill's mind gracefully drifted into the corridors of memory, unlocking the treasure trove of the day he exchanged vows with Dorothy. The vivid recollection transported him to a time when their love was fresh, vibrant, and full of promise.

The aroma of blooming tulips lingered in the air, weaving a fragrant tapestry that adorned the venue. Bill could practically smell the sweet fragrance, a sensory reminder of the vibrant tulips that adorned their wedding day. The vivid whites and pinks of the flowers seemed to dance in harmony with the emotions that enveloped the couple.

The sun painted the sky with hues of warmth and hope as they stood beneath its benevolent gaze. Bill's eyes met Dorothy's, and in that moment, time stood still. He could feel the soft touch of her hand in his, the gentle pressure of their entwined fingers symbolizing the unity of their souls.

As they exchanged vows, Bill was captivated by the sincerity in Dorothy's voice. The words "I do, take you Bill to be my beloved husband till death do us part" echoed in his ears, etching themselves into the fabric of his being. Each syllable carried the weight of a promise, a promise to navigate life's journey together, come what may.

Their first tender kiss as a married couple was a sweet revelation, a moment of pure connection that resonated in Bill's memory. The joy on Dorothy's face, the subtle taste of her lips, and the applause of their loved ones formed an indelible mosaic of that precious instant.

As Bill opened his eyes, he was back in the present, looking at Dorothy with a genuine and affectionate smile. The memory of their wedding day served as an anchor, a reminder of the enduring love that had weathered the passage of time. Despite the challenges of dementia casting shadows on his recollections, the essence of that beautiful day remained intact a love story eternally imprinted on Bill's heart.

As the morning routine continued, the mundane task of brushing teeth became an act of love. Bill's quizzical look as he held the toothbrush mirrored his growing confusion, yet his smile was a constant, a beacon of recognition even in the darkest corners of his mind. Dorothy, using her walker for support, leaned in to kiss him gently, guiding the toothbrush to his mouth with infinite tenderness. "Darling, this is your toothbrush," she whispered, a lifeline cast to a man adrift in the sea of his own thoughts.

Before parting ways, Bill's eyes twinkled with mischief as he made an invitation that would seal Amina's role in their unfolding love story. "After breakfast, won't you come to our room? I have a story to share, the tale of how we met and fell in love." Amina's smile held the promise of a heart open to stories, a heart ready to be touched by a narrative that had spanned decades and woven lives together.

The dining hall of the facility was a place of both warmth and nostalgia. Sunlight streamed through large windows, casting a gentle, golden glow over the room. The walls were adorned with framed photographs, capturing moments of joy from the residents' lives before dementia had taken hold. The tables were meticulously set with fresh flowers, each one carefully chosen to brighten the room and evoke memories of gardens and meadows.

Residents slowly made their way to their designated seats, guided by the familiar routines of the facility. Each person who inhabited a chair held a unique story, a testament to the lives lived within these walls. The room buzzed with a mixture of smiles and laughter, but there was an undercurrent of sadness that ran through the conversations.

Angel Living, a sanctuary for those grappling with dementia, is infused with love and compassion. The facility is thoughtfully designed to offer a sense of continuity and comfort. Each resident has a cherished chair and table in familiar communal spaces, creating a routine that serves as a lifeline against the erasure of memories.

In this haven of love, daily life unfolds with intentional consistency. Staff members, understanding the silent battles fought by residents, guide them through activities that evoke positive memories. The routine becomes a means of preserving identity and fostering emotional connections.

For those facing the relentless thief of dementia, Angel Living is more than a residence; it's a place where love is woven into every detail. The familiar surroundings, daily rhythm, and caring gestures create a haven where residents can find stability and comfort, holding onto the fragments of their past with the support of compassionate caregivers.

Amina with a smile on her face moved gracefully among the residents, her heart heavy with empathy for the challenges they faced. She checked to ensure that everyone had made it to breakfast, offering a warm smile and a reassuring pat on the shoulder to those who needed it.

As she approached Mr. Yang, who had already forgotten her role in waking him up that morning, he greeted her with a genuine smile. His eyes sparkled with a sense of recognition, even if it was fleeting. Dorothy, ever the anchor in her husband's shifting reality, gently reminded him of Amina's presence. Her touch was filled with affection, a silent promise that she would always be there to guide him through the fog of his fading memory.

Amidst the well-lived lives of these residents, Amina couldn't help but reflect on how challenging life had become for them. It raised a poignant question that lingered like a whisper in the air: How daring must one be to steal away the most generous gift of all time - our brains, the precious memory storage that sets us apart from other mammals? To forget the small joys, like savoring a cup of coffee or wielding a spoon, Alzheimer's disease felt like a relentless monster.

Standing there, watching, ready to lend a helping hand if needed, Amina's eyes welled up with tears as she gazed at Miss Janet. She observed the once-beloved breakfast before her, now a puzzle. Amina stepped closer, her heart filled with empathy, and gently asked, "Miss Janet, may I help you with your meal? I think you might enjoy trying this."

Dorothy's eyes locked onto Amina's, and a shared smile passed between them. As Amina continued to assist Miss Janet with her meal, her tender gaze would occasionally shift to Dorothy, who cared for her husband with the same unwavering love, wiping his chin or offering a sip of his drink.

Amina couldn't help but feel a deep respect for the love that bound Mr. and Mrs. Yang together. It was a love that transcended the limitations of memory and time. With a radiant smile, she promised to return to their room later to continue the story of how they had met, the story that had become the cornerstone of their shared history.

Before leaving, Amina kindly inquired about their breakfast preferences, offering a small touch of normalcy in their world. She understood that in this place, where the battle against dementia was fought daily, these small gestures of care and kindness held immeasurable value.

As Amina finished assisting Miss Janet and the dining hall grew quieter, Dorothy couldn't help but reflect on the journey that had brought her to this moment. Her eyes followed Amina's graceful movements as she moved on to help another resident. A warmth spread through Dorothy's chest, a feeling that had become all too familiar since she and her husband had moved here.

She watched her beloved husband, once so vibrant and full of life, now sitting beside her, his gaze distant, lost in the labyrinth of his memories. The ravages of Alzheimer's had stolen much from him, but not the love that had bound them together for a lifetime. She reached out and took his trembling hand, giving it a gentle squeeze. His eyes met hers, and for a brief moment, a flicker of recognition sparked in them. In that moment, Dorothy felt their connection, their shared history, and their enduring love, stronger than ever.

Tears welled up in Dorothy's eyes, and she whispered softly to her husband, "We'll get through this together, my love, just like we always have." He might not remember every detail of their life together, but Dorothy was determined to make each day they had left as beautiful and meaningful as possible.

With Amina's compassionate presence and the support of the community around her, Dorothy knew that they were not alone on this journey. The chapter of their life in this place was still being written, and she felt a renewed sense of hope and determination as she looked forward to the pages yet to come, where love would always be the guiding force.

Redmond Washington - 1940's

B ill's story began in 1940 in the quaint town of Redmond, Washington. This picturesque town, nestled amidst rolling hills and lush greenery, was a place where horses still played a significant role in daily life. It was in this tranquil setting that Bill entered the world, born in the comfort of his family's home with the guidance of a midwife.

From his very first cry, Bill's presence filled the house with joy. With a full head of hair and a robust cry that startled birds near the window, he was a cherished addition to his family. As the firstborn child, he seemed destined for a life of leadership and protection.

Even at a tender age, Bill exhibited a deep fascination with the world above. He would often venture into the backyard, gazing at the sky in wonder as airplanes soared overhead. His affinity for flight extended beyond man-made machines; he was an avid bird watcher, finding solace and happiness in the graceful creatures that shared the skies with him.

By the time he reached the age of ten, Bill knew exactly what he wanted to be when he grew up: a pilot. The very sound of an airplane's engine could coax a smile from his lips. It was as if the call of the skies was imprinted on his very soul.

Bill's dream of attending West Point and becoming a pilot was not just a goal, it was a relentless pursuit that demanded unwavering determination. The journey to achieve this dream required a disciplined and focused approach.

High school became a pivotal phase for Bill. Every assignment, every exam, and every extracurricular activity took on new significance as he realized the weight of his ambitions. The broad smile on his face in the classroom wasn't just a reflection of academic success; it was a testament to the steps he was taking toward his future in the skies.

Preparation for the exams to gain acceptance to West Point was intense. Bill immersed himself in rigorous study sessions, tackling complex subjects and mastering the skills required for the demanding entrance exams. His commitment went beyond academics; physical fitness became a daily regimen as he trained to meet the rigorous standards expected of West Point cadets.

Letters of recommendation were carefully sought from mentors who could attest to Bill's character, leadership potential, and determination. Each recommendation letter became a piece of the puzzle, highlighting his strengths and underscoring why he was the right fit for West Point.

As he worked tirelessly, Bill's dreams were not just about individual achievement but about serving his country. The path to becoming a pilot involved not only excelling academically but also demonstrating leadership, discipline, and a profound sense of duty.

Enrolling in college marked a significant milestone, bringing him one step closer to the realization of his dreams. The journey to West Point and the skies beyond was a testament to Bill's tenacity, a journey where every small victory in the classroom and on the training, ground propelled him toward the day when he would soar among the clouds.

Bill's passion was well-known among his peers and teachers. He spoke about planes and birds with a fervor that was infectious. While his friends started to take an interest in the opposite sex, Bill was more captivated by the magic of wings and flight. He would often be found sketching pictures of airplanes and birds, channeling his admiration into art.

Despite his teenage years, Bill didn't participate in the usual rites of passage. He didn't attend parties or pursue romantic interests. Instead, he was on a quest to discover the secrets of flight. While his peers explored teenage life, Bill chose to stay close to home, aiding his mother and caring for his two younger sisters.

The portrait of Bill's family is one of warmth, love, and a strong sense of unity. Bill, the firstborn, stands as the pride of his father an only son and the designated man of the house. His role transcends that of a sibling; it's a position of responsibility and leadership within the family dynamic.

The family is made up of two beautiful younger sisters: Jane, the middle child, and Sarah, the youngest and, as Bill's best friend, a cherished companion. Together, the siblings create a harmonious trio, each contributing to the family's collective tapestry in their unique way.

Bill's father, a dedicated fisherman whose work takes him to the vast waters of Alaska for extended periods, entrusts Bill with a profound sense of responsibility. In his father's absence, Bill seamlessly steps into the role of the man of the house. His dedication to protecting and providing for his sisters and mother is not just a duty; it's a reflection of his unwavering commitment to the well-being of the women who hold a special place in his heart.

The family, despite the physical distance imposed by the demands of Bill's father's work, remains emotionally connected. Bill's efforts to fill his father's shoes go beyond mere obligation, they are rooted in love, respect, and a deep understanding of the sacrifices his father makes for their collective future.

In the heart of this family, there exists a bond that transcends roles and responsibilities. The love between siblings is evident in the laughter they share, the support they offer one another, and the understanding that permeates their interactions. Bill's commitment to being the protector and provider during his father's absence reflects not only his strength of character but also the values instilled in him by a family that thrives on love and mutual support.

By the age of 16, Bill had already learned how to drive, and he willingly took on the role of chauffeur when his sisters needed a ride. It was more than a duty for him; it was a pleasure to witness the happiness in his sisters' eyes as he chauffeured them to their destinations.

Bill's character was a beacon of kindness and humility that endeared him to the people of Redmond. As he continued to grow and pursue his dreams, his genuine and compassionate nature became increasingly evident, leaving an indelible mark on the hearts of those around him.

In the close-knit community of Redmond, Bill dedicated his free time to selflessly serving others. Volunteering at the local community center, he became a familiar and reassuring presence, especially for the elderly residents. His acts of kindness extended beyond the center as he assisted them with groceries and ran errands, embodying the spirit of neighborly care and support.

Redmond, with its charming streets and tight community bonds, became a canvas where Bill painted strokes of goodwill. His interactions with others were characterized by warmth, respect, and a genuine desire to make a positive impact. Bill didn't just reside in Redmond; he actively participated in its heartbeat, contributing to the collective well-being of the community.

The town, where everyone knew one another, embraced Bill for the sincerity of his smiles and the authenticity of his greetings exchanged freely on the sidewalks. His genuine interest in people's lives, coupled with a willingness to lend a helping hand, created an atmosphere of camaraderie that permeated the town.

Beyond the human connections, Bill found inspiration in the natural beauty that surrounded Redmond. The town's landscapes became a constant source of motivation, reflecting the harmony he sought in both his personal and communal life.

In the eyes of the people of Redmond, Bill was more than a resident; he was a pillar of kindness and humility, an embodiment of the community spirit that made Redmond a special place. His genuine care for others and his dedication to fostering connections painted a portrait of a man who, amidst chasing his dreams, never lost sight of the importance of being a good neighbor and a compassionate human being.

Bill, being the kind and generous soul that he was, was known throughout Redmond as a young man with a heart of gold. He didn't just dream of flying; he soared in his commitment to help others. It appears the same wings he longed to embrace had bestowed upon him a sense of responsibility and compassion.

In a town where the rhythm of life was often marked by the steady clopping of horses' hooves, Bill was a rare gem. His neighbors saw him as a reliable and caring friend, always willing to lend a hand without expecting anything in return.

As he continued to excel in his studies and work toward his dream of becoming a pilot, Bill's connection to Redmond only grew stronger. The town, with its serene landscapes and close community bonds, remained his anchor, reminding him of the importance of kindness, humility, and the pursuit of one's dreams.

Redmond had not just witnessed Bill's growth but had played a pivotal role in shaping the man he was becoming. It was a place where dreams were nurtured, where hard work was celebrated, and where the heart of a small town beat strongly. Bill, with his dreams and his dedication to his community, was a testament to the values that Redmond held dear, and he carried those values with him as he prepared to spread his wings and take flight into the wider world.

Bill, in his youth, was not just a Redmond son; he was the embodiment of pride for the entire town. He was the boy every girl dreamed of marrying, a beacon of excellence at Redmond High School. Bill was not only the star captain of the baseball team but also the chairman of the Aviation group, a shining example of leadership. Moreover, he was a perennial scholar, consistently earning a coveted spot on the Dean's list and President's list.

Bill's relationships with his friends, John, and Mike, were marked by a deep sense of camaraderie and mutual support. In both academics and sports, Bill wasn't just a friend; he was a driving force that propelled his friends toward success. He believed in the collective strength of their friendship, understanding that he couldn't be better if his friends weren't thriving alongside him.

In the classroom, Bill was not only a diligent student but also a source of inspiration for John and Mike. He dedicated his time to helping them understand challenging concepts, patiently guiding them through their studies. His belief in the idea that their collective success was intertwined fueled a spirit of collaboration among the trio.

On the sports field, Bill's prowess wasn't just about personal victories. He was the teammate who motivated John and Mike to push their limits, fostering an environment where each one's success was celebrated as a shared triumph. His love for sports wasn't confined to competition; it was about the joy of playing together and the shared sense of achievement.

Beyond academics and sports, Bill's friendships were rich with laughter, goofy stories, and well-executed prank jokes. His infectious laughter became a soundtrack to their shared experiences, and his playful antics added a layer of joy to their lives.

What truly set Bill apart, however, was his unwavering humility. Despite academic achievements and athletic prowess, he remained down-to-earth, never seeking the spotlight for himself. To his friends and family, Bill was a source of admiration and love for a person whose genuine nature shone through in every interaction.

In the eyes of those close to him, Bill wasn't just a friend; he was a symbol of kindness and generosity. His humility was the foundation of his character, making him not only exceptional in his achievements but also extraordinary in his humanity. To encounter Bill was to encounter goodness, leaving an indelible mark on the hearts of all who were fortunate enough to know him a truly exceptional human being.

However, beneath his charming exterior, Bill harbored a depth that few could fathom. He was selective when it came to forming deeper connections with others, especially in matters of the heart. Bill wanted anyone who entered his life to understand that he held the utmost respect for them, and he was not willing to enter any commitment that did not nourish his soul.

Bill was a striking figure, a portrait of physical allure from head to toe. His ginger hair framed a face adorned with hazel eyes, adding a captivating depth to his gaze. Standing tall at 6 feet 1 inch, his physique bore the sculpted grace of a basketball player, each inch of his body a testament to athleticism and strength.

His hair, meticulously styled to complement the contours of his face, accentuated his features. The hazel eyes sparkled with warmth, possessing an innate ability to convey emotions, especially when paired with his signature smile. Bill's smile was nothing short of magnetic a radiant expression that could light up even the darkest of rooms. It wasn't just a curve of the lips; it reflected the kindness and joy that emanated from within.

His eyes, often described as "tickle eyes," held a playful glint that added an element of charm to his overall presence. When he smiled, those eyes would crinkle at the corners, giving a delightful hint of mischief. It was a smile that not only charmed but also made others feel a genuine connection.

Bill's physical allure, however, was just one facet of his being. For some, his selectiveness in matters of the heart became a source of heartbreak. He wasn't quick to offer his heart in love, recognizing the weight and significance of such a commitment. Those who didn't align with the path he sought to tread found themselves facing the reality of unrequited feelings, with Bill unintentionally becoming a heartbreaker, leaving behind tears and shattered dreams.

Yet, Bill held a profound belief in the sanctity of love. He understood that love, like everything else in life, should be cherished, nurtured, and built upon a foundation of mutual understanding, trust, and respect. His selective approach to matters of the heart wasn't born out of callousness but from a genuine desire to forge connections that stood the test of time. In the eyes of those who admired him, Bill was not just eye candy; he was a man who recognized the depth of love and approached it with the reverence it deserved.

Dorothy A Picture-Perfect Frame

The scene was set against the backdrop of a beautiful summer day in Redmond, a day so perfect it felt like it had been plucked from a dream. The sky stretched out in a brilliant shade of blue, casting a radiant light upon the town that nestled amidst lush, green hills.

Under the warm embrace of the summer sun, Bill, John, and Mike cruised through the charming streets in Bill's open-roof car, the wind playing with their hair as they made their way to the local fair. The promise of a day filled with whimsy and laughter hung in the air, but little did Bill know that destiny was about to add a touch of magic to their adventure.

As the trio approached the fairgrounds, the lively atmosphere heightened. Bill, at the wheel, couldn't help but feel the thrill of the wind rushing through the open car, a sense of freedom encapsulated in each breeze. The streets were alive with vibrant hues of laughter and excitement.

Meanwhile, Dorothy and her friends rode bicycles, their laughter and animated chatter creating a kaleidoscope of joy that painted the air around them. Dorothy, with her friends in tow, pedaled with carefree abandon, the summer sun casting a golden glow on their journey.

Amidst this tableau of merriment, as Bill's car and Dorothy's bicycle path intersected, time seemed to slow. The wind carried the lighthearted melody of the fair, and Bill's eyes were drawn to a group of beautiful girls, with Dorothy at the forefront. Her laughter and the shimmering radiance of her smile became the focal point of this enchanting scene.

Bill's open-roof car became a chariot of destiny, carrying him toward the unexpected encounter that awaited. The sunlit streets framed a romantic backdrop, and as Bill's gaze met Dorothy's, their worlds collided in a moment that echoed with the magic of serendipity.

Dorothy, pedaling on her bicycle with friends, added to the lively spectacle. The sound of their laughter became the accompaniment to this serendipitous dance between two souls, unaware that was about to unfold.

As Bill passed Dorothy on that summer day, her image imprinted itself on his mind like a delicate brushstroke of beauty and intrigue. Though he didn't know her name or anything about her, the girl he just glimpsed became a muse in his thoughts, a fleeting vision that sparked a cascade of emotions within him.

In Bill's eyes, Dorothy's youthful radiance shone through. Her petite figure, standing at 5 feet 1 inch, carried an undeniable grace and charm. Long waves of black hair danced in the wind, framing a face that held an ethereal quality.

His imagination painted a picture of her, clad in a pink T-shirt that accentuated the gentle curves of her figure. Her bust, elegantly outlined, and a well-rounded bump beneath a purple pair of shorts created a silhouette that seemed like a work of art. In his mind's eye, she possessed the allure of a runway model, a beauty so captivating that it could grace the pages of a magazine.

As Bill continued his journey to the fair, the image of Dorothy lingered in his thoughts. There was a tenderness in the way he perceived her, an appreciation for the beauty that transcended physical appearance. In that moment, Redmond felt like a small city with endless possibilities, and Bill silently vowed to hunt for another glimpse of this mysterious and enchanting girl.

Through Bill's eyes, Dorothy wasn't just a passing stranger; she became a symbol of the unexpected magic that life could unfold. His tender thoughts held the promise of future encounters, creating a connection that went beyond the superficial and resonated with the longing for a love story yet to be written.

His friends noticed his reaction and couldn't resist teasing him. "I told you there would be girls, and beautiful ones," John chuckled. Bill smiled and said, "I never said that I didn't like girls I just choose to focus on my studies."; he simply didn't want anything to distract him from his academic pursuits.

As they reached the fair, He parked his car and settled down with his book, paying little attention to the festivities around him. But life had other plans.

Laughter echoed through the air, and Bill, for the first time in his life, was compelled to look up from his book. There she was the girl with the bright smile, long black hair, and a complexion that seemed to glow in the sunlight. His heart raced as he watched her, utterly captivated.

Moments later, she approached him, her voice clear and inviting. "Hey, why are you sitting alone? Aren't you here for the fair?" she asked. Bill, momentarily stunned by her presence, stammered a response. With a voice that was almost too cheesy to bear, he uttered, "I was just a driver, but I think I like it more now that you're here." The words, laced with a charming awkwardness, carried a genuine warmth and a hint of playful vulnerability. In that simple sentence, he revealed a subtle shift in perspective, acknowledging that her presence had added a newfound joy to the ordinary role he played.

In response to his explanation that he had only come to drive his friends, she offered a different perspective. Her radiant smile illuminated the conversation as she gently reminded him that life encompassed various facets both play and study. With wisdom beyond her years, she emphasized the importance of balance, expressing that too much focus on one aspect could be harmful. Her words carried a subtle yet profound encouragement to appreciate the richness of life's experiences.

Bill couldn't contain his laughter, and he playfully asked about her age. "Okay, tell me again, how old are you?" Her response was a playful turnabout as she insisted that he should have first asked for her name. With a charming twinkle in her eye, she teased, "Boy, as beautiful as I am, you just ask my age without knowing my name, where I go to school, or if I even want to take you to prom?" With a hint of mischief, she finally revealed her name, introducing herself as Dorothy.

As their hands met in a tender shake, a subtle but unmistakable current passed between them. The touch, gentle yet charged, hinted at a connection that transcended the brevity of their meeting. In those fleeting seconds, a dance of unspoken emotions unfolded.

Dorothy's youthful energy radiated, and Bill couldn't help but be captivated not only by her beauty but also by the determination and self-assuredness that emanated from her. Their eyes locked in a moment, and in that shared gaze, there was an unspoken understanding of an uncharted territory of emotions that hinted at something more.

The click of their hands touching resonated like a heartbeat, a silent rhythm that underscored the chemistry forming between them. In those moments, the world around them seemed to fade as they shared laughter, their eyes speaking a language of their own.

Dorothy, possessing a maturity beyond her years, playfully took his book from him, teasing him about reading schoolwork instead of something more interesting. Their laughter became a shared melody, each chuckle weaving another thread into the tapestry of their connection. In that shared amusement, a bond was solidifying, and the spark of something special lingered in the air.

As their laughter subsided, the admiration in their eyes lingered a recognition that in this chance encounter, something profound was unfolding. The magnetic pull between them, from the touch of their hands to the laughter they shared, hinted at the potential for a love story that transcended the ordinary an unfolding tale of two souls drawn together by an invisible thread of destiny.

Soon, they were engrossed in conversation, and Bill learned more about this remarkable girl. She was fourteen, a sophomore in high school. "Yes, I know I am young, but I am smart and was able to skip a grade" she said with smiled on her face. Her aspirations were as high as the clouds he dreamed of reaching. She wanted to be a marine engineer, to travel the world, and to find the love of her life, the most handsome man in the world, and start a family.

Bill inquired about her school, surprised that he had never noticed her despite attending the same Redmond high school. Dorothy chuckled, explaining that he was often too absorbed in his books and birdwatching to notice the world around him. They both shared a laugh at his single-mindedness.

As the sun dipped below the horizon, casting a golden glow over the fare as it prepared to set, Bill's friends returned to his car. He looked at Dorothy, realizing that they needed a plan to meet again. She simply winked at him, a mischievous gleam in her eye, and told him that if he wanted to find her, he would.

Taking her bicycle and slowly riding it, then she stops and looked at Bill who was still looking at her as she rode away, "If you seek you will find. Bye, see you soon." Bill watched her disappear into the distance; her image etched in his heart.

His friends, seeing Bill's transformation in just a few hours, were amazed. His heart, once dedicated solely to the world of aviation, had taken its first fluttering steps into the world of romance, and it was a feeling he couldn't wait to explore further.

As Bill's friends chattered away in the car, their laughter and excited voices filling the space, Bill's outward demeanor remained calm. He pretended to be fully engaged in their conversation, but his mind and soul were adrift in the world of the perfect stranger he had just met.

Dorothy's image was imprinted on his thoughts. Her bright smile seemed to light up his world, her laughter echoed in his ears like the sweetest melody, and her words lingered in his heart like poetry. He couldn't help but steal glances toward the fairgrounds where he had last seen her, hoping for another glimpse of her enchanting presence.

It was as if a spell was casted upon him, a spell of curiosity, fascination, and an inexplicable connection. Bill had never felt this way before, a mix of excitement and nervousness that both thrilled and frightened him. His dreams of flight were momentarily eclipsed by the dreams of meeting Dorothy again.

Bill's friends, ever attuned to his usual lighthearted nature, couldn't help but notice the subtle shift in his demeanor. Playfully, they prodded him with a barrage of questions and teasing remarks, completely unaware of the storm of emotions that was quietly brewing within him.

John, with a mischievous twinkle in his eye, leaned in and said, "Hey Bill, you've been acting like you've just seen a ghost. What's going on?" Mike, equally mischievous, chimed in, "Or maybe a love potion? Did someone cast a spell on you?"

Their teasing banter continued, the camaraderie between friends turning the situation into a playful spectacle. Little did they know that the source of Bill's distraction wasn't a ghost or a love potion it was a girl with long black hair named Dorothy.

Bill, managing to summon a polite smile, played along with their banter, deflecting their questions with a skillful blend of humor and vagueness. Inside, however, his thoughts were consumed by the memory of Dorothy's radiant smile and the twinkle in her eye.

The deepest bonds of friendship were evident in this exchange, the kind where friends could tease one another relentlessly yet sense when something deeper was at play. As the banter continued, Bill's friends inadvertently became the supporting cast in the unfolding drama of his heart, unaware of the quiet revolution taking place within him.

In the midst of their playful banter, Bill's thoughts drifted back to Dorothy, and the storm of emotions within him raged on. Little did he know that this chance encounter had woven a thread of enchantment that would color the canvas of his friendships and add a new chapter to the tale of his heart.

He remembered the way her long black hair caught the sunlight, how her eyes sparkled with intelligence and warmth, and how her laughter had made the world seem a brighter place. He could almost feel the warmth of her hand in his as they had shaken hands, a simple touch that had sent a jolt of electricity through him.

As the car cruised through the streets of Redmond, Bill's thoughts continued to drift back to Dorothy. He envisioned future encounters, conversations that would deepen their connection, and moments that would etch their love story into the tapestry of time.

With each passing moment, Bill realized that he was falling for the idea of wanting more from Dorothy, the girl who had appeared like a shooting star in his life, leaving a trail of wonder and possibility. He knew that he needed to find her, to see her again, and to explore the uncharted territory of his heart.

As Bill's friends continued their playful teasing, they couldn't help but sense that something was different this time. John, always quick-witted, leaned in with a sly grin and said, "Bill, my friend, it seems you've met someone special. Spill the beans! How can we help you navigate the treacherous waters of love?"

Mike, equally invested in their friend's newfound intrigue, added, "Yeah, Bill, you've been the heartbreaker all this time. Now, it looks like the tables have turned, and you're the one smitten. We're here to help you set sail on this romantic adventure!"

Unbeknownst to his friends, Bill found himself on unfamiliar terrain. Unlike the past, when girls had come to him, this time the dynamics had shifted. Dorothy had left a lasting impression, and Bill was eager to find a way to get in touch with her.

With their collective wisdom, his friends brainstormed ideas, from casually bumping into her at familiar spots to orchestrating chance encounters. John, with a wink, suggested, "How about offering to show her around town? It's the perfect excuse to spend more time together."

Mike, ever the strategist, chimed in, "Or you could 'accidentally' leave something at the fair, and then you'll have a reason to see her again. Smooth, right?"

As they plotted and planned, Bill felt a mix of excitement and nervousness. The world of aviation, once the sole focus of his dreams, was now joined by a newfound passion the art of pursuing love. The canvas of his life expanded, and the colors of romance began to paint a picture that went beyond the blue skies and clouds.

In the realm of his heart, Bill was navigating uncharted waters, ready to dive deeper into this exhilarating adventure. The world was no longer just a place for aviation; it had transformed into a canvas where the brushstrokes of romance awaited. With the support and camaraderie of his friends, Bill was ready to embrace every shade and hue of this enchanting journey into the mysteries of love.

Quest to find Dorothy

On a Monday morning, raindrops cascaded from the heavens, washing away the sins of the weekend, and lending the air a refreshing aroma as it mingled with the scent of the awakening trees. The world outside seemed to come alive with the gentle pitter-patter of raindrops, a poetic overture to the unfolding drama in Bill's heart.

The blissful spring break had become a cherished memory, a chapter in the book of time that was now history. As the raindrops painted a canvas of renewal, Bill felt a stirring in his soul. The time had come to seek out the girl he had met at the fair, a girl named Dorothy, who had left an indelible mark on his heart.

Driven by a burning desire, for the first time since he had started high school, Bill made a decision that echoed with the resonance of determination. He chose to skip baseball practice, an activity that had once claimed his afternoons, to embark on a quest to find Dorothy.

As he roamed through the school corridors, raindrops clinging to his jacket, Bill's heartbeat with a sense of purpose. The rhythmic tap of rain on the roof served as a backdrop to his thoughts, each drop echoing his anticipation and resolve. The scent of rain-soaked earth filled the air, adding a layer of nostalgia to the moment.

Hours passed as Bill wandered through the labyrinth of hallways, peering into classrooms with a hopeful heart. His determination, like the rain that continued to fall, was unwavering. And then, like a ray of sunshine breaking through the clouds, he finally spotted her in her typing class, a glimpse of Dorothy that brought a surge of joy to his soul.

In that moment, amidst the sounds of rain and the scent of a Monday morning, the universe seemed to conspire to reunite two hearts. Bill's journey, fueled by love and determination, had led him to the object of his search. As he stood outside the typing class, rain-kissed and heartbeats quickened, the stage was set for a new chapter to unfold in the romance between Bill and Dorothy.

Bill quietly stood by the door, patiently waiting for her to finish. As she emerged from the classroom, Dorothy paid little attention to him, as a few girls vied for his attention, Bill politely excused himself from their clamor and hurried after Dorothy. With a smile that radiated warmth and affection, he called out, "Dorothy, I've been looking for you, Hold up!!

Dorothy, still amused by the group of admirers trying to capture Bill's attention, turned to him with a playful glint in her eyes. "It's very hard to speak with you when you're surrounded by your groupies," she teased, her gaze fixed on Bill. "Why were you looking for me?" She asked.

Bill, felt nervous, he realized that this was the first time he had ever asked a girl out. His uncertainty and trembling nerves were palpable. Dorothy looked at him with a tender touch, gently placing her hand on his. "I suppose you want to ask me out?" she inquired.

With a playful twinkle in her smart eyes, Dorothy led the dance of romance, effortlessly recognizing the happiness written all over Bill's face. Embracing the moment, she allowed him to follow her lead, their connection unfolding like tulips on a mountain hill.

Bill, caught in the enchantment of the situation, couldn't help but wear a grin that mirrored his overflowing joy. In the silent language of love, their smiles resonated, setting the stage for a tender and affectionate exchange.

"Yep, I came to ask you out," Bill confessed with a playful grin, adding an extra dose of cheese to his admission. Dorothy, still wearing her knowing smile, egged him on, teasingly encouraging him to spill the beans.

"Dorothy," he began with a cheesy flair, "would you do me the honor of joining me to watch the birds by Lake Sammamish?" The choice of a lakeside escapade, where nature itself whispered sweet nothings, added an extra layer of charm to his cheesy invitation.

Dorothy, with a delightful mix of amusement and affection, playfully mimicked Bill's voice, "Would you do me the honor of joining me to watch the birds by Lake Sammamish?" She teasingly declared that it was a bit too formal for a young man like him, and their laughter filled the air, a symphony of shared amusement.

In response, Bill, still wearing a grin, playfully touched his face as if searching for more casual words to ask her out. Before he could find them, Dorothy, with a mischievous glint in her eye, adopted a playful British accent and said, "I would be honored to join you watching the birds at Lake Sammamish." Their laughter continued, echoing through the space like a melody of joy.

Dorothy, unable to resist the opportunity for a playful touch, gave Bill a hard and playful handshake, saying, "Yes, sir, it is a date." In this whimsically cheesy exchange, their shared sense of humor and affection for each other became the vibrant hues in the canvas of their budding connection.

As Bill walked away from Dorothy, the school aisle seemed to transform into a corridor of dreams and emotions. The door where Dorothy stood became a portal to a world where hearts beat in unison, and the air was charged with the magic of budding romance.

The feel of the school aisle was a tapestry woven with the threads of hope, excitement, and the promise of something beautiful. Each step Bill took resonated with the echo of his heartbeat, the melody of a newfound connection playing in the background.

As he glanced back at Dorothy, a smile adorned his face, radiant with the triumph of a first victory. The weight of uncertainty lifted, replaced by the buoyancy of success. In that moment, the school aisle became a runway where Bill walked with the grace of a conqueror, his heart aflutter with the wings of newfound love.

Dorothy, standing by the door, winked at him, a silent acknowledgment of the shared joy that hung in the air. The exchange of glances spoke of a secret language between two hearts, a language that promised a journey into the unexplored territories of love.

Yet, in this romantic tableau, the school aisle was not without its observers. As Bill poured his heart out to Dorothy, the eyes of many girls were fixed on him. Some, enchanted by the vulnerability of his confession, admired him from afar. However, a few, standing in the aisle, did not share the sentiment. Their glances, fueled by envy, cast a shadow on the scene.

The anger in their eyes, however, was not directed at Bill, the promo king, the baseball player, or the debate captain. Instead, it turned towards Dorothy, the girl who had won the heart of the sought-after figure. In their eyes, she became a queen in her own right, the object of desire for someone they once considered out of reach.

Bill, oblivious to the silent drama around him, felt like a token that shone brightly, a symbol of a conquest that transcended the high school hierarchy. In his mind, he was not just the promo king; he was the queen of England, securing the first date with the girl who had captured his heart. The school aisle, now charged with the emotional currents of the moment, bore witness to the beginning of a love story that promised to unfold with grace and intensity.

The Lake Sammamish

On a Sunday evening, bathed in the soft, warm glow of the setting sun, Dorothy arrived at the lake, just slightly past their appointed time. She approached the bench where Bill was sitting, his gaze fixed on the gently lapping waves of the lake. Lake Sammamish, bathed in the hues of the setting sun, seemed to be in harmony with the emotions that swelled between them. The water glistened with golden reflections, mirroring the love that had flourished on its serene shores.

As the sun dipped lower on the horizon, casting a warm, golden glow across the lake, Bill and Dorothy settled onto the bench together. They watched in awe as the water shimmered like liquid gold, each ripple carrying a secret whispered by the setting sun. The air was filled with a gentle breeze, carrying the scent of the surrounding pine trees and the promise of a magical evening.

The symphony of nature enveloped them. The lake's gentle lapping against the shore provided a soothing backdrop, and the melodious chirping of birds added to the enchantment of the moment.

It was as though the avian world had gathered in harmony, their songs blending seamlessly into a love ballad composed just for Bill and Dorothy.

Bill couldn't help but steal glances at Dorothy, captivated by the way her eyes sparkled in the fading light. He felt a connection with her that ran deeper than words could express. As they gazed at the birds skimming the water's surface, a sense of tranquility washed over them. The world seemed to slow down, and time held its breath to savor their budding romance.

Dorothy, her heart aflutter, leaned in closer to Bill. Their shoulders touched, and a spark of electricity passed between them, igniting a fire in their hearts. Without a word, they knew they were meant to be together, two souls drawn together by the magnetic pull of love.

In that moment, Bill turned to Dorothy, his eyes locked onto hers, and he softly whispered, "Dorothy, this evening is just the beginning. I hope to share countless more moments like this with you, watching the birds, feeling the breeze, and developing a friendship with you.

Dorothy's heart swelled with emotion, and she replied, "Bill, I couldn't imagine a more perfect evening. And I can't wait to create many more beautiful memories with you."

Hand in hand, they watched as the sun dipped below the horizon, leaving the lake in the soft embrace of twilight. As the stars began to twinkle overhead, Bill and Dorothy knew that their love story had taken root, destined to blossom in the days and years to come.

As the sun dipped below the horizon, casting hues of orange and pink across the sky, the bench nestled by the tranquil shores of Lake Sammamish transformed into their sacred rendezvous point.

A gentle breeze carried the whispers of the nearby willow trees, and the serene ripples of the lake echoed the heartbeat of their burgeoning love story.

In the quiet stillness of those evenings, time seemed to lose its grip, allowing Bill and Dorothy to escape into their private world. The bench, weathered by the elements and witness to countless sunsets, became a silent spectator to the unfolding chapters of their romance.

Week after week, as the golden glow of the twilight enveloped the surroundings, Bill and Dorothy found solace in the familiarity of this spot. It was more than just a wooden seat; it was a repository of stolen glances, shared laughter, and unspoken promises.

Underneath the branches of an ancient oak tree that stretched its limbs protectively, Bill took Dorothy's hand in his. As the first stars emerged in the indigo canvas above, they made a vow a promise to meet again, right there on that weathered bench, where they had etched their names as a symbol of their growing connection.

The carving, a testament to their shared laughter and whispered confessions, stood as a silent guardian of their love. The initials intertwined, forever marking the wood with the echoes of their devotion.

And so, as the sun dipped below the horizon each weekend, casting its warm glow on the lake and the bench that had become an emblem of their affection, Bill and Dorothy continued to add new chapters to their love story. The tranquil shores of Lake Sammamish bore witness to the timeless romance that unfolded, one sunset at a time.

Under the soft caress of twilight, bathed in the ethereal glow of the setting sun, Dorothy and Bill would meet here. It was their place of solace, where the complexities of the world melted away, leaving only the simplicity of their love. As the gentle breeze whispered secrets of the lake, they would come together, hand in hand.

Dorothy, with her heartwarming smile and a twinkle in her eyes, would eagerly help Bill with his math homework. Despite being two classes behind him, Bill found her intellect enchanting. He believed that the magic of this place seeped into her, making her solutions as brilliant and awe-inspiring as the colors painted across the evening sky.

In return, this very bench became the canvas for Bill's passion. He would bring a treasure trove of bird pictures, each chosen with the utmost care. With a voice as tender as the evening itself, he would describe these birds to Dorothy, each word a brushstroke in the masterpiece of their love story. As the fading light cast a warm embrace around them, Bill's descriptions transformed into a symphony of love, painting vivid images that danced in their hearts.

With each passing weekend, their connection deepened, like the ever-changing hues of the lake's waters. Their conversations were more than just words; they were whispers of longing, laughter that echoed through the ages, and promises etched into the very fabric of the universe.

One enchanting evening, with the sky ablaze in shades of amber and rose, Bill looked into Dorothy's eyes with a love that transcended time. He realized that this bench, this lake, and the woman beside him were forever etched into the tapestry of his soul.

And as they held each other's gaze, the bench by Lake Sammamish transformed into an altar of love, a place where their hearts converged with the world around them. It was here, under the canvas of the setting sun, that their love story was written in the stars.

The Bench

In the gentle embrace of their unique connection, Dorothy and Bill shared a friendship that resonated with the soft cadence of love, yet it danced within the delicate boundaries they willingly upheld. Dorothy, a guardian of their unspoken rules, protected the fragile equilibrium they had carefully crafted, while Bill, ever respectful, navigated the subtle contours of their bond with a reverence that mirrored the depth of his feelings.

Their friendship, an enigma to the outside world, was a realm where love tiptoed along the edges, beckoning but never daring to overstep. It was a secret garden of shared glances, unspoken words, and the quiet hum of understanding that only they could decipher. No one in Bill's circle of friends or among Dorothy's confidantes comprehended the nuances of their connection. For Dorothy and Bill, however, it was a tapestry of emotions woven with threads of companionship and a silent promise that transcended the ordinary.

As the sands of time slipped through the hourglass, Dorothy and Bill found themselves entwined in a friendship, unlike any other.

A connection that defied categorization and eluded the constraints of conventional relationships. Theirs was a bond that bloomed like a rare flower in the garden of companionship, sheltered from the prying eyes of the world.

In the quiet corners of the library, amidst hushed conversations and shared notes, their friendship blossomed. Dorothy's patient guidance through the labyrinth of mathematics became a metaphor for the intricate pathways of their connection navigating through complexities with grace and understanding.

Their rides together, whether under the vast expanse of the evening sky or through the tree-lined streets of Redmond, solidified the unspoken pact between them. They reveled in the shared silences, the uncharted territory of emotions, and the unspoken question that lingered in the air: were they merely close friends or something more?

Time, relentless in its march, whispered its silent reminder. Before they fully grasped the transformation, a year had slipped through their fingers like grains of sand, leaving in its wake a friendship that had quietly metamorphosed into something profound. The lines between camaraderie and romance blurred, leaving Dorothy and Bill suspended in a beautifully ambiguous dance, a dance only they knew the steps to, as they continued to traverse the delicate balance of their enchanting connection.

In the soft glow of affection, Bill found himself standing at the precipice of possibility, urged on by the thoughtful prodding of his dear friend John. The air was charged with the promise of a near future where love might bloom, if only he could summon the courage to take the next step with Dorothy. John, a sage in matters of the heart, had warned Bill about the looming specter of the "friend zone," a place Bill was determined not to find himself trapped within. His feelings for Dorothy ran deeper than mere friendship; he yearned for her to become his confidante in matters of the heart, his partner in the dance of life.

Bill understood that to seize the moment, he needed to step beyond the comfortable boundaries of friendship. He wanted more than shared laughter and secret glances; he envisioned a future where Dorothy would be the one who held a special place in his heart. The mere thought of Dorothy existing solely in the realm of friendship was inconceivable to Bill, and the idea of losing her to the "friend zone" sent shivers down his spine.

Taking John's heartfelt advice to heart, Bill decided to orchestrate a momentous occasion, a date with Dorothy that would transcend the boundaries of friendship and set the stage for something deeper. With a tender smile, Bill approached his mother, revealing his intentions and seeking her assistance in crafting a romantic picnic basket. Bill's family, overjoyed at the prospect of his burgeoning romance, embraced the idea wholeheartedly. His sister, Sarah, knowing Dorothy well and fond of her, eagerly contributed their insights, eager to ensure that Bill's first date with Dorothy would be nothing short of unforgettable.

As the preparations unfolded, the anticipation in Bill's heart swelled. The prospect of expressing his true feelings to Dorothy filled him with a mixture of excitement and nervousness. He envisioned a picnic by the lake, under the same oak tree that had silently witnessed the evolution of their connection. Bill's intentions were clear to navigate the delicate balance between friendship and the uncharted territory of romance.

In this tender dance of emotions, Bill prepared to embark on a journey that held the promise of transforming their relationship into something extraordinary. The picnic, a canvas for their shared dreams and unspoken desires, awaited its protagonists' two friends on the brink of discovering a love that had quietly blossomed in the spaces between shared moments and stolen glances.

The air was thick with anticipation as Bill stood before the grandeur of Dorothy's ancestral home. A nervous excitement pulsed through him, magnified by the weight of the bouquet, he clutched a simple offering that carried the depth of his feelings. The doorbell echoed through the ornate halls, and soon, the imposing figure of Dorothy's father emerged to welcome him.

Dressed in the opulence befitting his family's legacy, Dorothy's father exuded an air of sophistication that spoke of old money, a lineage steeped in the richness of tradition and heritage. The walls of the house bore witness to the passage of time, adorned with portraits of generations past and artifacts that whispered tales of a storied history. Bill, acutely aware of the privilege encapsulated within these walls, felt a mixture of awe and trepidation.

With a quivering voice, Bill extended the bouquet, a silent offering that conveyed his respect and admiration. Dorothy's father, a man of stature and grace, chuckled warmly as he accepted the flowers. With an inviting gesture, he welcomed Bill into their home, where the fragrance of history mingled with the scent of polished wood and the soft notes of classical music that played in the background.

Inside, Bill found himself navigating the delicate dance of meeting Dorothy's parents. He was keenly aware of the responsibility that came with this encounter, determined to leave a lasting impression that extended beyond a mere first date. As he unfolded his plans for the upcoming picnic, Dorothy's father observed him with a discerning gaze agaze that seemed to delve beyond the surface.

The moment hung in the air, charged with the unspoken question that eventually materialized in Dorothy's father's firm inquiry, "What are your intentions with my daughter?" Bill, though momentarily taken aback, met the gaze with sincerity. He spoke of his genuine affection for Dorothy, of the shared laughter and dreams that had quietly woven their connection into the fabric of his heart.

The living room, adorned with timeless elegance, became the backdrop for a pivotal moment in Bill's journey into Dorothy's world. Dorothy's father, a figure of authority and love, offered advice that carried the weight of paternal concern. The air was charged with a mix of sternness and warmth as he conveyed his expectations to Bill.

"Son," he began, his voice a blend of stern authority and paternal care, "I expect you to treat my daughter with the utmost respect. Anything less won't sit well with me." His words, a silent directive echoing through the room, carried the weight of years of protectiveness for his cherished daughter.

Dorothy's father, with a no-nonsense demeanor softened by fatherly wisdom, laid down a clear set of guidelines. "I don't want you doing anything you wouldn't do in front of me. No liberties, no compromises. If you were me, you wouldn't even think about kissing her or doing anything that" His sentence hung in the air, unfinished, yet the weight of his gaze and the gravity in his voice spoke volumes.

Bill, standing at the precipice of this unspoken agreement, nodded in earnest understanding. His voice, though shaky, carried the sincerity of his intentions. "Yes, sir. I will be respectful, as I have always been. I promise," Bill assured, a subtle tremor in his words revealing the challenge of the promise he was making.

A smile softened Dorothy's father's stern expression, as if acknowledging the sincerity in Bill's response. "Good," he said, his gaze unwavering. And then, with a touch of humor that belied the seriousness of the moment, he added, "And one last thing, son. You break her heart; I break your legs. Understand?" The room seemed to hold its breath as the weight of those words settled, and Bill, his forehead glistening with nervous sweat, responded with a tremor in his voice, "Yes, sir." The unspoken pact had been sealed, and in that exchange, Bill not only received the keys to Dorothy's heart but also the implicit trust and protection of a father who cherished his daughter beyond measure.

Dorothy entered the room, and it was as if the very essence of sunlight had taken human form. Her radiant smile illuminated the space, and her presence exuded a warmth that enveloped Bill's senses. She was a vision of grace, dressed for the occasion in a flowing floral sundress that danced with the gentle breeze. The soft fabric cascaded around her, echoing the elegance of her movements.

Bill's eyes, filled with an unspoken admiration, traced the contours of Dorothy's form. In the gentle curve of her smile and the sparkle in her eyes, he found the reflection of a blossoming connection. Her hair, kissed by the sun's golden rays, framed her face like a halo, adding to the ethereal glow that captivated him.

As Bill took in the sight of Dorothy, her father observed the exchange with a prideful gleam in his eyes. The love and care he had poured into raising his daughter were mirrored in the way she carried herself a testament to the nurturing environment that had shaped her into the remarkable woman she had become.

Dorothy greeted Bill with a warm hug, her playful banter with her father adding a touch of familial charm to the moment. Bill, in awe of her beauty, felt a surge of gratitude for the privilege of sharing this day with someone as captivating as Dorothy. Her parents, watching the interaction unfold, couldn't hide their joy at seeing their daughter treated with such genuine admiration and respect.

As they embarked on their journey to Lake Sammamish, the car became a cocoon of shared smiles and easy conversation. The earlier nervousness dissipated with every passing mile, replaced by a growing sense of connection and anticipation. Bill, stealing glances at Dorothy, marveled at the serenity of the moment and the promise that lay ahead.

The Basket of Joy

In the soft glow of the late afternoon sun, Bill led Dorothy to a secluded spot by the lake, a tapestry of wildflowers surrounding them. The air was infused with the sweet fragrance of lavender and the gentle rustle of leaves, creating an ambiance that heightened the romance of the moment.

As Dorothy waited in the car, Bill, with a mischievous smile, prepared a surprise that would etch this day into the canvas of their shared memories. The picnic blanket unfurled like a canvas, and Bill carefully arranged an array of flowers, each chosen with precision. The vibrant hues of daisies, sunflowers, and roses mingled together, creating a kaleidoscope of colors that mirrored the love blossoming between them. The fragrance of the flowers, a symphony of scents, danced in the air, further enhancing the sensory experience.

The basket, a treasure trove of delights, held a carefully curated assortment of treats prepared by Bill's mother. From artisanal cheeses and freshly baked bread to succulent fruits and a selection of desserts, the contents spoke of love and thoughtful consideration.

Each item was chosen to delight Dorothy's palate, a reflection of the care and attention that had gone into crafting this romantic interlude.

Returning to the car, Bill blindfolded Dorothy, heightening the sense of anticipation. As they reached their destination, he gently removed the blindfold, unveiling a picturesque scene that took Dorothy's breath away. The blanket, adorned with carefully arranged flowers, welcomed them to a magical setting overlooking the serene lake.

Dorothy's eyes sparkled with delight as she beheld the romantic tableau before her. The sun's warm rays bathed the scene in a golden glow, casting a spell over the lake and the couple nestled within nature's embrace. They dined on the delectable picnic fare, savoring each bite and relishing the simple pleasure of being in each other's company.

As they conversed and laughed, their connection deepened, and the bond that had been quietly growing between them solidified amidst the beauty of the setting sun. The lake mirrored the changing hues of the sky, reflecting the warmth and magic of the moment. In this carefully crafted scene, love unfolded like the petals of the flowers surrounding them, creating a memory that would forever be imprinted on their hearts.

Dorothy thanked Bill for the wonderful time, her heart brimming with gratitude. Bill, overcome with emotion, gazed into her eyes and expressed his admiration for her wisdom, beauty, and intelligence. The connection between them deepened with every word, every shared smile, and every tender moment.

As the sun dipped lower in the sky, casting a warm, golden glow over the tranquil waters of Lake Sammamish, Bill and Dorothy decided to immerse themselves in the cool embrace of the lake. The air, thick with the fragrance of wildflowers and the whispers of the evening breeze, set the stage for a moment of enchantment.

Dorothy, with a playful glint in her eyes, surprised Bill by revealing a stunning blue swimsuit beneath the delicate folds of her dress. The silk fabric clung to her curves, accentuating the contours of her graceful body. Bill, momentarily entranced, felt his heart skip a beat at the sight of her. The color of the swimsuit mirrored the depth of the lake, and Dorothy's beauty, adorned in azure, became a living embodiment of the serene waters that surrounded them.

With a confident stride, Dorothy approached the water's edge, her every movement a dance of allure and grace. The silk swimsuit, kissed by the sunlight, shimmered like a sapphire gem against her sun-kissed skin. Bill, momentarily captivated by the vision before him, found himself speechless in the presence of such breathtaking beauty.

As Dorothy waded into the lake, the water embracing her with a gentle ripple, she playfully challenged Bill to a race. Her spirited nature, mirrored by the gleam in her eyes, drew Bill into the playful dance of their shared joy. The air was alive with the promise of laughter and the splashes that echoed their shared delight.

In the midst of the lake's cool embrace, Bill and Dorothy swam together, their laughter mingling with the soft lapping of the water against the shore. Bill, overwhelmed by the intense rush of emotions, swam closer to Dorothy. Gently holding her waist, he locked eyes with her, the reflection of the sunset painting a canvas of warmth and intimacy.

Their connection deepened with each stroke, the rhythmic dance of their bodies in the water a metaphor for the synchronicity of their hearts. The lake bore witness to a moment of pure, unbridled joy, a dance of love and laughter that unfolded beneath the canvas of the setting sun. In the midst of nature's embrace, Bill and Dorothy created a memory that would forever be etched in the tapestry of their shared romance.

In the soft embrace of the lake, the sun dipping below the horizon, Bill and Dorothy found themselves suspended in a moment that defied words. The air was charged with the tenderness of their hearts, an intimate connection that whispered promises of a love that transcended time. For Bill, the overwhelming feeling took root an unspoken certainty that Dorothy was the person he had been waiting for, the missing piece to complete the puzzle of his life.

As the desire to kiss her swelled within him, a gentle hesitation held Bill back. The echo of Dorothy's father's words, a stern warning tinged with humor, reverberated in his ears: "if you do anything to --- I will break your legs." With a heavy heart, Bill pulled away, the longing in his eyes betraying the unspoken words that lingered between them.

Dorothy, bewildered and hurt by his sudden withdrawal, questioned the rejection. Bill, his voice trembling with the weight of the promise he had made, explained the pledge he had taken not to overstep the boundaries set by her father. The air hung heavy with unspoken desires, a tension that neither of them anticipated.

However, Dorothy's playful spirit, ever resilient, took charge. Determined to bridge the gap, she decided to seize the moment. In a passionate and intense kiss, she expressed the emotions that words couldn't convey. Breathless and swept away, Bill found himself enveloped in a stolen moment of affection, a kiss that spoke volumes about the depth of their connection.

With a smile that held the sparkle of mischief and triumph, Dorothy playfully uttered, "Okay, now go tell him you have kissed his baby girl." In that shared understanding, they embarked on a new horizon, the resonance of their lips echoing the beginning of a love story that promised to be extraordinary.

As the sun dipped below the horizon, the golden sky giving way to dusk, Bill and Dorothy found themselves locked in a gaze that spoke of promises, dreams, and the uncharted journey ahead. The world around them seemed to fade into insignificance as they shared vows that echoed across the lake, an intimate ceremony witnessed by the sky above and the waters below.

This stolen moment marked the inception of a love story, a tale that would be etched into the fabric of their lives. With the lake as their backdrop and the sky as their silent witness, Bill and Dorothy stepped into a future where their love would be the guiding star, illuminating the path of their shared destiny.

Reluctantly leaving the enchanting shores of Lake Sammamish, Bill couldn't shake the feeling of being the luckiest man alive. Dorothy, his best friend and now the love he had discovered amidst the magic of the day, stood by his side. The car, a cocoon of shared warmth, carried them back into the embrace of reality.

As they settled into the car, Bill's heart brimming with newfound courage, he turned to Dorothy. Holding her hand in his, he looked into her eyes with a radiant smile. "Will you be my girlfriend? I think I love you. I mean, I know I am in love with you," he confessed, the words carrying a weight of sincerity.

Their laughter bubbled forth, a shared joy that spoke volumes. Dorothy, moved by the sweetness of the moment, hugged him tightly and whispered into his ear, "My darling, you were my boyfriend from the first day I met you. I was just waiting for you to realize it. Yes, I would be more than happy to be your girl."

Bill, overwhelmed by the confirmation of their feelings, was determined to make every moment with Dorothy as memorable as their first date. The car, now filled with the warmth of their shared laughter and the promise of a future together, carried them back home.

As they drove, their hands found each other naturally, fingers entwined in a silent yet powerful declaration of their newfound love. Their smiles, radiant as the setting sun, mirrored the warmth in their hearts. Bill and Dorothy, now officially a couple, embarked on the journey back home with a shared sense of joy, anticipation, and the knowledge that their love story had only just begun.

As Bill and Dorothy drove through the rolling hills of Redmond, Washington, in the enchanting era of the 1940s, the landscape unfolded before them like a timeless masterpiece. The horse town, nestled in the embrace of nature's bounty, revealed its beauty in every lush greenery-covered corner.

The hills, adorned with an array of vibrant colors, seemed to breathe life into the scenery. Majestic trees, standing tall and proud, their branches reaching towards the heavens, created a canopy of serenity. The leaves rustled in the gentle breeze, whispering secrets of love to the young couple as they traversed the familiar paths of their hometown.

Bill, with a twinkle in his eye, pointed out the landmarks that held a special place in his heart. Each sight, from the spot where he got his first haircut as a teen to the corner where the best ice cream parlor stood, now carried a unique significance. The horse town, with its charming streets and quaint buildings, became the backdrop for their journey into love.

As they drove, Bill shared stories of the town where he had taken his first breath, where childhood dreams had mingled with the sweet fragrance of blooming flowers. He recounted tales of gazing at the skies, dreaming of soaring like the birds that graced the heavens above Redmond. The very essence of the landscape seemed to echo the sentiment of their blossoming romance, a timeless dance between nature and love, with Redmond serving as the enchanting stage.

The sunlight filtered through the leaves, casting a warm glow over the town, and the air was filled with the nostalgic charm of a bygone era. The beauty of Redmond, in the 1940s, unfolded as a living testament to the simplicity and allure of small-town life, a perfect backdrop for the love story that was quietly blossoming between Bill and Dorothy.

Dorothy listened with rapt attention, her eyes never leaving Bill's face. She marveled at how this humble, kind-hearted young man had captured her heart. She realized that their love had been found in the most unexpected of places, just like the treasures hidden in the heart of their beloved Redmond.

The love they had discovered on the shores of Lake Sammamish had transformed their world. It was a love that would grow with time, nurtured by their dreams, their shared laughter, and their unwavering commitment to each other.

Dorothy listened with unwavering attention; her gaze fixed on Bill's face. In the tales of their shared hometown, she discovered the essence of a humble and kind-hearted young man who had effortlessly captured her heart. Their love story, much like the treasures hidden in the heart of Redmond, had unfolded in the most unexpected of places, turning their world into a canvas painted with the hues of love.

The shores of Lake Sammamish had become the sacred ground where their love had taken root, a love destined to grow and flourish with time. Nurtured by dreams, shared laughter, and an unwavering commitment to each other, their love was a beacon guiding them through the vast possibilities that lay ahead.

Their shared laughter echoed through the streets, a symphony of joy and promise. The open road stretched out before them, inviting them to embark on a lifetime of adventure and love. Bill and Dorothy, eager and thrilled, faced the horizon with hearts intertwined, ready to explore the vast expanse of their shared destiny.

As the sun dipped below the horizon, casting its final golden embrace on their love, Bill, and Dorothy's affection for each other ascended to new heights. The radiant glow of the twilight sky mirrored the warmth of their hearts, and with each passing moment, their love story continued to unfold a timeless narrative written in the language of shared dreams, laughter, and a love that promised to endure for all eternity.

High School Love

As the summer sun bid its farewell and the crisp air of autumn ushered in the beginning of a new semester, Bill and Dorothy stood as a power couple, a living testament to the beauty of both heart and mind. In the hallowed halls of Redmond High School, they echoed the aspirations and achievements that marked them as an extraordinary pair.

Bill, a beacon of accomplishment, captained the debate team, was hailed as the baseball player of the year, clinched a silver medal in a swimming competition, and maintained a stellar 4.0 GPA. His dreams of becoming a pilot were already taking flight with an internship at Boeing. His charisma and achievements made him the quintessential high school boy every girl wished to date.

Beside him stood Dorothy, a force of nature in her own right. A member of the science team and debate team, a track runner, and the epitome of beauty that struck like fire, Dorothy embodied brains and beauty harmoniously. Her excellence in academics and her prowess in various activities painted her as the best in her class.

In the hallways of Redmond High School, Bill and Dorothy were an undeniable force, a power couple whose presence radiated with love, intellect, and kindness. Their brilliance made them shine stars, casting a glow that drew admiration and affection from all who crossed their path.

Hand in hand, they embodied an undeniable optimism, a belief that their love was not only unbreakable but had the power to conquer any challenge life might present. Their commitment extended beyond the walls of their school; it was a shared promise to contribute to making the world a better place, infusing every moment with the potent blend of love, intelligence, and kindness.

Their story, etched in the tapestry of Redmond High School, was more than a love affair, it was a testament to the extraordinary heights that love, and compassion could reach. Together, they painted a canvas of dreams and aspirations, a future waiting to be colored by the strokes of their shared journey. As they walked hand in hand, their love was not just a bond between two souls; it was a beacon that illuminated the way for all those touched by their extraordinary presence.

As the fall semester unfolded, Dorothy embraced every opportunity to showcase her brilliance and passion, leaving an indelible mark on the academic landscape of Redmond High School. Her activities were not just a testament to her intellect but also a source of pride for Bill and their families.

Dorothy's participation in the debate team became a defining highlight of the semester. With eloquence that could rival the most seasoned orators, she stood on the stage, a beacon of confidence and intellect. Bill, sitting in the audience, gazed at her with a mix of awe and pride. The auditorium echoed with the sound of her persuasive arguments and articulate expressions, each word a testament to her dedication and prowess.

In the midst of the debate, Bill felt a surge of pride as Dorothy gracefully navigated the intricacies of her arguments. Her intelligence, coupled with a passion for public speaking, illuminated the room. The audience, including Bill's attentive eyes, marveled at her ability to articulate complex ideas with poise and conviction.

When Dorothy delivered her final statement, the auditorium erupted in applause. Bill, standing with pride, joined the thunderous applause, his hands clapping in unison with the audience. His heart swelled with admiration for Dorothy's achievements, and the joy that radiated from his eyes spoke volumes about the depth of their connection.

Dorothy's excellence wasn't confined to the debate stage alone. She continued to shine in the science team, running track with grace and speed that left spectators in awe. Her academic achievements, coupled with her athletic prowess, painted a picture of a well-rounded and exceptional individual.

In the quiet moments between events, Bill stood by Dorothy's side, a steadfast and unwavering pillar of support. Their connection, fortified by shared dreams and mutual respect, served as a source of strength, not just for Dorothy but for both. As the semester unfolded, their bond became more than a witness to success; it became a shared celebration of triumphs and joy.

While Dorothy navigated the challenges of the semester with determination and grace, Bill found himself actively participating in the joy of her success. The applause that echoed through the auditorium after her eloquent debate performances became a symphony of shared achievement. In those moments, Bill's heart swelled with pride, knowing that he was not only witnessing but contributing to Dorothy's accomplishments.

However, the dynamics of their support system weren't one-sided. Bill, a standout in his own right, became a central figure in Redmond High School's sports scene. In every home game, Dorothy's voice rose above the cheers of the crowd, echoing through the entire stadium. "Bill, you got this!" became a rallying cry that Dorothy initiated on stage, and the entire stadium followed suit. The roar of encouragement filled the air, creating an atmosphere of shared excitement and celebration.

Dorothy's unwavering support wasn't just confined to the stands. She moved beyond being a spectator, transforming into Bill's biggest cheerleader and motivator. Her presence added an extra layer of joy and motivation to Bill's high school experience. As he played his heart out on the field, he could feel the collective energy of the stadium, propelled by Dorothy's infectious enthusiasm.

Their love story was interwoven with the fabric of their high school experiences, and as the semester unfolded, Bill found himself savoring every moment of his last year in high school, accompanied by a girlfriend who would move mountains for him. The joy, the cheers, and the shared accomplishments became the building blocks of a memorable journey, a journey that spoke not just of individual success but of the profound impact that love and support could have on one's high school experience.

As the school year reached its triumphant conclusion, the echoes of shared triumphs and joy resonated through the halls of Redmond High School. Bill and Dorothy, inseparable throughout the journey, found themselves standing at the threshold of a memorable chapter that would linger in their hearts long after the cheers and chants of "Bill, you got this!" had faded into the corridors.

With the anticipation of the last prom night hanging in the air, there was no question as to who Bill's companion for this special occasion would be. Dorothy, the steadfast supporter, and love of his life, stood by his side as he prepared to don his best suit. The atmosphere was charged with excitement and the promise of a night to remember.

Bill, dressed in his finest attire, looked at himself in the mirror, a smile playing on his lips. The suit, chosen for this significant night, reflected a sense of both sophistication and celebration. As he adjusted his tie, his gaze shifted to Dorothy, whose eyes sparkled with admiration and love.

Dorothy, radiant in her prom dress, stood with a grace that matched the elegance of the evening. The dress, a canvas of beauty, accentuated her features, and her presence added an extra layer of magic to the moment. The shared anticipation of the night ahead was palpable, a culmination of the highs and lows of the school year.

Hand in hand, Bill and Dorothy made their way to the venue, their steps echoing the rhythm of their shared journey. The prom, a celebration of achievements and camaraderie, awaited them. The soft glow of fairy lights adorned the venue, creating a dreamlike ambiance that mirrored the enchantment of their love story.

As they entered the venue, the music and laughter enveloped them, creating a soundtrack for the final chapter of their high school experience. Bill and Dorothy, their hearts beating in unison, swayed to the music with a sense of shared nostalgia and excitement. The dance floor became a stage where their love story, woven with threads of support and shared dreams, took center stage.

In the moments between twirls and laughter, Bill looked into Dorothy's eyes, a silent exchange of gratitude and love passing between them. The memories of the debates, sports games, and shared triumphs flooded their minds. This last prom night encapsulated not just the end of a school year but the beginning of a new chapter in their lives.

As the night unfolded, Bill and Dorothy created memories that would be etched into the tapestry of their shared history. The echoes of laughter, the gentle sways on the dance floor, and the shared glances spoke of a love that had weathered the challenges of high school and emerged stronger than ever.

As the final notes of the last dance faded away, Bill and Dorothy stood hand in hand, their hearts full, ready to step into the future together. The school year might have come to an end, but their love story was just beginning a narrative of resilience, shared dreams, and the promise of a lifetime of love and companionship.

Graduation

As the valedictorian, Bill stood tall at the pinnacle of academic achievement, a picture of athletic prowess with a body sculpted by discipline and determination. The azure of hope radiated from his eyes, and his posture reflected a self-assuredness that hinted at a clear understanding of his identity and the path he was destined to tread. Graduation day unfolded as a culmination of dreams realized, an occasion that left everyone in awe of Bill's exceptional accomplishments.

Wearing his cap and gown, Bill stood with the confidence of someone who not only knew where he stood but also where he was headed. The scholarship to West Point in his hand symbolized not just an academic achievement but a commitment to a future steeped in purpose and service. The pride in his heart matched the brilliance of the future that lay ahead.

In the midst of the cheering crowd, Dorothy's voice soared above the rest, echoing with unwavering pride and joy for her beloved Bill. Her exuberant shouts reverberated through the stadium, a testament to the shared victories and dreams they had conquered together. As Bill's name was called, Dorothy couldn't contain her excitement, shouting, "You did it!" with infectious enthusiasm, ensuring everyone present shared their joy.

The stadium, a sea of proud families and friends, witnessed this significant milestone in the lives of the graduates. Bill's and Dorothy's families, once separated by distinctions of social class, found unity in the love and dreams of their children. Dorothy's parents and Bill's parents, alongside Bill's younger sisters and Dorothy's brother, stood together, a united front eager to celebrate the remarkable achievement of the young graduate.

As they stood side by side, the boundaries of class and background faded into insignificance. The love and pride emanating from both families were palpable, creating a harmonious blend of old and new, traditional, and contemporary. The air buzzed with shared anticipation and joy, as each family member contributed to the collective celebration of Bill's journey and accomplishments.

The graduation ceremony became a tapestry woven with threads of shared dreams, resilience, and the unbreakable bond between Bill and Dorothy. As they looked towards the future, the unity of their families mirrored the strength of their love, a love that had transcended boundaries and forged a path of its own. The stadium, filled with applause and cheers, bore witness to a moment that went beyond academic success, capturing the essence of unity, pride, and the limitless possibilities that lay ahead for the graduates and their families.

As Bill rushed toward his family and Dorothy, he felt like he was running toward a bright and promising future. Dorothy couldn't wait any longer; she ran to him, leaped into his arms, and Bill, with sheer strength and love, lifted her high off the ground. In that moment of joy and celebration, Dorothy boldly kissed Bill right in front of her parents, surprising everyone and leaving Bill with wide eyes and a nervous glance at her father.

But her father, with a hearty laugh, reassured Bill that it was allowed on such a momentous day. "Only today, son," he quipped, as they all shared a laugh before getting into their cars to head to a special graduation dinner hosted by Dorothy's family in newly open Texas steak house restaurant in downtown Redmond to honor Bill.

During the dinner, the two families chatted, laughed, and enjoyed their time together. The couple had plans for their future, dreams of conquering the skies and diving into the depths of the ocean, and their parents could not be prouder of their smart, purposeful children.

As the evening ended, the families separated, heading to their respective homes. Bill, however, had one more request: he wanted to walk Dorothy home instead of riding with their families. Her father agreed, with one condition: "Do not do anything that you couldn't do in front of us, understand?" Bill replied with a respectful "Yes, sir."

With heartfelt hugs and high-fives exchanged, the cars left them behind as they strolled hand in hand towards home. After a few minutes of walking, Bill gently pulled Dorothy closer, lifted her face towards him, and placed a tender kiss on her lips. They looked into each other's eyes, grateful for this moment and for their shared dreams.

In the warm glow of the evening, Bill and Dorothy shared a moment of profound connection, their dreams intertwining as they discussed the promising future that awaited them. Bill, brimming with happiness, expressed his eagerness for the day when Dorothy would finish high school, marking the beginning of their journey together.

Dorothy, equally proud of Bill's accomplishments, spoke with admiration in her voice, "Bill, you never cease to amaze me. Your star is burning my eyes." Laughter, sweet and genuine, echoed between them, a melody of shared joy and affection. With a loving smile, Dorothy continued, "Simply, I am super proud of you, my darling."

In response to her heartfelt words, Bill sealed the sentiment with a tender kiss, halting her words with the sweetness of their love. The connection between them spoke volumes, a language of shared dreams and unwavering support. With a loving smile, Bill encouraged Dorothy to pursue her dreams, referencing the Titanic, urging her to dive as deep as she desired.

As they neared Dorothy's house, the embrace between them tightened, and Bill confessed his fear of leaving her behind. The vulnerability in his words reflected the depth of his emotions, a testament to the profound impact their love had on his heart. Dorothy, understanding the weight of his sentiments, reassured him with a gentle touch and whispered words of comfort.

The journey toward Dorothy's home took on a magical quality, as if the street they strolled along was a path paved with hope and promises. Bathed in the soft glow of streetlights, the surroundings seemed to conspire with the couple, whispering secrets of love and whispered promises of a future they were eager to embrace.

Hand in hand, Bill and Dorothy walked together, their steps synchronized with the rhythm of their hearts. The world around them faded into the background, leaving only the warmth of their shared journey and the anticipation of the boundless potential their love held. As they approached Dorothy's home, the sense of hope and promise lingered in the air, creating a canvas upon which their love story continued to unfold, painting a picture of a future filled with dreams, shared aspirations, and the enduring strength of their connection.

Their steps were in sync, a tangible reflection of their shared dreams and aspirations. With each stride, the world around them faded into the background, and all that mattered was the connection between them. Their fingers were interlocked, a symbol of their commitment to walk this path of life together, hand in hand.

The cool evening breeze carried the scent of blooming flowers from nearby gardens, creating an enchanting atmosphere around them. The gentle rustling of leaves in the trees overhead provided a soothing backdrop to their conversation.

In the twilight of the evening, Bill, and Dorothy, lost in the cocoon of their love, engaged in heartfelt conversations about their future. Their words echoed with the history of their love and the promises they were making to each other.

Bill, with a dreamy glint in his eyes, pictured himself as a captain flying Boeing planes, with his lovely wife by his side. Dorothy, embodying her spirit of independence and adventure, expressed, "I want to be a co-pilot, not just a wife." A warm embrace followed, sealing their commitment to navigate the journey of life together.

"Dorothy, in this life, you will be my co-pilot each and every day," Bill whispered with sincerity and a twinkle of laughter in his eyes. As they continued their conversation, they delved into every aspect of their shared future. Bill playfully imagined himself as the father of three girls with an amazing wife, while Dorothy envisioned herself as a marine engineer, mother of a son and two daughters, with a handsome husband.

Their words carried the weight of sincerity and the promise of a love that would endure the test of time. They spoke of supporting each other's ambitions, celebrating individual successes, and providing unwavering love and comfort in times of hardship. Each vow strengthened the foundation of their relationship, laying the groundwork for a future filled with shared dreams and aspirations.

Their voices, soft and filled with emotion, created an intimate space where dreams were shared, and promises were made. The street they walked along seemed to shimmer with the energy of their love, as if the very pavement beneath their feet was celebrating the union of two hearts. The houses they passed by stood as silent witnesses to their love story, their windows radiating warmth that mirrored the love emanating from Bill and Dorothy's hearts.

As they continued their walk, the world outside faded away, leaving only the two of them immersed in the magic of their affection. Time stood still, allowing them to savor every moment of this shared journey.

Their walk home wasn't just a physical journey; it was a journey of the heart, a testament to their love, shared dreams, and unbreakable bond. With each step, they solidified their commitment to each other, promising to be there through all of life's twists and turns. The night, adorned with the soft glow of streetlights, witnessed the unfolding of a love story that transcended time, leaving an indelible mark on the canvas of their shared history.

By the time they reached Dorothy's home, they felt like they had embarked on a new chapter of their lives, one filled with love, hope, and the unwavering promise to be there for each other, now and always. Their love story had taken root, and as they stood at the doorstep, they knew that their journey together had only just begun.

In a heartwarming exchange filled with promises and love, Bill and Dorothy pledged to support each other's dreams and remain committed to their shared journey. Standing at the threshold of Dorothy's house, Bill, with a mischievous twinkle in his eyes, almost touched the doorbell before turning to her with a spontaneous idea.

"Do you want to go for a road trip to Mount Rainier, the most beautiful mountain in Washington, a snow gem of the land?" he asked, his enthusiasm palpable. Dorothy, wrapping her arms around him in a tight hug, looked into his eyes and replied, "I would love to. Will you let me drive?"

Bill chuckled, "Not quite yet, but as your co-driver, yes, I will let you drive as long as you follow the rules." A sweet kiss on her forehead sealed the agreement. With a shared laugh, Bill pressed the doorbell, and Dorothy's mother warmly welcomed him into their home.

As Dorothy entered her house, she promised to visit Bill the next day for driving lessons, ensuring that they could spend more precious time together. The anticipation of new adventures and shared experiences added an extra layer of excitement to their love story.

With a final wave and a heart filled with love and gratitude, Bill walked away from Dorothy's house. The glow of the streetlights seemed to echo the warmth in his heart, knowing that their love was a treasure worth cherishing, and their futures were intricately intertwined. Each step away from the door marked the beginning of a new chapter, where the road ahead held the promise of countless adventures, shared laughter, and a love that would only grow stronger with time.

Ride With Me

Bill and Dorothy's love had deepened after graduation, growing into something that felt both profound and eternal. As they embarked on a road trip, leaving behind the familiar streets of Redmond, they carried their love with them like a cherished treasure.

The beauty of the state of Washington unfolded before them, a panorama of stunning landscapes and rolling hills. Dorothy navigated the winding roads with a sense of awe, her eyes taking in the rolling hills, lush forests, and picturesque lakes that stretched out before them.

Bill gazed out of the window, his heart swelling with gratitude for the beauty of the world around him and the woman beside him. He turned to Dorothy, his eyes filled with adoration, and expressed the sentiment that had been brewing in his heart: that perhaps Washington had received a special touch from God, an extra dose of beauty and wonder that made it unique. "I bet Washington is the most beautiful place in the world."

Dorothy smiled at his words; her heart warmed by the depth of his observation. She knew that Bill had a way of finding beauty in the everyday, in the grandeur of nature and in the simplicity of a shared moment. His appreciation for life's wonders resonated deeply with her.

As the wheels of their journey turned, the idyllic road trip to Mount Rainier took an unexpected turn. Bill, seated with the map in hand, diligently studied the directions, his focus intent on navigating the way. On the other hand, Dorothy, behind the wheel, seemed carefree and less inclined to listen to the plotted course.

Their young love was woven with moments of misunderstanding, and this journey was no exception. Dorothy, uninterested in the map, was more driven by her instincts, often leading to divergent routes that challenged Bill's sense of direction. The car became a battlefield of differing opinions, and the clash of perspectives soon escalated into their first real argument.

As the tension filled the car, Dorothy's inability to conceal her feelings added fuel to the flames. Bill, recognizing the fragility of the moment, assumed the role of a mediator, attempting to control the situation. Their bickering showcased the common struggles faced by many young couples, grappling with communication barriers and the art of compromise.

In this disagreement over driving, they confronted the reality of their differences, and the emotional depth of their connection was laid bare. However, in the midst of the heated exchange, a resilient undercurrent of love and understanding emerged. They navigated through the storm of anger, finding the strength to forgive and empathize with each other.

This moment of discord became a pivotal steppingstone in their relationship, a lesson in growth, resilience, and the importance of effective communication. Their ability to reconcile and move forward marked a milestone in their journey, strengthening the foundation of their love.

As they continued their road trip, the landscape around them seemed to mirror the emotional terrain they had just traversed. The mountains ahead stood as silent witnesses to the ebbs and flows of their relationship. The car, once a battleground, transformed into a sanctuary where forgiveness and understanding prevailed.

Their shared laughter and playful banter allowed them to recover from the argument quickly. Bill's lighthearted notetaking during their argument and Dorothy's witty retort spoke volumes about their ability to find joy in even the most challenging moments. Their relationship was marked by a sense of playfulness and a shared desire to navigate life's ups and downs as a team.

Their road trip took them to the majestic Mount Rainier. As they hiked the trails, hand in hand, they felt the unity of their spirits, strengthening their connection.

As the sun began its descent, casting a warm glow over the landscape, Bill and Dorothy knew that their journey was not just about the road trip itself. It was about the journey of their hearts, the road they had walked together, and the road that lay ahead. They understood that relationship was not just about grand gestures but also about the willingness to navigate the twists and turns of life together.

Bill's gaze never wavered from Dorothy, his eyes tracing the contours of her face, etching the memory of her beauty into his heart. He felt a fondness for her like a river flowing through his veins, and he could not imagine his life without her by his side.

The sun began its gentle descent, casting a warm golden glow over the landscape as Bill and Dorothy embarked on their journey back to Redmond, Washington. The road ahead held the promise of both adventure and challenge, a metaphorical path mirroring the twists and turns of their relationship.

In a playful exchange of keys, Dorothy, with a smile that sparkled in the fading sunlight, took the reins of the car. The vehicle, a vessel of their shared dreams, hummed with the anticipation of the future, and the rhythmic beating of their hearts echoed in tandem with the road beneath them.

Dorothy, embracing the thrill of the open road, couldn't resist the temptation to press the pedal a little harder, making the car glide down the highway at a speed that made Bill uneasy. The wind, a playful accomplice, rushed through the open windows, tousling their hair, and the surrounding landscape became a vibrant blur of colors.

However, Bill, with a strong sense of responsibility, recognized the importance of adhering to speed limits for the safety of the road. He gently requested Dorothy to slow down, concern evident in his voice, but she responded with mischievous defiance, laughter filling the car as she continued to revel in the exhilarating speed.

For the first time in their relationship, a crack appeared in the facade of their tender love. Bill's patience wore thin as the tension simmered between them. His voice, once gentle, took on a firmer tone as he raised his concern again. Dorothy, thinking it was a game, playfully disregarded his words.

As the miles passed, the tension escalated into a heated argument. Bill, feeling a responsibility to protect them both, raised his voice, demanding that Dorothy pull over and let him drive. "For God's sake, Dorothy, can you slow down?" he yelled, the urgency evident in his tone. However, Dorothy, her stubbornness doubling down, chose to stop the car in the middle of the road.

Without a word, she stepped out of the car, the fading sunlight casting a glow on her silhouette as she began to walk along the side of the road. Bill, left in the vehicle, watched her with a heavy heart, a mix of worry and regret settling in. This argument, escalating beyond their control, unfolded in the quiet hum of the car's engine.

Bill, his pleas growing louder, followed her slowly with the car, begging her to come back. The reality of their fight was palpable in the fading light, a poignant moment where love and frustration collided. The road, once a symbol of shared journeys, now stretched before them as a challenging path, and the echoes of their heated exchange lingered in the air.

For almost 30 minutes, she walked in silence, their hearts heavy with the weight of their disagreement. The world around them seemed to fade away as they navigated the distance that had unexpectedly grown between them. The road felt longer, the silence more profound, and the landscape that had once held such beauty now seemed devoid of color.

Finally, Dorothy stopped walking and sat down by the side of the road. Bill pulled over and joined her, the urgency in his heart driving him to apologize. He looked into her eyes, the depth of his love reflected in his gaze, and said, "Darling, I'm so sorry. I'll never, ever yell at you again."

As the sun dipped below the horizon, casting a warm glow over the landscape, Bill and Dorothy found themselves still sitting on the roadside, surrounded by the beauty of nature. The soft sounds of passing cars hummed in the background, creating a gentle melody to accompany their tender moment.

Dorothy's eyes, initially filled with frustration, softened as she took in the serene surroundings. The anger that had gripped her heart began to melt away, but she remained steadfast in her desire for mutual respect in their relationship. In a voice that carried both vulnerability and strength, she expressed, "We have to learn how to fight."

Bill, realizing the weight of his actions, responded quickly, "I promise to be better. We'll learn together; we have a whole life ahead of us." Dorothy's features softened further, and a small, forgiving smile graced her lips. In that moment, they both understood the importance of growth and learning from their conflicts.

Embracing each other, their hearts sought solace in the warmth of their connection. With a playful tone, Bill reached into his pocket and pulled out a notebook. Chuckling, he told Dorothy that he was going to write down this moment as their first fight, a reminder of the challenges they had faced and overcome together.

"We've had so many arguments, but this is our first fight," he said with a hint of humor. Their laughter, like a soothing melody, mingled with the soft breeze, creating a symphony of love, and understanding. The world around them, bathed in the hues of the setting sun, seemed to come alive once more, echoing the resilience of their tender relationship.

As the sun dipped lower on the horizon, bathing them in a warm, golden glow, Bill and Dorothy knew that love was not just about the smooth roads but also about navigating the occasional bumps and detours with understanding and forgiveness. Their love, forged in the fires of passion and evaluated by the trials of the road, was stronger than ever, and they embraced each other with a renewed sense of devotion, their hearts entwined in a love that could weather any storm.

Approaching Redmond's city speed limits, Bill stole a glance at Dorothy, his heart heavy with regret. He knew he needed to make things right. With a sigh, he promised her, "Dorothy, that fight was a mistake, and I promise you, it will be our first and our last. Those thirty minutes of you not wanting to talk to me felt like thirty years."

Dorothy turned her gaze toward him, her eyes dancing with a hint of mischief. She could not help but find humor in their situation. "Bill," she said with a playful smile, "I can't guarantee that we won't have disagreements in the future, but what I can promise is that I'll learn how to fight with you." Her voice filled with warmth as she continued, "Fighting is a normal part of any relationship, but the real key is learning how to forgive, forget, and truly understand the reasons behind our disagreements. That's what will make us last forever."

Bill could not help but be enchanted by her wisdom, her intelligence shining through even in the midst of their first disagreement. He marveled at her maturity, which seemed far beyond her tender age. "You're so incredibly mature," he whispered, his admiration for her overflowing. They locked their eyes, sharing a moment of profound gratitude for each other, as the weight of their disagreement lifted, leaving behind a deeper understanding and an even stronger connection between them.

The Ring

As Bill stood on the brink of a new chapter in his life, two days away from departing for the East Coast to embark on his college journey, a mix of emotions surged through his heart. The unknown future lay before him, but it was a single, profound desire that occupied his thoughts, the longing to make a commitment that would echo the depths of his love for Dorothy.

In the quiet moments of introspection, his heart swelled with intense enthusiasm. The idea of expressing his devotion to Dorothy filled him with a sense of purpose and meaning. The values instilled in him by his parents, the essence of responsibility and compassion, now sought a tangible form in this commitment to the woman who had captured his heart.

He couldn't shake the tender, unknown feeling deep inside a blend of excitement and anticipation, a poignant awareness that he was about to take a step that would forever bind their destinies together. His mind replayed the shared laughter, the whispered promises, and the challenges they had faced as a couple. It was a journey they had undertaken hand in hand, and now, he was ready to solidify their connection in a way that transcended the physical distance that awaited them.

Bill sought the counsel of his best friends, Mike, and John, sharing the sentiments swirling within him. They, too, had been witnesses to the blossoming of his relationship with Dorothy, and they encouraged him to seize the moment. Their advice echoed in his mind, fueling his determination to make this commitment before embarking on the next chapter of his life.

As he contemplated the impending departure, Bill's heart brimmed not just with the excitement of college adventures but with a deep-seated passion to make Dorothy a central part of his journey. The East Coast held the promise of new beginnings, but in his heart, he carried the promise he was about to make, a testament to the enduring love that would bridge the miles and bind their hearts together across the expanse of time and space.

Each moment he spent with her felt like a precious gem in the mosaic of his life, and he could not bear the thought of leaving her without expressing how much he loved her. The very idea of being apart from her, even temporarily, tugged at his soul.

Bill knew that love was more than words; it was a commitment to stand by each other through life's twists and turns. It was a promise to be there, no matter the miles that separated them, to be the steady anchor in each other's lives. And so, with a heart brimming with tenderness and a deep, unwavering love for Dorothy, he felt the time was ripe to take the next step in their journey together.

Bill approached his parents, explaining his intentions of wanting to marry Dorothy. He knew that he might not be financially ready, but he also understood the value of showing his unwavering commitment to her. The idea of being separated by miles and miles, with Bill heading to the East Coast for his education while Dorothy remained on the West Coast, filled him with worry. He feared that without a formal commitment, the distance might open the door for someone else to win her heart.

Bill's parents, understanding the depth of his emotions, asked how they could assist him in this important step. His mother, with a warm smile, agreed to buy him a ring, a symbol of their love. But his father, wise and supportive, advised Bill to take one more step before purchasing the ring. He suggested that Bill speak to Dorothy's parents and ask for their blessing. If they gave their approval, then he would buy the ring.

In a moment of honor and pride, Bill, fueled by determination, seized the opportunity to make a meaningful commitment to Dorothy. With a smile lighting up his face, he extended his hand, and Bill's father, with a silent understanding, tossed the newly acquired open-roof Benz key into the air. It arced gracefully before landing securely in Bill's waiting hand. There was no need for words; the look in his father's eyes spoke volumes go get the love of your life.

Embracing the symbolism of the moment, Bill hopped onto the sleek new car, the engine humming with anticipation. The open road beckoned, and with each second, he propelled himself forward with a sense of urgency to reach Dorothy's house.

Upon arrival, he found Dorothy's father in the front yard, a man he had respected for years. Bill, with a mixture of nervousness and sincerity, greeted him with a firm handshake. This encounter marked a significant moment of transition, a shift from the boy who once sought approval to the man ready to stand as an equal.

For the first time, Bill looked directly into the eyes of the man who had played a crucial role in Dorothy's life. Man to man, without fear and with a voice that carried the weight of conviction, Bill began to pour out his heart. The spoke of his deep love for Dorothy, the woman who had become the center of his world. He explained how, in just two days, he would be heading off to West Point, leaving behind the love of his life.

With genuine sincerity, Bill expressed that, for the past years, he and Dorothy's father had stood as two men, their hearts imprinted with the love they shared for Dorothy. The words carried the resonance of commitment and honor, a pledge that transcended the passage of time and the distance that would soon separate them. In this moment of vulnerability and authenticity, Bill sought not just approval but the blessing of a man who understood the depth of his love for Dorothy.

Dorothy's father, a wise and caring man himself, looked into Bill's eyes. He saw the sincerity and love in this young man's heart. With a smile that spoke of understanding and acceptance, he extended his hand to Bill and shook it firmly. He told him that he would be honored to have him as a son-in-law.

Bill, filled with gratitude and joy, asked Dorothy's father to keep this conversation a secret from Dorothy for now. He wanted to surprise her with his intentions. With a heart full of hope and a smile on his face, Bill drove back home, knowing that he had just taken a significant step towards a future with the love of his life.

Later that day, Bill and his father drove to Seattle downtown, to carefully select a beautiful ring for Dorothy.

As Bill and his father walked into the jewelry store in downtown Seattle, the gleaming showcases held a dazzling array of rings, each one vying for attention with its unique sparkle and design. They were on a mission to find the perfect ring that would symbolize Bill's unwavering love and commitment to Dorothy.

After a few minutes of exploring the various options, a particular ring in a velvet-lined tray captured Bill's attention. It wasn't the largest or the most ornate ring in the store, but there was something about it that drew him in. It was a ring with a simple, timeless elegance that seemed to embody the essence of and beauty of his lovely Dorothy.

The ring featured a delicate band made of white gold; its shimmering surface caught the soft store lights. It held a single, brilliant-cut diamond at its center, surrounded by smaller accent diamonds that gracefully extended down the sides of the band. The central diamond was a masterpiece of nature, with its facets expertly cut to maximize its brilliance. It radiated a pure and timeless beauty, much like his beloved Dorothy.

What made this ring truly unique, however, was the setting. It wasn't the traditional prong setting that you often see. Instead, the diamond was nestled within a vintage-inspired bezel setting, which gave the ring a distinct character and a touch of old-world charm. The bezel not only secured the diamond but also seemed to cradle it, symbolizing Bill's desire to protect and cherish Dorothy for all time.

Bill could not take his eyes off the ring. Its uniqueness and the feelings it evoked in him made it the perfect choice. It spoke of their love, one that was classic, enduring, and surrounded by a sense of timeless elegance.

Yet, as he held the ring in his hand, Bill could not help but feel a mixture of excitement and trepidation. He knew that the moment he would propose to Dorothy would be one of the most significant in his life. He wondered if she would say yes if she would accept this symbol of his commitment and love. Bill couldn't escape the fear that lurked within him, the fear of the unknown, the fear of her response.

But amidst the fear, there was also a deep well of hope. He believed in the love they shared, a love that had grown over three precious years. And as he looked at that ring, he knew that it represented not only his love but also his dreams and aspirations for their shared future.

With the ring securely in its box, Bill and his father left the jewelry store. Bill began to plan for the upcoming days where he hoped to present this symbol of his love to Dorothy, the woman who had captured his heart so completely.

Ready To Board

As the two days slipped through his fingers like sand, Bill found himself grappling with the weight of the ring in his pocket and the fear that nestled in the corners of his mind. The question he longed to ask Dorothy hovered on the tip of his tongue, yet the fear of her response paralyzed him. In the quiet moments, he wished for more time in Redmond, a sanctuary where he could prolong the inevitable departure and the uncertainties that lay ahead.

Bill meticulously painted pictures of the perfect moment the words he would speak, the expression on Dorothy's face, the joy that would envelop them both. But when the decisive moment arrived, his lips seemed to betray him, unable to articulate the sentiments that swirled within his heart. Time, elusive and relentless, marched forward, leaving Bill in a state of contemplation and indecision.

The day of departure came, and his family drove him to the airport, the ring a silent companion in his pocket, holding the weight of unspoken intentions. Each passing moment brought him closer to the reality of leaving everything he knew and loved behind.

Despite his inner turmoil, Bill clung to the hope that perhaps, at the airport, he could summon the courage to express his feelings to Dorothy.

Unknown to Bill, Dorothy had requested her father to take her to the airport, eager for a chance to say a final goodbye to him. When Bill and his family arrived at the airport, there she was, perched on top of her father's car, a beacon of anticipation and love, waiting for the moment when their worlds would collide one last time before the departure. The airport, a place of comings and goings, held within its walls the crossroads of fate for Bill and Dorothy, where a single question had the power to shape the course of their shared future.

As Bill prepared to embark on his journey, there was a bittersweet aura enveloping the day. The air was thick with a mix of emotions in anticipation of the bright future Bill was about to embrace, and the somber realization that his absence would leave an undeniable void in the lives of those who loved him.

His sisters clung to him tightly, tears glistening in their eyes as they whispered their love and farewells. In the midst of their sorrow, Bill, always the caring big brother, reassured them with words of comfort. He reminded them that this departure was just a chapter, and his heart would always be connected to theirs, no matter the physical distance.

And then, there was Dorothy, standing by her father's car, a beacon of light amid the tearful goodbyes. Bill's heart skipped a beat as he rushed towards her, his arms opening wide to envelop her in a warm and passionate hug. In that embrace, he sought solace, finding comfort in the familiarity of her presence.

Amidst the chaotic symphony of farewells, Bill and Dorothy shared a moment that transcended words. Their embrace spoke volumes, a silent exchange of love, assurance, and the promise that their connection would endure the challenges of distance. As Bill held Dorothy close, he couldn't bear the thought of leaving without imprinting the memory of her warmth on his heart. The hug was a testament to the profound love they shared, a love that could withstand the test of time and miles.

Dorothy handed him a notebook, a treasure trove of love. It contained letters, poems, and heartfelt messages that she had poured her heart into, a tangible piece of her that he could carry with him. "Whenever you miss me," she said softly, "open it and read, my voice will be in your ears." Bill's eyes glistened with tears of love for this extraordinary woman in his life.

But the most significant moment was yet to come. As their parents watched, a circle of love surrounding them, Bill knelt before Dorothy, the woman who had captured his heart completely. His voice trembled with emotion as he poured out his feelings, the words of a promise and commitment that would shape their future together.

"Dorothy, you have been my friend, my confidante, my darling. Yet it's not enough for me. I want you to be mine, and only mine, Dorothy. My love, will you marry me, please?"

Dorothy's eyes glistened with tears; her heart filled with love of their shared future. She looked at her parents, who nodded in approval, their eyes brimming with joy. Then, her gaze fell upon Bill, who remained on one knee, waiting for her answer.

"I will always be yours, forever and ever," she whispered, her voice filled with love and a deep sense of commitment. "Yes, I will marry you, darling."

Ecstasy coursed through Bill's veins as he leaped to his feet, his joy echoing through the terminal. He turned toward his parents, shouting with unbridled enthusiasm, "She said yes! She said yes!" It was a moment of pure elation, a celebration of love that filled the airport with warmth and hope.

As swiftly as the euphoria of celebration had enveloped them, the harsh reality of departure descended upon Bill. The security gate stood as a somber threshold, marking the inevitable separation. With tear-streaked cheeks, Bill walked away from the woman he had just pledged his future to. Though his heart was heavy with the weight of parting, he carried his head high, fueled by the unwavering promise of a shared tomorrow. In a poignant farewell, he waved to Dorothy, who stood there, her heart aching with love, watching her beloved disappear into the sea of departing travelers. The bustling crowd swallowed Bill, leaving Dorothy with a mix of emotions and an emptiness that echoed in her soul.

Recognizing the depth of Dorothy's longing, her father approached and wordlessly offered his support. He guided her toward the car, understanding that this moment marked not just a departure, but the beginning of a journey filled with yearning. Sarah, Dorothy's friend, approached the car and gently suggested that they ride together. With a nod and a soft smile, Dorothy's father welcomed the idea, knowing that a special dinner awaited them at home.

As Sarah embraced Dorothy tenderly, she conveyed a sense of belonging, welcoming her into the familial fold. Amidst the bittersweet parting, she extended an invitation for dinner, a gesture meant to soften the edges of the emotional turbulence. Dorothy, still gazing at the fading figures in the distance, accepted the offer. The car, now carrying a medley of emotions, pulled away from the airport, leaving behind the echoes of tearful goodbyes and carrying with it the anticipation of a heartfelt reunion. The journey home became a bridge between the pain of separation and the solace of shared moments with those who understood the ache of love left behind.

The Smith household radiated warmth and joy, infused with the festive spirit of the celebration they had prepared for Dorothy. As she stepped into the house, the air was filled with the comforting scent of home-cooked meals and the inviting glow of carefully arranged decorations. The walls echoed with laughter and the clinking of utensils, creating an atmosphere that embraced Dorothy like a familiar hug.

Festive decorations adorned the living room, reflecting the Smith family's excitement and enthusiasm for the special occasion. Colorful streamers hung gracefully, and soft fairy lights twinkled, casting a gentle glow on the walls. The scent of fresh flowers wafted through the air, adding a touch of nature's beauty to the festivities.

The dining table was a masterpiece, meticulously set with elegant China, gleaming silverware, and crystal-clear glasses. Each place setting was a testament to the care and consideration that went into welcoming Dorothy into their family. The table centerpiece, however, left an intentional void, a symbolic acknowledgment of Bill's absence. A framed picture of Bill smiling warmly served as a poignant reminder of his presence in spirit.

Sarah, Bill's sister, had taken it upon herself to ensure that the evening unfolded seamlessly. She and Dorothy shared a camaraderie that extended beyond the realms of sisterhood. Together, they laughed and chatted as they arranged the table, their bond evident in the joyful atmosphere they created. The house, with its inviting ambiance and thoughtful details, embraced Dorothy, making her feel not just welcomed but cherished.

As the dinner progressed, the atmosphere was filled with love, laughter, and heartfelt conversations. The Smiths family and Dorothy's parents shared stories of Bill, highlighting his remarkable journey from childhood to the remarkable young man he had become. They spoke of his dreams, his unwavering determination, and the love he held in his heart for Dorothy.

Sarah, with a twinkle in her eye, could not resist sharing some of Bill's quirks and childhood anecdotes, eliciting laughter from the entire table. It was clear that they cherished Bill, and their shared stories were a testament to the profound impact he had on their lives.

The conversation flowed effortlessly, and the room was filled with joy and a sense of togetherness. Dorothy sat among them, feeling the warmth of their embrace, not just as Bill's girlfriend, but as a cherished member of this extended family. It was a love that extended far beyond the confines of a romantic relationship; it was a love that embraced her with open arms and enveloped her heart.

As the evening continued, Dorothy realized that this love was not solely about Bill and her. It was a love that transcended their individual lives, a love that had the power to bring two families together. She felt grateful for the acceptance and love she had found in this remarkable union of hearts.

The dinner became a beautiful symphony of love, laughter, and acceptance. It was a celebration of not just Bill and Dorothy's love, but also the love that had woven their families together, a love that would continue to grow and flourish as they embarked on this new journey as one united and loving family.

Love Letters

In the tender threads of letters exchanged, Bill and Dorothy's love flourished with a depth and uniqueness that only distance could inspire. The words they wrote held the weight of their longing and the promise of their future together. Each letter was a testament to the unbreakable connection they shared, despite the miles that separated them.

Bill's letters were like windows to his new world on the East Coast. He described the unfamiliar surroundings, the distinct accents, and the subtle differences in cuisine. He confided in Dorothy about the challenges he faced, but he also shared the victories and successes that came his way. Every word he wrote was infused with his unwavering commitment to her and their shared dreams.

Dorothy eagerly awaited each letter, finding solace in the fact that no matter the distance, their love remained steadfast. On a serene Sunday evening, she ventured to Marymoor Park with Bill's cherished picnic basket, a symbol of their shared memories. As she read his latest letter, her heart swelled with a mixture of joy and longing.

Bill's words painted a picture of their future together, a house by the lake where their love had bloomed, a promise of success and a life filled with shared dreams.

My Dearest Dorothy,

With every passing day, the anticipation of reading your latest letter has filled my heart with uncontainable joy. The thought of returning to you, the love of my life and the keeper of my dreams, has been my guiding light, propelling me forward even when the days of training grow tougher, and the intensity of my classes seems insurmountable. Knowing that you are patiently waiting for me, my love, that is the beacon of hope that ignites my spirit.

As I immerse myself in the rhythm of life on the East Coast, the accents and the slogans of this place never fail to bring a smile to my face. It's different from our beloved Pacific Northwest, but it's a delightful change. And oh, my darling, I have a confession to make – I think I'm falling in love with bagels. Yes, the very ones I used to scoff at. A touch of cream cheese makes them a heavenly delight. Yet, I must admit, nothing here compares to the taste of our home's smoked salmon. I've tried it, but it simply doesn't hold a candle to the flavors we know so well. But enough of my trivial grumblings; I ought to count my blessings.

Now, my love, let's shift the focus back to you. How is your schooling going? What's new in your world? I yearn to hear about your adventures and the moments that have painted the canvas of your life since we last spoke.

Darling, I must bring this letter to a close for now, but rest assured, my thoughts and love are always with you. I promise to write to you very soon, my light, my love, and the mother of our future children.

Yours, now and forever,
Bill

Dorothy's smiled, she felt his presence in his words, as if he was right beside her, whispering sweet nothings in her ear.

With pen in hand, Dorothy poured her own feelings onto the paper. She shared the challenges of her last semester of high school, her brave leap into drama class, and her unwavering dedication to her studies. But beneath her words lay the ever-present feeling of longing, the anticipation of the day they could finally be together.

The exchange of letters wasn't just about keeping each other updated on their lives; it was a declaration of their love, a reminder of the promises they held, and an affirmation of their unbreakable bond. Dorothy's words carried the essence of her heart, assuring Bill that he was the only one who would ever touch her lips, the only one who would ever possess her love.

My darling future husband,

As I sit here beneath the azure skies of our beloved Washington state, I cannot help but feel the depth of my love for you. The birds serenade me with their sweet melodies, but their songs only serve to remind me of your voice, which is the sweetest music to my ears. With every note they sing, I am transported to our shared moments, where your laughter is my favorite symphony, and your whispered promises are my cherished lullaby.

The gentle caress of the breeze on my skin is a fleeting reminder of your touch, which I crave with an intensity that words can scarcely express. I long for the warmth of your embrace, the reassuring strength of your arms around me, and the tender love that envelops us when we are together. Every gust of wind that brushes against my face carries with it a whisper of your name, and in those moments, I feel your presence beside me.

The vibrant colors of the flowers surrounding me pale in comparison to the kaleidoscope of emotions you evoke within me. You have painted my world with the hues of love, passion, and devotion. Each petal that dances in the wind is a reminder of the delicate beauty of our love, and how it blooms with every passing day.

future husband, I am the luckiest girl in the world to have you in my life. Your love has become the very air I breathe, the heartbeat of my existence. Every day without you feels incomplete, like a beautiful melody missing its final note. But even in your absence, I am filled with an overwhelming sense of gratitude for the love we share.

Please, take care of yourself, my love. Your safety is my utmost concern, and I eagerly await the day when you return to me, whole and unharmed. Our love is a flame that burns eternally, and distance can never diminish its intensity.

Until that day arrives, know that I am thinking of you with every beat of my heart, with every breath I take. I am counting down the moments until we are reunited, and I can hold you close once more.

Your future wife is waiting for you, my love, with open arms and an even more open heart. Until then, please carry my love with you, as I carry yours with me, always.

Forever yours,

Dorothy

As the sun descended in the western sky, casting its golden embrace over the world, Dorothy's heart was aglow with warmth and love. With her treasured letter safely sealed and tucked away, she felt as if her emotions were carried on the very breeze that brushed against her skin.

Mounted on her trusty bicycle, Dorothy rode along the familiar path with a radiant smile gracing her lips. The basket, which had held their picnic delights, now rested by her side, a silent witness to the affectionate exchange that had taken place during her solitary sojourn.

The gentle cadence of her pedaling mirrored the rhythm of her heart, which beat with a lightness that defied the distance separating her from her beloved. With every turn of the wheels, she carried with her the memories of their shared moments, the laughter that echoed through the park, and the sweet promises of a future together.

The world around her seemed to shimmer with a newfound beauty, as if nature itself celebrated their love. The trees whispered their secrets in the wind, and the flowers, bathed in the warm, golden light, nodded in approval. Dorothy felt as though the entire universe conspired to remind her of the love that bloomed within her heart.

With each passing moment, she was drawn deeper into the cocoon of their affection, a place where time and space held no dominion. It was a love that transcended distance and defied separation, one that only grew stronger with every passing day.

As she approached her home, the familiar sights and sounds of her surroundings took on a new significance. The chirping of the birds, the rustling of leaves in the gentle breeze, and the fragrance of blooming flowers all whispered tales of love and longing. Dorothy knew that she carried a piece of her heart within her, a heart forever entwined with her future husband's.

With a sense of contentment and anticipation, she knew that no matter how vast the physical distance that separated them, their love was a bridge that spanned any gap. As she parked her bicycle and made her way inside, she held onto the smile that adorned her face, a radiant testament to the enduring power of their love, which thrived despite the miles that lay between them.

Sarah & Dorothy

In the enchanting realm of their friendship, Sarah and Dorothy discovered a connection that went beyond the typical sister-in-law dynamic. With Bill immersed in his studies and physical distance separating them, their bond evolved into something truly magical. The absence of Bill, rather than creating a void, became the catalyst for a profound connection between these two women.

As they navigated the ups and downs of life, Sarah found in Dorothy not just a sister-in-law but a kindred spirit, a confidante who understood the nuances of their shared experiences. Their conversations became a sanctuary where they could freely express their thoughts, dreams, and fears. Whether seated at the dining table, surrounded by the warmth of family, or in the quiet corners of the house, their talks were filled with laughter, shared secrets, and the unspoken understanding of missing someone they both held dear.

Dorothy, with her wisdom and kindness, became a source of support for Sarah. The bond they shared wasn't just about their mutual love for Bill; it was a friendship built on genuine affection and shared moments. Dorothy's presence brought a unique joy and comfort to Sarah's life, making her feel understood and valued in a way that transcended the familial ties.

Their friendship wasn't bound by the physical proximity of Bill; instead, it blossomed independently, creating a space where Sarah and Dorothy could celebrate, commiserate, and navigate the complexities of life together. In the tapestry of their connection, the threads of sisterhood, friendship, and shared love for Bill intricately wove a bond that added depth and richness to their lives.

Despite the physical absence of Bill, Dorothy never felt lonely. Sarah's presence filled any void, and their days were painted with the colors of harmonious togetherness school lessons, shared homework sessions, and seamless transitions between their two families. It was as if the two households had merged into one, and they reveled in the warmth and unity it brought.

Dorothy hailed from a family of old money, renowned for their globe-trotting adventures. They embarked on journeys to far-flung corners of the world, and when the opportunity arose, Dorothy approached her father with an idea that would forever etch a memory into Sarah's heart a graduation gift of unparalleled magnificence. She proposed that Sarah join them on their upcoming Serengeti safari tour.

To Dorothy's delight, her father readily agreed to the plan, recognizing the immense value of such an experience. The mere thought of witnessing thousands of magnificent creatures roaming freely in the Serengeti filled Sarah with uncontainable excitement.

One evening, while dining with Bill's family in their cozy home, Dorothy couldn't keep her thrilling secret any longer. A radiant smile graced her face as she shared the exhilarating news of her father's generous gift. Sarah's joyful exclamation filled the room, reverberating off the walls.

Overwhelmed with gratitude and emotion, Sarah stammered, "You know, Bill may not always get everything right, but choosing you is the best thing he's ever done." Laughter filled the air, a harmonious symphony of joy, and they continued to savor their dinner together.

Their conversation danced around the topic of their upcoming graduation plans; from the cuisine they would indulge into the dress code they would follow. During it all, they schemed gleefully about how to surprise Bill upon his return for their graduation party.

Their birdwatching expeditions by the lake became a cherished tradition. On sunny mornings, they would pack a picnic basket with sandwiches, fruits, and lemonade, and head to their favorite spot by the water. The lake, with its shimmering surface, was a sanctuary of serenity, where the songs of birds intertwined with their own laughter and conversations.

Dorothy's stories about Bill, his passion for birds, and the tender moments they had shared at this very lake wove a beautiful tapestry of memories for Sarah. As she learned more about Bill through Dorothy's anecdotes, Sarah's admiration for her brother grew, and she could not wait for the day he would return home.

One brisk morning, as they sat by the lake, sipping hot cocoa from thermos flasks, Sarah turned to Dorothy with a twinkle in her eye. "You know, Dorothy, you and Bill are so alike in some ways. "Your love for birds, for instance."

Dorothy nodded, a fond smile gracing her lips. "Yes, Sarah, Bill and I share many interests. But more importantly, we share the same love for the people in our lives, especially those we consider family."

Their hearts warmed in the crisp morning air as they discussed their shared love for Bill and their plans for his return. They couldn't wait to welcome him back with open arms and share all the beautiful memories they had created in his absence.

Dorothy became Sarah's confidante in matters of the heart and advice on life's complexities. Together, they navigated the joys and challenges of their teenage years, their friendship providing a steadfast anchor in the ever-changing sea of adolescence.

With each passing day, their connection grew deeper, their friendship stronger, and their hearts more intertwined. The enchanting realm of their friendship had evolved into a sanctuary of unwavering support, shared dreams, and a love that transcended time and distance.

With just two days left before the eagerly anticipated graduation ceremony, a letter arrived for Dorothy. She reclined on Sarah's bed; the room filled with the soft glow of evening sunlight and began to read the heartfelt words of her fiancé. Sarah, playfully seizing the letter from Dorothy's hands, read it aloud with great enthusiasm, each word resonating with the shared excitement that bound them together. In that moment, as they basked in the warm embrace of their friendship, they could not help but feel that life had graced them with something truly beautiful and precious.

"To my dearest soon-to-be wife,

As I pen this letter, my heart races, and my hand trembles. But my heart is resolute in pouring my love onto this page. I trust you are well; here, everything is going as planned. Training has been rigorous, but my instructor has faith in me. Last week, I soared solo for the first time with a mix of anxiety and exhilaration. I know I'm in capable hands, and God watches over me. I can't wait to share more when I'm at your graduation.

I've been granted just four days in Washington, brief but delightful. I yearn to see you, my love. How's Sarah? Don't let her steal you away from me. She wrote to me last week; in short, my sister adores you. She told me about your Africa trip. I'm eager to hear all about it upon your return.

Darling, I miss you beyond words. Your last letter gave me strength and a daily reason to smile. Farewell

for now, see you soon."

Yours and only your love Bill

Dorothy laughed and reclaimed her letter from Sarah. "Your brother is truly remarkable. I adore him," she declared. Sarah chuckled and teased, "He's just okay, nothing special." Their laughter filled the room as they left, hand in hand, to assist Bill's mother in preparing dinner.

As the days passed, Sarah and Dorothy's friendship became a source of boundless joy. They discovered an unspoken connection that transcended words, a shared laughter that echoed through their homes, and a support system that felt unbreakable. Whether it was giggling over inside jokes during their late-night chats or sharing secrets under the starlit sky, their bond deepened with every passing moment.

They celebrated each other's victories and offered solace during moments of doubt. Sarah found comfort in Dorothy's wisdom and grace, while Dorothy admired Sarah's resilience and unwavering positivity. Together, they formed a dynamic duo, ready to face the world with open hearts and beaming smiles.

Their joy extended to their shared dreams and aspirations. They would often sit on Sarah's porch, gazing at the horizon, and talk about their plans. They dreamed of exploring the world together, just as Dorothy's family did, but with their own unique twist. They vowed to create a lifetime of memories filled with adventure, laughter, and unwavering friendship.

Their laughter was infectious, bringing warmth and happiness to everyone around them. Bill's parents often marveled at how Sarah and Dorothy's friendship had transformed their household. The air seemed lighter, and the world appeared more colorful in their presence.

One thing was clear to everyone who knew them: Sarah and Dorothy's friendship was a beacon of joy in their lives, a treasure they cherished and nurtured every day. It was a testament to the extraordinary bond that two people could share, filling each other's lives with love, laughter, and the promise of a beautiful future together.

Good Bye High School

On that chilly Friday evening, amidst the gentle rain and cold breeze sweeping through, "Juneuary" Redmond High School, Sarah and Dorothy stood together, their maroon graduation gowns contrasting beautifully with their light blue dresses and black high heels. Their families watched proudly as they made their way to their seats, the anticipation of the ceremony palpable.

For Dorothy, the day was bittersweet. As the valedictorian, she took the stage, but her heart ached with the absence of her beloved Bill. She longed for him to be there, to share this monumental day with her. As she approached the podium and took a deep breath, her emotions swelled, but she managed to get a warm smile.

"Did you see this day coming?" she asked her fellow graduates. "We've been waiting for this moment since the first day we walked through these halls, imagining what it would be like." Dorothy glanced at her notes but then turned her gaze to her family. And there, in that crowded auditorium, her eyes met Bill's, holding a bouquet of flowers. For a few precious moments, the world seemed to stand still, and it was as if only the two of them existed. A radiant smile graced her lips as she continued her speech.

"Over the past four years, we've given our all. We've worked tirelessly to chase our dreams, whatever they may be. I want you all to know that your dreams are valid, don't ever stop pursuing them." Dorothy's voice was filled with conviction. "Life after today will bring change, but change is a part of life. Just as the seasons change, so do our lives, and with the knowledge we've gained here, we're well-equipped to face whatever comes our way. Some of us will venture far from this beautiful state for college, while others will continue chasing their dreams right here in the evergreen state. No matter where you go, know that the sky is not your limit; you are your own limit. You have wings, you can fly and fly high, thank you "

As Dorothy left the stage, Bill's booming cheers filled the auditorium, drawing the attention of everyone. "That's my girl! I'm so proud of you, baby girl!" Dorothy waved to him, her heart bursting with joy at the sight of her beloved fiancé.

After the ceremony, as the graduates made their way to their families, Dorothy couldn't contain her excitement. She rushed toward Bill, who looked striking in his uniform. With his towering six-foot frame, he effortlessly lifted her and planted a passionate kiss on her lips. "A man in uniform, and he is all mine" Dorothy romantic whispers on his ears. Bill passionately kisses her again, this time, there was no fear of her father's disapproval. It was official Dorothy was going to be his wife.

Dorothy accepted the bouquet of flowers Bill had brought, savoring their fragrance, her eyes shimmering with tears of joy. "For a few minutes, I was afraid you wouldn't make it," she confessed. Bill kissed her again, his love evident in his eyes. "My dearest, I wouldn't have missed this for the world. You're not just my star, my love; you're my entire galaxy."

As they walked hand in hand, they joined Sarah and their families, who couldn't help but tease Bill about being late. "Bill my brother, I bet you going to be late on your own funeral" Laughter filled the air as they made their way to their cars, heading to the graduation party that both families had meticulously arranged.

As Bill's time in Redmond was limited, they spent the next two days creating lasting memories together. They spoke excitedly about their upcoming trip to Africa and the adventures that lay ahead.

After the lively graduation celebration, as the night sky stretched out above them, Dorothy and Bill decided to take a leisurely stroll by the serene Sammamish Lake. The moon cast a soft, silvery glow over the water, creating a romantic atmosphere that seemed tailor-made for the promises they were about to make to each other.

Hand in hand, they walked along the shore, the gentle lapping of the water against the rocks providing a soothing soundtrack to their journey. The stars above sparkled like distant diamonds, as if nature itself was celebrating their love.

Dorothy nestled closer to Bill, feeling the warmth of his presence beside her. The cool breeze tousled their hair, and the scent of the lake filled the air. They exchanged smiles that held a thousand words, for in that moment, words seemed insufficient to capture the depth of their feelings.

Finally, under the tender gaze of the moon, Bill stopped and turned to face Dorothy. His eyes, illuminated by moonlight, held an intensity that took her breath away. He spoke from the depths of his heart, his voice a soft, sincere melody in the night.

"Dorothy," he began, his voice a gentle whisper, "from the moment I met you, my life has been filled with more love, joy, and purpose than I ever thought possible. You are my guiding star, my muse, and my heart's deepest desire. As I stand here beside you, under this enchanting moonlight, I promise to cherish and protect you, to stand by your side through every storm and every sunrise. I vow to be your unwavering support, your confidant, and your greatest love."

Dorothy's eyes glistened with tears of happiness, and she responded in kind, her voice filled with emotion. "Bill, you are the love of my life, my partner in every adventure, and the one who has brought endless laughter to my days. Under this moonlit sky, I promise to love you with all my heart, to be your sanctuary in times of trouble, and your greatest source of joy in times of happiness. I pledge to build a life together that is filled with love, respect, and shared dreams."

As they sealed their promises with a tender kiss, the moonlight seemed to intensify, casting a brilliant glow around them.

The Serengeti

Standing at the entrance gate to the majestic Serengeti, Dorothy felt a surge of emotions welling up inside her. The large words, "The Serengeti shall never die," adorned the gate, a testament to the enduring beauty and significance of this incredible place. She took a deep breath, inhaling the unique blend of earthy scents, and let her gaze wander across the expansive savannah that stretched before her. In that moment, she could not help but imagine returning to this breathtaking land with Bill by her side, sharing this awe-inspiring experience together.

After her father had captured the moment with a photograph, they embarked on their journey to explore the heart of the Serengeti. The land seemed to stretch on endlessly, an open canvas teeming with life. Animals of all kinds roamed freely, creating a bustling city of wildlife that rivaled even the busiest scenes of New York Square Garden.

As they ventured deeper into this natural wonder, their luck shone brightly on the first day of their safari. They were privileged to witness the entire Big Five the lion, leopard, elephant, buffalo, and rhinoceros all in a single day. The sight of these magnificent creatures left them in awe. Each animal, with its unique presence and grace, contributed to the symphony of life that was the Serengeti.

The Serengeti, bathed in the warm hues of the setting sun, transformed into a breathtaking canvas of nature's splendor. The vast expanse of the land stretched before them, adorned with the silhouettes of acacia trees and the gentle sway of grasses, as if nature itself was choreographing a symphony of beauty.

The horizon, painted in shades of gold and crimson, was a mesmerizing panorama that seemed to embrace the soul. The air was filled with the chorus of wildlife, each creature adding its unique melody to the harmonious orchestra of the African plains. Lions roared in the distance, zebras and wildebeests grazed peacefully, and the occasional trumpeting of elephants resonated through the air.

The Serengeti, with its untamed beauty, was a testament to the divine craftsmanship of creation. As the stars began to twinkle overhead, casting a celestial glow upon the land, Sarah and Dorothy found solace in the serenity of their surroundings. The Serengeti night was alive with the magic of the wild, a lullaby that cradled the weary earth in a tranquil embrace.

Inside their cozy tent, the soft glow of a lantern illuminated the faces of Sarah and Dorothy. The sounds of the Serengeti outside whispered tales of the untamed, echoing the vastness of God's creation. The canvas walls of the tent seemed like a thin veil between them and the wild beauty that surrounded them.

In this sacred space, under the Serengeti sky, gratitude filled their hearts. They marveled at the intricate tapestry of life, at the interconnectedness of every creature under the heavens. The beauty of the Serengeti wasn't just a visual feast; it was a spiritual experience that stirred a deep sense of awe and reverence.

As they lay under the African stars, Sarah and Dorothy whispered words of gratitude to the Creator, thanking Him for the privilege of witnessing such majesty. The Serengeti, with its wild symphony and celestial wonders, became a sanctuary where they connected not only with nature but with the divine presence that graced this sacred land.

Dorothy, however, couldn't resist the urge to capture her thoughts and emotions in a letter to her future husband, Bill. She took out a piece of paper and a pen, her heart still filled with the wonder of the Serengeti.

"My Dearest Future Husband,

As I sit here under the vast, open African sky, I find myself struggling to convey the profound beauty that surrounds me. It's as if nature itself has conspired to reveal its most magnificent secrets to me, and yet, I know that even my most heartfelt words can only scratch the surface of the breathtaking grandeur that is the Serengeti.

The Serengeti stretches out endlessly, a boundless canvas painted with the brushstrokes of Mother Nature's finest work. I may not have seen the entire world, but this place has already revealed to me the incredible beauty that our planet holds. Every day here feels like an exploration of a world untouched by time. Today, a spectacle unfolded before our eyes that words alone cannot do justice. Thousands of majestic creatures embarked on the treacherous journey of crossing the river. It was a testament to their determination, unity, and the relentless pursuit of life itself. In that moment, I couldn't help but draw parallels to our own journey, my love, and the unwavering commitment we share.

We've been blessed to encounter most of the Big Five, and I now understand why they hold such a special place in the hearts of those who are fortunate enough to witness them in their natural habitat. The zebras, my love, they walk with undeniable pride, as if aware of their unique beauty, each stripe telling a story of strength and individuality. And the giraffes, oh Bill, they move with a grace that is both mesmerizing and enchanting. It's as if they're participating in an American beauty competition, their long necks swaying with a delicate elegance as they reach for fresh, springtime leaves.

In these moments, I can't help but feel your absence more profoundly. I imagine you by my side, your hand in mine, as we share in the wonder of this place together. My heart aches with the desire to have you here, to witness this incredible journey alongside me.

My love, if I were to choose a place for our honeymoon, the Serengeti would undoubtedly be at the top of my list. I long for the day when we can stand side by side and watch in awe as nature's most majestic creatures grace us with their presence. Until then, I'll continue to write, to paint pictures with my words, so that you may experience the wonder of the Serengeti through my eyes.

Yours, now and forever,

Dorothy"

With her letter complete, Dorothy carefully folded it, placed it in an envelope, and slipped it into her handbag, where it would be a tangible reminder of the love, wonder, and dreams she had experienced in this extraordinary place.

Before drifting off to sleep in the peaceful Serengeti, surrounded by the soft rustling of leaves and distant sounds of wildlife, Dorothy allowed her imagination to carry her away into a realm of deep romantic thoughts.

Under the vast, star-studded African sky, she pictured herself and Bill strolling hand in hand along the savannah. The moonlight bathed them in a gentle, silvery glow, casting a luminous aura around their figures. The air was filled with a symphony of nocturnal sounds the distant calls of lions, the rhythmic chirping of crickets, and the occasional rustling of grass by unseen creatures.

As they walked, their fingers intertwined, Dorothy could feel the warmth of Bill's hand in hers, a comforting and reassuring presence. They did not need words to express the depths of their love; it was woven into the very fabric of their being. Their connection was like an unbreakable thread that bound their hearts, and in this magical place, it felt more profound than ever.

The gentle breeze caressed their skin, carrying with it the scent of the African night earthy, wild, and untamed. It was a scent that filled their senses and made them feel intimately connected to the natural world around them.

Dorothy looked into Bill's eyes, and in their depths, she saw the reflection of the Serengeti's timeless beauty and the eternal love they shared. In that moment, they knew that their bond was as enduring as the land they stood upon, and their love was as boundless as the African horizon.

As sleep finally claimed her, Dorothy held onto these romantic thoughts, knowing that tomorrow would bring more adventures and that her heart was forever entwined with Bill's, both in the Serengeti and in the world beyond. With a contented smile on her lips, she surrendered to dreams filled with love, connection, and the promise of an everlasting future together.

November 1965 brought a phone call that would forever alter the course of Dorothy and Bill's lives. As the phone rang and Mr. Hall picked it up, his face etched with concern, Bill's voice on the other end quivered with uncertainty and a sense of urgency. Bill needed to return to Washington immediately and marry Dorothy before he was deployed to Vietnam. The prospect of their love being tested by distance and war was a reality they couldn't ignore.

Mr. Hall, torn by the situation, gave his blessing once more, recognizing that love and duty were calling Bill in opposite directions. He knew there was no other choice, and he handed the phone to Dorothy so she could speak with her fiancé.

With trembling hands, Dorothy took the phone and listened to Bill's heartfelt words. His voice, filled with emotion, reassured her that he would return to her safely. Tears welled up in her eyes as she gave her consent, her love for Bill shining through in every word. In that moment.

After hanging up, Dorothy turned to her father, and the tears flowed freely as she leaned on his shoulder for support. Her mother walked into the kitchen, seeing the emotional scene unfold, and joined in the shared sorrow without knowing the reason.

Dorothy shared the news of Bill's imminent deployment, and the decision was made to plan a wedding in just two days. The families came together for an impromptu wedding planning meeting, organizing a quick wedding at Dorothy's family vacation house in the mountains. Her grandmother's wedding dress, which had been lovingly preserved, would be worn by the bride, and John would be the best man, with Sarah as the maid of honor.

Dorothy's wedding dress was a masterpiece, a timeless heirloom that had been passed down through generations. The gown, carefully crafted from the finest silk and chiffon, seemed to whisper the stories of love and union that had unfolded within its delicate threads.

The bodice of the dress was adorned with intricate lace detailing, a testament to the artistry of the hands that had carefully sewn it. Tiny pearls and delicate sequins sparkled like stars, catching the light with every step Dorothy took. The silhouette embraced her figure gracefully, creating an ethereal aura around her.

The gown's sleeves, sheer and billowy, cascaded down to her wrists, adding a touch of romantic elegance. The skirt, flowing like a cascade of soft petals, trailed behind her, creating a regal and enchanting effect. As Dorothy walked, the dress seemed to dance with the gentle breeze, a living testament to the time-honored beauty of her family's traditions.

The color of the dress was a soft, ivory hue, symbolizing purity, and the beginning of a new chapter. Delicate floral embroidery adorned the edges of the gown, incorporating the beauty of nature into its design. The flowers, meticulously stitched with threads that held a history of love, added a touch of whimsy to the ensemble.

In her hands, Dorothy held a bouquet of blooms that mirrored the colors of a summer garden. Roses, lilies, and delicate baby's breath intertwined, creating a fragrant symphony that filled the air with the sweet aroma of romance. The bouquet was wrapped in satin ribbon, a subtle touch of sophistication against the vibrant hues of the blossoms.

As Dorothy walked down the aisle, the scent of her bouquet lingered, leaving an indelible mark on the hearts of those who witnessed this union. Bill, captivated by the vision of his soon-to-be wife, felt a surge of emotion. Sarah, standing by his side, whispered words of encouragement, reminding him of the love that surrounded them on this momentous day.

Dorothy's dress wasn't just a garment; it was a legacy, a manifestation of love that transcended time. As she reached the end of the aisle, where Bill eagerly awaited her, the dress became a symbol of the union between past, present, and future, a testament to the enduring power of love and the beauty of generations coming together.

The ceremony was filled with love and joy, witnessed by friends and family. As the sun set and rain began to fall, the guests departed, leaving the newlyweds to spend their first night together in the serene family vacation home.

As Sarah and John left the house, Dorothy and Bill stood together, embracing the quiet moments of their first evening as husband and wife. Bill held his wife close, whispering romantic promises into her ear under the soft glow of the moon. Their love was a force to be reckoned with, and they knew that, no matter the distance or challenges ahead, their love would endure.

"You are my life, my everything," Bill whispered tenderly. "I promise to love you through thick and thin, in sickness and health." Dorothy gazed deeply into Bill's eyes; her heart full of love. "And I promise to stand by your side always, for better or worse, in sickness and health."

As they sealed their promises with a kiss, they knew that their love was unbreakable. Playfully, Bill scooped Dorothy into his arms and carried her to their bedroom. It was a night of anticipation, where they chose to save the consummation of their love for their wedding night.

As they lay together, their love making was filled with tenderness and care. Dorothy felt a mix of sensations, some pain, but most importantly, an overwhelming feeling of joy and love that Bill bestowed upon her. He was patient, trying every trick he had heard from friends to ensure she felt the same euphoria he did. Eventually, they discovered the right rhythm, and Dorothy experienced her first orgasm, tears of joy streaming down her cheeks. "I've never felt this way before," she confessed, her body still trembling. "I want you more and more, my love."

Over the next few days, they indulged in each other's bodies and souls, creating memories of passion and love that would sustain them during Bill's deployment. Their love was a fire that burned brightly, and they cherished every moment they spent together.

Their sojourn in the cabin nestled among the majestic mountains unfolded as a whirlwind of passion and undying love, a modern-day tale echoing the timeless romance of Juliet and Romeo. In the embrace of nature's sanctuary, Dorothy and Bill's connection deepened, transcending mere mortal constraints.

As dawn painted the heavens with hues of blush and gold, Bill, enchanted by the ethereal beauty of his beloved, would rise with the first light, a willing servant to the symphony of their love. Each morning, he ventured into the dew-kissed meadows, gathering not just flowers but tokens of eternal devotion. His hands, guided by a love as ancient as time, wove delicate blooms into a kaleidoscope of colors, a fragrant love letter left on Dorothy's pillow, promising a love that would endure beyond the ages.

The ritual of breakfast in bed became an intimate affair, a communion of souls entwined in a dance of stolen glances and tender caresses. Bill, the culinary maestro, would craft a feast fit for gods, each morsel a testament to the intensity of his love. With every bite, they tasted the sweet nectar of passion, their laughter mingling with the melodies of nature serenading them through the open window.

In the languid afternoons, under the caress of the sun's golden rays, Dorothy, inspired by the spirit of true love, would assemble a rustic picnic basket, a treasure trove of delectable delights. Hand in hand, they ventured into the heart of the wilderness, guided by the whispers of ancient trees and the secrets shared only between kindred spirits.

As the sun dipped below the horizon, casting the world in hues of fiery passion, they returned to their sanctuary, the cabin's hearth a witness to the inferno burning within their hearts. Their shared culinary endeavors became a love potion, their laughter a symphony that echoed through the ages, an echo of Romeo and Juliet's timeless ardor.

Underneath the celestial canopy, with stars shimmering like witness tomes of their love story, they would retreat to a secret corner of their garden. In those stolen moments, surrounded by the beauty of the night, they counted not just stars but the beats of their entwined hearts, their whispered confessions echoing the eternal vows of love that Romeo and Juliet had once shared.

And as the midnight hour approached, they sought solace in the seclusion of their chamber, where the flickering candlelight cast shadows upon the tapestry of their desire. In the hallowed intimacy of the night, they surrendered to a love as profound as any Shakespearean sonnet, their bodies merging into a sacred union that defied mortal constraints. In the tender embrace of the night, they became timeless lovers, their passion a flame that burned brightly in the annals of love's rich tapestry.

As the time drew near for Bill's departure, their final family dinner was a bittersweet affair. Laughter and tears intermingled as they recounted cherished stories and relived moments of togetherness. The weight of uncertainty hung in the air, a stark reminder that the future held challenges and separations they could not predict.

For Dorothy, the prospect of Bill's absence stirred deep emotions. She had never felt so vulnerable, wondering if he would touch another woman as he had touched her. The mere thought of sharing Bill with anyone else tore at her heart, and tears flowed like a relentless river from her eyes. She gazed at him, her eyes filled with a mixture of love, longing, and fear.

"My darling," she whispered, her voice quivering with emotion, "the idea of sharing you with another woman would be unbearable. Promise me, Bill, promise me that you will never give your heart or your touch to another."

Bill, touched by her vulnerability, cupped her tear-stained cheek, and kissed her gently. "You are the only woman I have ever loved, and you always will be, my dearest. I promise that my heart and my touch belong to you, and you are alone."

Their promises sealed with tender kisses, Bill reluctantly walked into the airport, turning back to catch one last glimpse of his beloved Dorothy. She stood there, tears streaming down her cheeks, a vision of love and devotion.

Sarah, ever the protective sister-in-law, enveloped Dorothy in a comforting hug until she felt strong enough to return to the car. They drove back to Redmond, where Dorothy would now be living with her new family. In the room once occupied by Bill, she would begin her new life as a wife.

When spring arrived, Dorothy and Sarah would move to the university dorms in Seattle. They planned to take the same classes and be roommates, ensuring they would continue to be each other's rock in the absence of their beloved Bill. The arrangement brought comfort to Bill, knowing that his sister would always be there to protect and provide companionship for his wife, their connection and love deepening as they faced the challenges of separation together.

Bill's letters from Vietnam were like a lifeline, connecting him to his loved ones back home and filling their hearts with both relief and longing. Dorothy cherished each word, finding solace in the ink on paper that carried his thoughts and love across the vast distance that separated them.

Seated in their shared dorm, Dorothy unfolded the latest letter with a smile that couldn't be contained. Bill's words were a testament to his deep affection.

" *My Dearest wifey Dorothy,*

Amidst the relentless chaos and unforgiving terrain of Vietnam, I find myself transported back to our cherished days in the mountains. Each night, as I lay beneath the starry Vietnamese sky, I ache with the fervent desire that courses through my veins. The memories of our stolen moments together burn in my heart, like a beacon guiding me through the darkest of times.

In this war-torn land, where the very air is thick with tension and uncertainty, your presence is a distant, cherished memory that fuels my spirit. The touch of your hand, as gentle as a whisper, still tingles upon my skin, and your voice, like a soothing melody, reverberates in my ears, providing solace amidst the deafening cacophony of battle.

The longing to be with you, to hold you close and share our love, consumes me with an intensity that surpasses the fiercest battles. I yearn for the simple pleasures of being by your side, of losing myself in the depths of your love as if it were an oasis in this arid desert of conflict.

As I face the trials of war, I often wonder about your life back home. Are you excelling in your studies, my brilliant love? I have no doubt that you continue to shine brightly in every endeavor you pursue. Have new friends had the privilege of experiencing your warmth and kindness? And dear Sarah, I hope she continues to watch over you as a guardian angel, just as I would if I were there.

Vietnam is a world apart from the tranquility of our life together, and I beg you not to let the burdens of the news weigh down your tender heart. It is not within my power to assure you that all is well here, but please know that I am vigilant and cautious, for I have a million reasons to return to your loving embrace.

Every moment spent in this foreign and hostile land feels hollow without you, my beloved. My heart yearns for the day when I can hold you close, as if trying to make up for all the lost time in a single, passionate embrace. You are the heartbeat that sustains me, the light that guides me through the darkest of nights, and I love you with a depth that transcends the boundaries of time and space.

Yours forever,

Bill

Dorothy held the letter close to her heart, feeling Bill's presence through his words. She had stopped counting the days until his return, focusing instead on the love that bound them across the miles.

With a sense of longing in her heart, she carefully folded the letter and placed it back in the envelope. As she reached for a pen and paper to respond, her thoughts turned to her beloved husband, thousands of miles away, facing the unknown.

"My Dearest Husband,

The longing for your presence consumes me with each passing day. My heart aches with a deep, profound yearning for the warmth of your embrace, and my thoughts are constantly filled with images of your face, your smile, and the way your eyes light up when you look at me.

Every moment without you feels like an eternity, as though a vital part of my soul is missing. I find myself tracing the contours of your letters, imagining that your fingers are intertwined with mine, even when they're miles apart. Our connection, the bond we share, remains unbroken despite the vast distance that separates us.

Please, my love, take the utmost care of yourself in that treacherous land. I pray to the heavens every day, beseeching them to watch over you and protect you, so you may return to us unharmed. I can't bear the thought of anything happening to you, for you are not only the love of my life but also the father of our child, a precious life growing within me.

As I read these words, I feel the fluttering of our baby inside me, a tiny beacon of hope that reminds me of the beautiful future we will share as a family. You now have another reason, a precious one, to be cautious and return to us. Our child, whom we have created out of our boundless love, eagerly awaits the day they can feel your love and warmth in person.

On this side of the world, life goes on, but it's shrouded in the shadow of your absence. The rain falls relentlessly, much like the tears that sometimes escape from my eyes when I think of you. But despite the gloomy weather, I hold on to the promise of our reunion, when the rain will turn to sunshine, and our hearts will once again beat as one.

Until that day, my dearest husband, please know that you are loved beyond measure, and your absence is felt in every corner of our home. We are bound by an unbreakable love that transcends time and distance, and nothing in this world or the next can diminish the flame that burns for you in our hearts.

With all my love,

Dorothy

As she penned her letter, Dorothy's thoughts were filled with the shared dreams of a family, a future together, and the deep, abiding love she and Bill shared. She placed the letter in an envelope, sealed it with a loving kiss, and held it close to her heart.

Just as she finished, Sarah entered the room, carrying two cups of hot chocolate and a plate of cookies. The sisters-in-law shared a quiet moment together, seated by the window with a view of Lake Washington and the gentle rain outside. It was a simple, comforting moment amidst the uncertainty, a reminder of the beauty of nature and the strength of their bond as they awaited Bill's return. The rain outside seemed to echo the emotions in the room.

As Dorothy sat by the window, watching the rain pour down in a soothing rhythm, her thoughts drifted away, carried by the pitter-patter of raindrops against the glass. She longed for Bill, her beloved husband, who was thousands of miles away in the tumultuous land of Vietnam. The sound of the rain seemed to echo the tears of longing in her heart.

With a soft sigh, she imagined herself outside, in the midst of the downpour, feeling the cool raindrops cascade over her skin. In her mind's eye, she danced gracefully, twirling, and spinning beneath the gentle rain. The raindrops clung to her hair and traced their way down her cheeks like tender caresses.

As her imagination painted this romantic scene, Dorothy's hand instinctively moved to her growing belly, where a precious life was taking shape. She wished with all her heart that Bill could be there to share this intimate moment with her, to feel life within her, and to experience the miracle of their child growing inside her womb.

Tears welled up in her eyes, not from sadness but from the overwhelming depth of love and vulnerability she felt. She whispered softly to herself, "Oh, Bill, how I wish you were here with me, sharing this beautiful moment. I can't help but imagine your gentle touch on my growing belly, your hand in mine, and our hearts beating in unison as we embrace our future together."

In that vulnerable moment, as the rain continued to cascade outside, Dorothy's love for Bill deepened even further. She held onto the hope that soon, the rain would subside, and they would be reunited to experience all the joys and wonders of parenthood together.

A Baby On The Way

The passage of time was a poetic dance, a symphony of light and darkness, a celestial waltz conducted by the sun, moon, and the whimsical winds. Days seemed to slip through their fingers like grains of sand, and the seasons painted the world with their ever-changing hues. Time, that elusive thief of moments, stole away with their hours, yet in its relentless march, it bestowed upon them moments of immeasurable joy and love.

In the quiet halls of academia, where rules and traditions dictated the course of a young woman's life, Dorothy found herself navigating a delicate dance between expectation and reality. In an era where societal norms deemed pregnant women unfit for the rigors of education, she had to conceal the burgeoning secret within her womb.

As her pregnancy journey unfolded like a gentle river, Dorothy faced the stark reality that societal norms could cast shadows on the dreams she held close to her heart. The vibrant threads of her academic pursuits were momentarily woven into the fabric of secrecy, as she gracefully concealed the evidence of impending motherhood beneath loose-fitting garments.

The gentle sway of her skirts and careful choice of attire became a strategic dance, a choreography of concealment designed to shield her growing belly from the watchful eyes of teachers and peers alike. Dorothy, determined and resilient, masked the physical transformation occurring within her with a grace that mirrored the still waters of the lake near her home.

Her commitment to education and the dreams she shared with Bill remained unwavering, but the societal constraints of the time forced her to navigate a path where discretion became her ally. Only a select few, trusted friends, and confidantes were privy to the tender secret she carried.

Despite the challenges, Dorothy stood resolute, her determination fueled by the promise of a brighter future for her child and the unyielding love she held for Bill. The tranquil haven of her father's house by Lake Sammamish became a cocoon where she could embrace both the joys of impending motherhood and the pursuit of knowledge.

In the quiet moments between classes and clandestine movements through the hallways, Dorothy's heartbeat in sync with the rhythm of life growing within her. The lake, with its timeless wisdom, mirrored her strength and resilience, offering solace amid the societal whispers that sought to dim the brilliance of her aspirations.

As she moved forward, navigating the challenges of concealing her pregnancy, Dorothy's spirit remained unbroken. The threads of love, family, and education intertwined in a delicate dance, weaving a tapestry that defied societal norms. And in the quiet sanctuary of

Lake Sammamish, where the lullaby of rippling waters embraced her, Dorothy found the courage to face the world and protect the precious life she carried within.

Two weeks after settling into their new lakeside home, Dorothy brought forth a beautiful baby girl into the world, a gift of life and love in the midst of tumultuous times. She named her daughter Bella, a name that echoed Bill's own, a tender reminder of the man she longed for every day.

Sarah couldn't help but tease her sister-in-law about the choice of the name, and Dorothy's response was filled with a love that transcended words. She simply wanted a name that held a piece of Bill within it, a name that would keep his memory alive and close.

Bella was a remarkable baby, a bundle of serenity who rarely shed a tear without good cause. Her cries were reserved for the simple needs of hunger or a wet diaper, and the rest of the time, she cocooned herself in peaceful slumber within the cozy confines of her room.

The nursery, with its large window overlooking the tranquil Sammamish waters, held a special place in Bella's heart. The rhythmic lull of the lake's gentle waves served as a soothing lullaby, cradling her little soul into the sweetest dreams.

As Bella drifted into her peaceful dreams, Dorothy would softly approach, her footsteps barely audible on the nursery's plush carpet. With loving care, she retrieved the cherished box that held Bill's letters, a testament to their enduring love. The delicate rustle of paper filled the room as she reverently unfolded the handwritten words penned by her beloved husband.

With each reading, Dorothy immersed herself in the emotions and memories conveyed within those letters. It was a ritual, a connection to Bill that transcended the distance between them. The scent of his words, the texture of his thoughts, and the love that flowed from his inked expressions enveloped her.

And then, as Bella slept peacefully, her mother would take pen and paper in hand. In the quietude of the night, she would compose her own words, pouring out her heart and soul onto the pages, reaffirming her love and longing for the man she held dear. It was in these moments that the family, though separated by miles, found solace in the written words that bound them together across the expanse of time and space.

My Dearest, hubby

As I watch our precious Bella grow day by day, I'm filled with an overwhelming sense of gratitude and love. Every time I look into her eyes, I see you, my darling. She has inherited your eyes, your hair, and that enchanting smile of yours. It's as if you are here with us, a part of her very being. She's growing into a kind and gentle soul, much like the man she was named after, and she cries only a few times a day, just like you did.

I want to express my heartfelt gratitude for the letter you sent, the words that bridge the gap between us, and for choosing me to be the mother of our beautiful daughter. Your love has filled our lives with a warmth and light that words can barely capture. It's a gift I cherish every day.

I placed the pictures we took last week when Bella turned four months in this envelope. Can you believe it, my love? Our little baby, our daughter, is now four months old. She's growing so fast, and each day she brings us more joy than we ever imagined.

I long for the moment when you'll return home and hold your child in your arms, as she smiles back at you with those precious features, she inherited from you. Until then, my love, I'll hold our little one close, and we'll continue to create beautiful memories together. I am thankful, beyond words, that you are forever mine.

With all my love,

Dorothy

As Dorothy settled in for the night, the soft glow of the lamp casting a warm ambiance across the room, she took the old letter in her hands, its pages worn from countless readings. Her heart swelled with both love and longing as she revisited the beautiful words written by her husband.

"My darling wife," she whispered to herself, savoring the endearment that always made her heart flutter. The imagery of him sitting under a starry sky, his words weaving a connection between them across the miles, resonated deeply within her.

"The night is very quiet, yet the sky is lit bright with all-star shine under me," Dorothy imagined the serene night he described, feeling as though she could almost see those stars herself.

Her eyes welled up with tears as she continued reading, her fingers tracing the lines. "These past few weeks have been very crazy," he had written, and Dorothy's heart ached for him. She understood the weight of his words, the sacrifices he was making, and the loss of friends that left a profound mark on his soul.

She couldn't help but be moved by his selflessness. "I am not worried about me, my love," he had said, his concern solely focused on her and their new baby. Dorothy's love for him swelled as she imagined his return and the promise of a future together, free from the burdens of responsibility.

With a deep sigh, Dorothy closed her eyes, holding the letter close to her heart. His words were a lifeline, a reminder that their love could withstand any distance or hardship. As she turned off the lamp and settled into her bed, she whispered softly to the empty room, "I love you to the moon and back," before drifting into dreams where her husband's presence filled the void of their separation.

In the soft glow of the moonlight reflecting off the tranquil lake outside her window, Dorothy sealed her letter to her beloved husband with a loving kiss. The paper, now imbued with her affection and longing, was a testament to their enduring love.

As tears of joy welled up in her eyes, she couldn't help but smile. It was a bittersweet moment, thinking of her husband so far away, but the connection they shared through their letters was a lifeline that kept her heart afloat.

Just as she finished reading, the sound of Bella's cries filled the room. Dorothy gently lifted her daughter into her arms, cradling her close, and settled into the swing breastfeed chair. She looked out at the moonlight dancing on the surface of the lake, its gentle ripples mirroring the emotions swirling within her.

With Bella nestled at her breast, feeding contentedly, Dorothy gazed at her daughter's tiny, perfect face. In this serene moment, under the watchful eye of the moon, mother and daughter were bathed in the soft, silver light, sharing an unspoken bond that transcended words. Their love, like the moonlight on the lake, was pure and timeless, a testament to the enduring strength of their family.

Vietnam

The news from Vietnam cast a shadow over their days. The headlines told tales of loss and sacrifice, leaving many to question the reasons behind the ongoing war. It was a time of uncertainty, a period marked by sleepless nights and anxious days. Yet, with the unwavering support of her family, Dorothy found the strength to navigate this challenging path.

She continued attending classes and caring for her beloved Bella, their bond growing stronger with each passing day. Bella, with her bright eyes and infectious smile, seemed to carry a piece of Bill within her. She would sit on her swing outside, giggling at the melodious songs of birds and gazing up at the sky, as if understanding the language of the planes that crossed the heavens.

Bill's letters became a lifeline, each one a testament to his deep love and enduring spirit. They were not just letters but a symphony of emotions, a connection that spanned thousands of miles. Dorothy held onto them tightly, reading and rereading his words, finding solace in the knowledge that, even in his absence, he was always with her.

As the months rushed by like a river in full flow, Bella grew, not just in stature but in spirit. She inherited her father's smile and her mother's strength. The love and laughter they shared in their lakeside home became a testament to the resilience of the human heart, a reminder that even in the darkest of times, love had the power to illuminate the path forward.

The lonely nights were a silent symphony of solitude and love for Dorothy and Bella. The moon, their faithful companion, would cast its gentle glow upon them as they sat by the window, cradled in the tender embrace of night.

Dorothy would hold her precious daughter close, their hearts beating in unison, as Bella nursed at her breast. It was a sacred moment, a mother's lullaby whispered in the quiet of the night, a connection that transcended words. As Bella fed, Dorothy would gaze down at her with a profound sense of wonder and gratitude, marveling at the life they had brought into the world.

In one hand, she held the letters from Bill, their pages filled with his thoughts, fears, and hopes. On the other hand, she lovingly caressed Bella's soft, downy head, feeling the warmth of their shared love radiate through her. The letters were a lifeline, a bridge that connected her to the man she longed for, the father of her child.

Outside the window, the lake shimmered like a liquid tapestry, its waters reflecting the moon's silvery face. The lake was their constant companion, a source of solace and strength. Its gentle ripples whispered tales of love, patience, and waiting.

Dorothy would often find herself lost in the dance of moonlight upon the water, tears welling up in her eyes. The lake held memories of her past with Bill, of shared moments and dreams of a future together. It was a bittersweet sight, for the same waters that brought her comfort also reminded her of the distance that separated them.

In the soft and comforting glow of the lamp, Dorothy immersed herself in Bill's letters, each word a lifeline connecting her to the man she loved, even across the vast expanse of miles that separated them. Emotions swirled within her like a tempestuous sea, tugging at her heartstrings. His words were a soothing balm, a testament to the enduring strength of their love.

With each page she turned, her lips curled into a tender smile, and her eyes glistened with tears of both joy and longing. These letters were more than just ink on paper; they were a profound declaration of their unwavering commitment to one another, a love that refused to waver despite the challenges of time and distance.

In those quiet, solitary nights, when the world outside slumbered, Dorothy and Bella found solace in each other's presence. They formed an unbreakable bond, a connection that transcended words. And in those cherished letters, they discovered the key to keeping their family united, even in the absence of their beloved husband and father.

Outside, the lake stretched under the moonlight, a silent witness to their love story. It whispered tales of hope, resilience, and the enduring connection between a mother, her child, and a father who, though far away, remained a steadfast presence in their hearts. Theirs was a love story for the ages, one that grew stronger with every passing day, fueled by the written words that bound them together.

The Silence

The silence that followed was deafening, its weight pressing down on Dorothy's heart like a leaden shroud. It was a silence that spoke of longing, of the absence of the words that had been her lifeline. In its void, desperation crept in, like a chilling shadow that refused to be dispelled.

Day by day, that creeping desperation grew, gnawing at her soul with relentless persistence. The tender fear of losing Bill had transformed into a constant, haunting presence in her life. It was a fear that clung to her like a second skin, a reminder of the uncertainty that now defined their existence.

The war, once a distant and abstract concept, had become an all-encompassing reality, looming over her like a relentless storm cloud. Its presence cast a pall of anxiety that refused to dissipate, coloring every moment of her life with uncertainty and dread.

In the midst of this silence, Dorothy clung to the memories of their love and the letters that had connected their hearts. She held their daughter Bella close, finding strength in the precious bond they shared. And though the future remained uncertain, she vowed to keep the flame of hope alive, believing in the enduring power of their love to overcome even the darkest of times.

Every morning, as the sun timidly rose, Dorothy would awaken with Bella in her arms and a flicker of hope in her heart. She would make her way to the mailbox, her footsteps echoing with anticipation, yearning for the sight of a letter from Bill. It had been six long, agonizing months since the last letter arrived, and each day without his words felt like an eternity.

The absence of his letters left a void in her life, a silence that seemed to scream with the unspoken words of love and longing. The world outside was changing, and the news reports only added to her despair. The war was escalating, and the casualties were mounting like a relentless tide. Each evening, the television would blare with grim announcements of lives lost, further fueling the uncertainty that gripped her heart.

The nation itself seemed divided, torn between those who questioned the purpose of the war and those who stood by their convictions. Dorothy felt adrift in a sea of conflicting emotions, her hope and fear locked in a bitter struggle.

In her desperation, she reached out to official channels, hoping for any scrap of information about Bill's whereabouts and well-being. She wrote letters, made calls, and knocked on countless doors, her determination unwavering. But the doors of bureaucracy remained locked, her pleas falling on deaf ears. The officials could offer no solace, no answers to the questions that tormented her.

Each night, as she cradled Bella to sleep, Dorothy would gaze at the moonlit sky through the window, her heart heavy with worry. She wondered where Bill was, if he was safe, and if he too lay awake at night, thinking of her and their daughter. The night, once a peaceful respite, had become a tormenting reminder of their separation.

Dorothy lived in a world where time seemed to stand still, where uncertainty and fear were her constant companions. She clung to the memory of Bill, the last letters he had sent, and the love that had brought them together. In the midst of despair, she held onto hope, a fragile flame in the darkness, praying for the day when the letters would once again find their way into her mailbox, and she could finally breathe a sigh of relief.

Bella, though too young to comprehend the complexities of the world, was surrounded by a mother's unwavering love and the enduring memory of her father. Dorothy made sure that even in Bill's absence, his presence remained a cherished part of their lives.

Every day, as Bella lay in her crib or played on her blanket, Dorothy would tell her about her father, painting a vivid picture with her words. She would speak of his handsome smile, the warmth of his embrace, and the love that radiated from his eyes. Bella, with her innocent gaze, seemed to listen intently, as if trying to grasp the essence of the man she had yet to meet.

Dorothy would take out photographs of Bill, showing them to Bella with a tender smile. She would let her tiny fingers trace the contours of his face, as if through touch, Bella could bridge the gap between them. Hours would pass as mother and daughter looked at those pictures together, as if seeking solace in the images of their beloved.

In addition to their daily ritual, Dorothy continued to write letters to Bill, pouring her heart onto the pages. She would share with him their daughter's every milestone, from her first giggle to the way her eyes sparkled when she saw the photographs of her father. The letters became a journal of their life, a testament to the love that transcended the miles.

Each evening, as the sun dipped below the horizon, Dorothy would carefully seal the letter and send it on its way, carrying her words and her love across the vast expanse that separated them. It was an act of faith, a lifeline that kept their connection alive.

Bella may have been too young to understand the depth of her mother's devotion, but she grew up in an atmosphere of love and longing. She would smile at the photographs, as if recognizing her father's presence, and her laughter would fill the room as Dorothy recounted tales of their love story.

Through her actions and her words, Dorothy ensured that Bill remained an integral part of their lives. She wanted Bella to know that her father was not just a distant memory but a living, breathing presence in their hearts. And as Bella grew, she would come to understand the profound love that bound their family together, even in the face of separation and uncertainty.

The Storm

In the hushed stillness of the early morning, the world seemed to hold its breath as the rain cascaded from the heavens. Bill, dressed in his olive-green flight suit, stood on the precipice of what was supposed to be his final flight before returning home. His emotions churned within him like a turbulent storm, a tempest of hope, longing, and trepidation.

The raindrops, falling with a gentle insistence, splattered against his flight suit like liquid memories. Each drop carried with it the weight of countless days spent yearning for the embrace of his beloved daughter, Bella. They mirrored the rhythm of his heartbeat, a poignant reminder of the precious moments he had missed in her life, moments that could never be reclaimed.

In that early morning stillness, vulnerability enveloped Bill like a heavy shroud. The rhythmic patter of raindrops against the metal exterior of the aircraft seemed to mirror the turbulent emotions swirling within him. A deep sense of trepidation gnawed at his core as he prepared for what was supposed to be his last flight before finally heading home.

The rain, though a physical manifestation of nature's tears, could never wash away the longing he felt for his family. Bill's heart ached for the moment when he would hold Bella in his arms and make up for the lost time, when he would reunite with Dorothy, and together they would find solace in the warmth of their love.

As he climbed into the cockpit and prepared for takeoff, his gaze lingered on the rain-slicked runway. In that moment, he held onto the hope that this flight would bring him one step closer to the embrace of his beloved family, and that the storm of uncertainty would soon give way to the calm of their reunion.

Bill and his unit stood in somber unison, packs meticulously secured, their hearts weighed down by the weight of anticipation mixed with the profound longing to reunite with their loved ones. Each drop of rain felt like a reminder of the tears he'd held back, a testament to the sacrifices he had made in service to his country.

As Bill and his co-pilot went through the pre-flight procedures, his fingers trembled slightly as they touched the photograph of Bella. She looked up at him with innocent eyes and a heartwarming smile, a beacon of love and hope in the midst of the storm that raged both inside and outside the aircraft. Bill pressed a gentle kiss to the picture, his voice a hushed whisper, "I can't believe she'll soon turn 2. I haven't seen my baby girl."

His co-pilot, a trusted friend and comrade, caught the tremor in Bill's voice and offered a warm and reassuring smile. "Remember, this is our last route before heading home. You'll make it home in time to celebrate her second birthday," he said, attempting to infuse some semblance of comfort into the heavy atmosphere that hung in the air.

As the plane continued its journey through the skies, the transition from the pristine clarity of the air to an unsettling murkiness unfolded gradually. The once-clear horizon now became shrouded in ominous, darkening clouds that gathered like a brooding storm. The azure expanse transformed into a foreboding canvas, as if nature itself was painting a prelude to impending catastrophe.

The air, once crisp and invigorating, took on a heavy quality. A subtle shift in temperature sent shivers down their spines, the atmosphere carrying an unspoken warning of the turbulence that awaited them. The aircraft, which had glided smoothly through the heavens, now felt the resistance of the encroaching storm.

The first droplets of rain descended, initially light and hesitant, tapping rhythmically on the plane's exterior. Within moments, the gentle percussion escalated into a torrential downpour. The raindrops, now driven by an unseen force, pelted the aircraft with relentless force, creating a symphony of chaos that drowned out the comforting hum of the engines.

Bill's grip on the controls tightened, his knuckles turning white as he wrestled with the unpredictable nature of the tempest. The cockpit, once a haven of control and precision, now felt like a fragile capsule at the mercy of forces beyond their command.

The co-pilot's earlier smile, a beacon of reassurance, waned in the face of this unexpected onslaught. His eyes mirrored the concern etched on Bill's face as they exchanged a silent acknowledgment of the precarious situation. The camaraderie that had sustained them through countless flights now faced its greatest test.

The transition from clear skies to the tempest unleashed a cascade of emotions from disbelief to anxiety, each raindrop seemed to carry the weight of impending doom. The atmosphere within the cockpit grew tense, the air charged with a palpable sense of urgency and uncertainty. In this relentless onslaught of nature's fury, the aviators struggled against the elements, their journey transforming into a battle for survival against the wrath of the storm.

Bill dared not show his co-pilot the vulnerability he felt, the creeping fear that whispered in the recesses of his mind. This was a moment of rare vulnerability, an emotion he had concealed behind a façade of strength throughout his military career.

The rain, once a mere inconvenience, now became a relentless torrent. Desperation settled in as they desperately sought a place to land, but there was no haven in sight. Their voices faltered as they exchanged silent glances, a wordless acknowledgment of their shared peril.

The winds, capricious and unrelenting, wrested control of the plane from their grasp, pushing them further into the unknown. Fear gripped Bill as he looked down, the world outside a chaotic maelstrom of elements that defied their mastery.

With heavy hearts, they made the agonizing decision to eject from the plane, to let go of their faithful companion that had carried them through countless missions. Bill was the first to act, to break free from the confines of the doomed aircraft, while his co-pilot, faced with the same excruciating choice, remained trapped.

As Bill watched the plane descend and be consumed by fire, his heart ached with a mixture of sorrow and helplessness. His co-pilot, a friend and comrade, had been left behind, a sacrifice to the merciless tempest that engulfed them.

Bill's parachute, his lifeline to safety, should have brought relief, but it refused to open. Panic surged within him as he plummeted through the storm, the world spinning in a disorienting whirlwind. His voice, once steady and unwavering, now held a note of fear he had seldom known.

Then, in a cruel twist of fate, the parachute remained stubbornly closed. Bill's descent into uncertainty became a harrowing freefall, the ground below an unforgiving abyss.

As he hurtled toward an uncertain destiny, his life dangled by the thinnest thread. Vulnerability consumed him as he wrestled with the merciless elements, a mere pawn in the tumultuous game of nature.

The world around him blurred into a maddening chaos. With every passing moment, he felt the weight of vulnerability pressing down on him, a reminder that even the strongest of spirits could be humbled by the uncontrollable forces of nature.

In the end, it was nature's capricious hand that determined his fate, as the winds carried him away from the wreckage and into the embrace of a small fishing village, nestled alongside a tranquil rice farm.

There, amidst the tranquil beauty of rural life, Bill's journey took an unexpected turn, plunging him into a world where vulnerability and fate held him in their grasp. He lay there, a lone figure on the brink of life and death, unknowingly intertwined with the lives of those who would soon discover him.

Bella's Birthday Party

The atmosphere was charged with a mix of joy and sorrow as guests and family members gathered to celebrate Bella's second birthday. It was a day meant for laughter, games, and sweet memories, but there was a heavy cloud that hung over Dorothy's heart. Bill, her beloved husband, had been absent from their lives for months, his silence a tormenting mystery that gnawed at her soul. She couldn't help but wonder why he hadn't written, hadn't reached out to reassure her of his safety. The weight of unspoken questions pressed upon her, but she clung to the belief that no news was sometimes good news.

Bella, the center of attention, radiated innocence and charm in her purple and pink dress, adorned with a matching flower on her head. Her bright eyes sparkled with excitement as she stood before the birthday cake, anticipation coursing through her tiny frame.

Sarah, her ever-loving aunt, carried the cake to the table, and the room erupted in a chorus of "Happy Birthday."

Dancing and laughter filled the air, as family and friends reveled in the celebration. Bella's grandfather doted on her, showering her with affection and warmth. It was a moment of fleeting happiness, a respite from the shadow that loomed over them.

Dorothy's eyes followed the two men as they stepped out of the car, their uniforms adorned with crisp, pressed creases, and their military caps casting ominous shadows over their faces. Their steps were measured, synchronized, as if they were navigating a solemn march. Every detail about them bespoke a sense of duty and gravity that sent shivers down her spine.

Their uniforms were immaculate, though faint traces of dust clung to their boots, a testament to the long journey they had undertaken to deliver this dreadful news. Their demeanor was stoic, their faces etched with lines of experience that hinted at the difficult conversations they had held with others before her.

As they approached, Dorothy couldn't help but notice the dark, stormy clouds that seemed to gather overhead, casting an eerie shadow on the day's celebrations. It was as though the very heavens mourned in anticipation of the sorrowful tidings they carried.

The men's voices were steady, their words carefully chosen, yet laced with the weight of the message they bore. Their accents hinted at distant origins, adding an air of mystery to their presence. When Dorothy offered her nervous greeting, they reciprocated with solemn nods, acknowledging the gravity of the moment.

As they entered the cozy living room, they moved with a practiced, mournful grace. Dorothy couldn't help but feel a sense of foreboding as they gestured for her to sit, their gestures deliberate and gentle. She settled onto the sofa, her heart racing, her mind racing even faster.

Their eyes, framed by stern brows, locked onto hers, and for a moment, time seemed to stand still. A deep sigh escaped their lips, heavy with the burden they were about to reveal. With a shared, unspoken understanding, they exchanged a glance that conveyed the depth of the tragedy they faced.

Dorothy's voice quivered as she implored them for news of Bill, her husband. Their response hung in the air, laden with sorrow and dread. The plane, Bill's plane, had met a catastrophic fate in the unforgiving mountains, and the remains of his co-pilot had been found, charred and lifeless. Her beloved Bill, however, had not been located.

"We are doing everything in our power to ensure his return home," they assured her, their voices filled with a sense of duty and determination. Yet, despite their reassurances, the words felt hollow as they echoed through the room, leaving Dorothy's world shattered, cloaked in disbelief and despair.

As they continued to speak, their voices a distant murmur, Dorothy stared out of the window, her gaze locked on the gathering storm clouds. It was as if the very heavens wept alongside her, sharing in her anguish and loss.

As the two men left, leaving behind a house filled with celebration and shattered dreams, Dorothy stood at the door, her heart broken and her spirit crushed. For a few moments, she was unable to cry or speak, the weight of the news bearing down on her like an insurmountable burden.

When she finally turned to face her family and friends, her expression said it all. The pain, the anguish, the raw and overwhelming sorrow could not be concealed. She collapsed, the strength leaving her body, and her loved ones rushed to her side, their own faces contorted with shock and grief.

As they gathered around her, concerned voices asking what had happened, Dorothy could not find the words. Overwhelmed by a sense of loss that felt insurmountable, she slipped unconsciously. Her family acted swiftly, rushing her to the hospital, where the emotional storm that had been building within her finally found its release in anguished tears and heartrending sobs.

The hospital room was a stark contrast to the celebration that had been taking place just moments ago. Dorothy lay on the bed, her eyes closed, her face pale, and her heart heavy with the weight of unbearable news. Her family surrounded her, their expressions a mix of worry, grief, and helplessness. Bella, oblivious to the gravity of the situation, clung to her mother's hand, her innocent eyes reflecting the concern in the room.

As the minutes ticked by in agonizing silence, Dorothy's breathing grew shallow, her consciousness slipping away. Her thoughts were a jumble of fragmented memories and fears about Bill. She had heard the words of the two men at the door, but they felt surreal, like a nightmare from which she hoped to awaken.

The room seemed to hold its breath, suspended in time, until finally, Dorothy's eyelids fluttered open. She blinked, disoriented, her gaze shifting from one worried face to another. Her mother, her father, Sarah, and other family members were all there, their eyes filled with unshed tears.

With a tremor in her voice, Dorothy managed to utter the words that had haunted her since the two men had arrived. "The plane... Bill... they couldn't find him." Her voice cracked, and her eyes filled with tears. The reality of her words hung heavily in the air, a painful confirmation of her worst fears.

In that moment, the hospital room transformed from a place of sorrow into a sanctuary of shared grief. Family members embraced one another, tears flowing freely, as they sought solace in their mutual support. Their love for Dorothy, and for Bill, bound them together in this time of anguish.

Bella, sensing the tension in the room, clung to her mother, her small frame trembling with emotion. She might not have understood the gravity of the situation, but she knew that something was amiss.

Dorothy's mother held her daughter close, offering comfort in her warm embrace. Her father, a pillar of strength, wiped away his own tears before they could fall, determined to be there for his family. Sarah, who had always been Dorothy's confidante and companion, stood by her sister-in-law's side, holding her hand as if willing some of her own strength to flow into her.

In that hospital room, they were united by their love for Bill and their shared pain. As the tears flowed and they held each other close, it was clear that their bonds of family ran deeper than any tragedy that life could throw their way. They would face this uncertainty together, drawing strength from one another and clinging to the hope that Bill would return to them.

Bella, at just two years old, was a living echo of her father, Bill, even though she had never met him. The resemblance was striking, not just in her physical features, but also in her quirks and mannerisms. As the family coped with the pain of Bill's absence, they found solace in Bella's presence, a precious reminder of the man they all loved.

Sea Of Sorrow

Dorothy found herself adrift in a turbulent sea of sorrow. The anguish that gripped her heart was like an undertow, pulling her deeper into its dark, unforgiving depths with each passing day.

At first, she clung to the hope that Bill might still be alive, that somehow, against all odds, he would return to her arms. But as the days turned into weeks, and the weeks into months, that glimmer of hope began to wane, leaving her stranded in an endless expanse of despair.

Her once-vibrant spirit had withered like a flower deprived of sunlight and water. The things that had once brought her joy held no allure anymore. The world outside her window, with its vibrant colors and cheerful sounds, seemed distant and foreign. It was as if she inhabited a separate realm, one shrouded in shadows and haunted by memories of happier times.

Dorothy's daily routine became a monotonous procession of empty hours. She would wake up each morning with a leaden heart, burdened by the knowledge that another day would stretch before her, empty and void of purpose. Her appetite dwindled, and even the simplest tasks felt like insurmountable obstacles.

Amid the somber backdrop of their lives, Sarah remained Dorothy's steadfast companion. She was not only a sister-in-law but a dear friend who had shared countless moments with Dorothy and Bill. Together, they weathered the storm of grief, offering each other solace and a shoulder to lean on.

Sarah's grief for her brother was profound, but her love for Dorothy ran just as deep. She couldn't bear to see her friend wither away in the shadow of sorrow. Sarah became Dorothy's anchor, grounding her when the waves of despair threatened to pull her under.

They spent countless hours talking about Bill, reminiscing about the man they both loved. Sarah shared stories that were equal parts laughter and tears, preserving Bill's memory as a living, breathing presence in their lives. These recollections were not just tales of the past; they were a lifeline, a connection to the love that had once filled their days.

As time passed, they realized the importance of ensuring that Bella knew about her father, even though they had never met. They spoke to Bella about Bill, painting vivid pictures with their words, showing her photographs that captured his warmth and vitality. They wanted her to feel the essence of her father's spirit, to understand the love that had brought her into this world.

Bella, with her innocent curiosity and her uncanny ability to mimic her father's gestures and expressions, provided a source of comfort to the grieving family. Her smile bore a striking resemblance to Bill's, a heartwarming reminder that his legacy lived on. She embodied his adventurous spirit, his sense of wonder, and his boundless kindness.

Through Bella, they found a way to keep Bill's presence alive. She became a living tribute to the man they had lost, a testament to the enduring power of love. As they navigated the turbulent waters of grief together, their family love became a lifeline, a reminder that even in the darkest of times, love could be a source of strength and healing. It was a love that transcended loss, a love that bound them together, offering hope that someday, the shadow of sorrow would recede, and the light of love would shine brightly once more.

Bella had a special connection with Bill's mother, her grandmother. They spent countless hours together at the flower park, where Bella would chase butterflies and listen intently to the birds singing. It was an uncanny similarity to Bill, who had also been fascinated by birdsong from a young age. The birds seemed to speak to Bella's heart, calming her and drawing her attention whenever they sang.

Bill's mother couldn't help but shed tears as she watched her granddaughter. She often found herself lost in thought, reminiscing about the times when Bill was Bella's age. Just like Bella, he had loved chasing butterflies, but the beauty of birdsong had always captivated him. "Apple doesn't fall far from the tree," she would whisper to herself. "Bill, my son, I miss you so much. I wish you could meet Bella. She is just like you."

For the family, Bella had become a cherished token of their memories of Bill. When they missed him most, they only needed to look at Bella and see his spirit living on through her. She was a ray of hope, a reminder that their love for Bill would endure, even in his absence.

At the tender age of two, Bella's fascination with the world around her was a reflection of the deep bond she shared with her father, Bill. Just as the beauty of nature had captivated Bill's heart, it now held his daughter in its gentle embrace. The parks of Redmond, Washington, with their lush greenery and singing birds, became a playground for Bella's senses and a canvas for her budding curiosity.

Whenever the melodious notes of birdsong filled the park's air, Bella's eyes would light up with wonder. Her tiny fingers would point toward the sky, as if trying to touch the very source of that enchanting music. Beside her on a weathered park bench, her grandmother would sit, a fountain of knowledge about the avian world. She would point out different bird species and share stories of their habits and characteristics. Bella's eager attention and her genuine love for the natural world touched her grandmother's heart in profound ways.

It was during these moments, amidst the blooming flowers and the melodies of nature, that a connection formed that transcended words. They communicated through shared glances, smiles, and the gentle touch of their hands. In the tranquil serenity of the park, they were not just grandmother and granddaughter; they were kindred spirits, connected by their love for Bill and their shared appreciation of the world he had cherished.

Bella's grandmother often found herself lost in thought, her gaze drifting toward the open sky. She couldn't help but reflect on her own son's love for the outdoors and the boundless beauty of the world. In Bella's eyes, in her boundless curiosity, and in the joy, she found in the simplest of things, she saw Bill's legacy living on.

Their time together in the park was not solely about creating memories for Bella, although it certainly did that. It was also about finding solace and healing for themselves. Through Bella, they felt the continued presence of Bill, as if his spirit lived on in their cherished granddaughter. Bella's laughter, her wonder at the world's marvels, and her loving relationship with her grandmother became a soothing balm for their grieving hearts.

In Bella's presence, they discovered that love could transcend the boundaries of time and space. It flowed seamlessly from one generation to the next, a testament to the enduring power of family and the beauty of their shared connection. As they continued to explore the wonders of Redmond, Washington, and embrace the beauty of nature together, they knew that Bill's memory would forever be intertwined with the love they held for one another.

Past Intertwine Present

While in Redmond Washington, the name of Bill starts with the late Bill in his new world his is a man with no name. Has been months since Bill was rescued in Laos. Laying in the swamp not knowing who he was and why he was there.

The secluded hut near the rice farm had become Bill's sanctuary, a place where time moved slowly, and his past remained a shrouded mystery. The elderly woman and her compassionate granddaughter, Natal, had taken him in without question, offering their care and protection. Bill had no memory of his name, his life before, or why he was there, and he relied on their kindness for his daily existence.

Every day was a struggle for Bill. His legs still bore the scars of his ordeal, making it difficult for him to walk unaided. He communicated only through silent expressions of gratitude, his eyes speaking the words he couldn't find. Natal and her grandmother had become his lifeline, tending to his wounds, feeding him, and helping him regain his strength.

As evening descended, Natal would accompany Bill on walks under the ethereal glow of the moonlight. She would sit beside him as they gazed at the stars, her voice a soothing melody as she shared stories of constellations and the secrets of the night sky. Bill remained a silent listener, his eyes reflecting the wonder he felt.

Natal found herself drawn to this enigmatic stranger she was caring for. She couldn't explain the connection that had formed between them, a bond that transcended words and reason. Her heart swelled with compassion, and she couldn't help but attend to his every need, ensuring his comfort and well-being.

Her grandmother, perceptive to the unspoken feelings between Natal and Bill, would tease her gently. "Are you falling in love with him, my dear? You know he's a white man, and when he can walk and talk again, he'll return to his home. Be careful; you may end up with a broken heart."

Natal dismissed her grandmother's warnings with a smile, convinced that fate had brought this man into her life for a reason. "Grandmother, he may have been lost, captured, or killed, but I believe God meant for me to find him," she would reply, laughter dancing in their eyes as they shared a moment of playful camaraderie.

After ensuring Bill was comfortably asleep, Natal would quietly exit his room, leaving him in the peaceful embrace of the night. Each day passed with her tending to him, the connection between them growing stronger, and the hope of discovering his identity becoming more distant.

Lost & Found

In the heart of a tranquil farm village, nestled amidst the lush, emerald fields of rice paddies, Bill awoke each morning in his modest dwelling, his gaze drawn to the expansive vista beyond his window. The sprawling landscape stretched for miles, a sea of green undulating under the gentle caress of the morning light. As he stood at the threshold of his world, a sense of disquiet gnawed at his core, his soul adrift amidst the vast expanse of uncertainty.

The chorus of birdsong filled the air, a symphony of nature's creation, yet within Bill's heart, there echoed a profound silence. Each morning, Natal, the tender-hearted caretaker of his sanctuary, would bring offerings of warmth and sustenance, her eyes a mirror to his own inner turmoil. Though words eluded him, their shared language transcended the barriers of speech, a silent communion of souls bound by the unspoken yearning for understanding.

In the embrace of the tranquil village, where time flowed like molasses and the rhythms of life pulsed with ancient wisdom, Bill found himself grappling with the echoes of his own existence. Lost amidst the verdant tapestry of nature's bounty, he wandered the labyrinth of his thoughts, a solitary voyager in search of the elusive shores of self-discovery.

The scent of fertile soil mingled with the delicate perfume of blossoming flowers, a kaleidoscope of fragrances that spoke of renewal and growth. Yet, within the recesses of his being, there lingered a sense of displacement, a poignant reminder of his fragmented identity lost amidst the expanse of the unknown.

Each day dawned with the promise of new beginnings, yet within Bill's heart, there lingered a shadow of uncertainty, a silent plea for solace amidst the vast expanse of the unfamiliar. In the quietude of the village, where the rhythms of life echoed in harmonious cadence, he sought refuge in the timeless embrace of nature's embrace, a solitary pilgrim on the journey of self-discovery.

The people of the village were the heartbeat of this serene landscape. Their faces bore the weathered lines of years spent tending to the land, cultivating life from the soil. With hearts as warm as the golden sun that bathed the fields, they welcomed each day with a spirit of resilience and unity.

Within this idyllic village, the secluded hut near the rice farm became Bill's refuge. It was a place where time seemed to slow to a crawl, a sanctuary where his past remained veiled in shadow. The elderly woman, wise and gentle, had opened her home and her heart to the enigmatic stranger who had appeared at their footstep. Her compassionate granddaughter, Natal, was equally kind-hearted, and together they had taken Bill in without question, offering their care and protection.

For Bill, the passage of time had blurred into a hazy continuum. He had no memory of his name, his life before, or why he had been found in the swampy embrace of the rice fields. The villagers whispered tales of a man with no name, a wanderer who had emerged from the murky waters like a mystery from the depths.

Every day was a relentless struggle for Bill. The scars on his legs, souvenirs of an unknown ordeal, made walking an arduous task. He communicated not with words but through silent expressions of gratitude, his eyes a wellspring of unspoken emotions. Natal and her grandmother had become his lifeline, their hands gentle as they tended to his wounds, their voices soothing as they offered him comfort.

In the quiet of the village, Bill's presence remained a closely guarded secret. He was a solitary figure, a white man in a community that had already endured the ravages of war and conflict. The villagers understood that exposing him to the outside world would invite danger, so he stayed hidden, seeking solace in the simplicity of the life the elderly woman and Natal had graciously extended to him.

In this peaceful enclave of the world, where the scent of the earth and the warmth of its people embraced him, Bill embarked on a journey of self-discovery. He may have been a man with no name, but he had found a home, and in the heart of the farm village, he began to rebuild not only his strength but also his sense of self.

Under the shimmering veil of moonlight, the rice farm transformed into a dreamscape, a place where time seemed to stand still. As the evening descended, Natal and Bill would embark on their nightly journeys through the fields, guided by the soft glow of the moon. The rice paddies, glistening with dew, stretched out in all directions like an endless sea of silver.

Natal's presence was a soothing balm for Bill's troubled soul. She walked beside him in companionable silence, the tranquil symphony of the night filling the spaces between them. The moon hung low in the sky, casting a gentle, silver light that painted the world in ethereal hues. It was in these moonlit moments that Natal shared her knowledge of the heavens, her voice a melodic whisper against the backdrop of the night.

Seated amidst the rice stalks, they would gaze up at the stars, each one a tiny beacon in the vast expanse of the universe. Natal's voice, filled with the reverence of a storyteller, wove tales of constellations and their secrets. She spoke of ancient myths and celestial wonders, her words an enchanting narrative that transported them to realms beyond their own.

Bill, a man burdened with the weight of forgotten memories, remained a silent listener. His eyes, like mirrors to his inner world, reflected the wonder he felt in Natal's presence. In those moments, he wasn't a man with no name, no voice, and no past; he was a soul adrift in the beauty of the universe, seeking solace and connection.

Natal, too, found herself drawn to this enigmatic stranger who had become a part of her world. She couldn't explain the profound connection that had formed between them, a bond that transcended words and reason. Her heart swelled with compassion, and she couldn't help but attend to his every need, ensuring his comfort and well-being.

As they walked together in the moonlight, a silent love story unfolded, a tale of two souls entwined by destiny. Bill may not have known who he was, but he knew the beauty of Natal's soul, and Natal may not have understood the mysteries of Bill's past, but she knew the love that had blossomed between them. In their shared moments under the luminous embrace of the moon, they were falling in love without knowing, and the heart's deepest emotions transcended the boundaries of words.

Natal's grandmother, wise and perceptive, had a way of gently teasing her granddaughter about the unspoken emotions that simmered between Natal and Bill. As they sat together under the moonlight, sharing their stories and their hearts, the elderly woman couldn't help but notice the connection that had woven itself between the two.

With a knowing smile, she would nudge Natal gently and ask, "My dear, are you falling in love with him?" Her voice carried a hint of concern, tempered with the wisdom of experience. "You know he's a white man, and when he can walk and talk again, he'll surely return to his home. Be careful, my love; you may end up with a broken heart."

Natal, however, dismissed her grandmother's warnings with a smile of her own, her eyes filled with conviction. She had an unwavering faith in the purpose behind Bill's presence in their lives. "Grandmother," she would reply, her voice filled with a blend of assurance and playfulness, "he may have been lost, captured, or even left for dead. But I believe God meant for me to find him."

In those moments of shared laughter and affection, they acknowledged the complexities of their situation. Natal's heart, brimming with compassion, had found solace in Bill's company. She believed that their paths had crossed for a reason, that their connection transcended the boundaries of race and circumstance.

As they looked up at the moonlit sky, they knew that the road ahead was uncertain, filled with challenges and questions. But in their shared determination to navigate this journey together, they found a bond that was stronger than any obstacle. Natal was resolute in her belief that love had a way of transcending boundaries, and even if their paths diverged in the future, the love they had discovered in each other's company would remain an enduring testament to the power of fate and the beauty of connection.

Under the velvet embrace of the night sky, Natal and Bill shared a profound connection that transcended words. It was on one of those starlit evenings when Natal decided to take Bill to the bonfire, a cherished tradition in their village.

They sat side by side, the crackling flames casting dancing shadows upon their faces. Natal's eyes were alight with the fire's glow as she began her enchanting ritual. "You see," she said softly, "each star up there has its own name, its own story."

With a sense of wonder, Natal pointed to the first twinkling star. "This one," she began, "is Altair, the brightest star in the Aquila constellation. It's said to be the abode of a lovelorn weaver. Legend has it that he weaves a bridge of stars to reunite with his true love, Vega."

Bill's gaze followed Natal's delicate finger as she traced the celestial patterns. She continued, "And over there, that's Orion, the great hunter. He's chasing the Pleiades, the Seven Sisters, across the heavens."

As Natal named each star, her voice held the cadence of a love poem, and her eyes sparkled with adoration for the night sky. "Sirius," she whispered, "the Dog Star, the brightest star of all. It's my favorite. It's the herald of a new day, the harbinger of hope."

Bill remained a silent observer, his eyes locked on the tapestry of stars above. He listened to Natal's stories with rapt attention, though he could not respond in words. But his presence, his unwavering gaze, spoke volumes about the connection they shared.

Time seemed to stand still as they sat by the bonfire, immersed in the beauty of the cosmos. Natal's heart swelled with love, not just for the stars but for the man beside her, who had become an irreplaceable part of her life.

When the night had whispered its secrets and the bonfire had dwindled to embers, Natal gently rose from rice's hay. She offered Bill a tender smile, her hand extended to guide him back to the small hut where he had found refuge.

In silence, they returned to the quiet sanctuary of their shared existence, their souls connected through the magic of the night sky and the unspoken feelings that bound them together.

After ensuring Bill was comfortably asleep, Natal would quietly exit his room, leaving him in the peaceful embrace of the night. Each day passed with her tending to him, the connection between them growing stronger, and the hope of discovering his identity becoming more distant.

The Voice

The awakening of Bill's voice was a moment that rippled through the air like a lilac wave, carrying with it a tidal surge of emotions. For so long, Natal had grown accustomed to the silent presence of the man who had become an integral part of her life, a man she had come to care for deeply. But now, as his voice graced the morning air, a newfound connection began to blossom, and their world seemed to shift on its axis.

With a smile that radiated gratitude and humility, Bill uttered his first words, and they hung in the air like a delicate, fragrant blossom. "Good morning," he spoke, his voice a tentative melody that danced upon the morning breeze. Natal stood there, momentarily stunned by the sound, her heart racing with surprise and elation. It was as though the entire universe had conspired to gift her this extraordinary moment.

Summoning her courage, Natal replied in a hushed tone, her voice trembling with a mixture of curiosity and anticipation. "You can speak. What is your name?" She had long yearned to know the identity of the man whose life she had helped to save, the man who had become a mystery she was determined to   unravel.

Bill's response was gentle, his voice like a lilac breeze, caressing the senses with its tenderness and vulnerability. "I don't know what my name is," he confessed, his voice quivering with uncertainty, "I don't know who I am, and I don't know where I am." The weight of his words hung in the air, a heavy fog of questions that had haunted him for months.

Natal, now sitting beside him on the bed, looked deeply into his eyes, her own filled with empathy and understanding. Her voice, like a warm embrace, was kind and reassuring as she provided the little information she had. "You are in Laos," she began, "but I don't know who you are or where you're from. We found you in the swamp water near our rice farm, and we have no idea how you got there." Her words carried a sense of shared bewilderment, a recognition that they were both navigating uncharted territory.

Bill's fingers brushed against Natal's hand, a gesture that spoke volumes of gratitude and a burgeoning connection that transcended words. He whispered, his voice a fragile echo of sincerity, "Thank you for saving my life." In that simple expression of gratitude, their friendship was forged, built upon the foundation of trust, care, and the mysteries of the past that were yet to be unraveled.

In the hush of that intimate moment, as their voices mingled in the quiet space between them, they realized that their connection ran deeper than circumstance or memory. It was a connection forged in the crucible of adversity and nurtured by the tenderness of their hearts. The lilac wave of emotion that enveloped them was a testament to the profound love that was growing, unspoken but deeply felt, between two souls brought together by fate.

As tears welled up in Bill's eyes, glistening like raindrops against the morning sunrise, he extended his arms and embraced Natal tightly. The hug was a wordless expression of gratitude, a heartfelt thanksgiving for the kindness and compassion she had shown him. He held her close, his emotions spilling over into silent tears that spoke of a profound sense of relief and connection.

With a trembling voice, Bill managed to say, "Thank you, Natal. I may not remember who I was, but I will always remember your kindness and your family's generosity." His words were a mixture of gratitude and vulnerability, a reflection of the gratitude that swelled within him.

Natal, in that moment, became both a comforting presence and a beacon of reassurance. She gently stroked his back, offering solace in the form of her touch. "You're welcome," she replied softly, her voice carrying a warmth that enveloped them both. "We will let you stay with us until you figure out who you are."

Their connection deepened as they leaned on each other for support and understanding. They became friends, their shared journey of self-discovery strengthening the bond that had formed between them. Natal was a source of unwavering encouragement, patiently helping Bill piece together the fragments of his lost past.

In the weeks that followed, they embarked on a mission to unlock the mysteries of Bill's forgotten life. Natal tirelessly shared stories of their village introduced him to their way of life and introduced him to the people who had become like family to her. Bill, in turn, absorbed every detail with a thirst for knowledge and a growing sense of belonging.

As they walked the path of rediscovery together, their connection evolved into a profound friendship. They became confidants, sharing their hopes, fears, and dreams. Bill's memories remained elusive, but with each passing day, he felt a little more at home in their village, and a little more at ease with the person he was becoming.

The love and connection between Bill and Natal continued to blossom, a testament to the power of compassion and the strength of their shared journey. They were no longer merely caretaker and patient; they were companions on a path of self-discovery, and their friendship was a beacon of hope that illuminated the way forward.

Natal, with unwavering dedication, became Bill's guide through the labyrinth of his forgotten past. Each morning, they would walk hand in hand towards the rising sun, the golden light casting a romantic aura around them.

Natal had vowed to help him remember who he was, just as he had vowed to stand by her side. Their bond grew stronger with each passing day. As they walked, they would often pause to lean into yoga postures, Bill's body gradually regaining its strength and flexibility under Natal's patient guidance. Together, they would meditate, finding solace in the tranquil surroundings, their hearts beating in unison with the rhythm of the earth.

In the quietude of these moments, Bill felt his connection with Natal deepening. Her kindness, her wisdom, and her unwavering support became a balm for his fractured soul. With every shared breath, he was drawn further into the enchantment of her presence.

One day, as they toiled in the rice fields, their hands covered in the fertile earth, Bill spoke softly, "Natal, I cannot continue to be known a man without a name. Will you help me choose one?" Natal looked at him, her eyes sparkling with warmth, and with a chuckle, she replied, "I could see you as Yang."

Bill's heart swelled with gratitude and newfound hope. "Yang," he repeated, savoring the sound of his new name on his lips. It was the beginning of a new chapter in his life, marked by a name that Natal had chosen, a name that held the promise of a brighter future.

As the days melted into weeks and the weeks into months, Bill, now known as Yang, found himself drawn to Natal in ways he couldn't comprehend. Their shared moments grew increasingly intimate, and the lines between friendship and something deeper began to blur.

One of their most cherished rituals was sitting by the bonfire under the velvet canopy of stars. The night sky became their canvas, and the stars their storybook. Natal would name each constellation, and Yang would listen, his eyes fixed on her face, as if she were the brightest star in the universe. With each passing night, their conversations became more personal, sharing their dreams, fears, and the fragments of their lives.

In the daylight hours, they toiled side by side in the verdant rice fields. Yang marveled at Natal's strength, grace, and unwavering determination. Her laughter, like the tinkling of wind chimes, became the melody that accompanied their labor. They reveled in the simplicity of life on the farm, finding solace in the shared rhythm of their work.

But it was during the quieter moments that Yang's heart began to unravel. As they sat together, gazing at the shimmering stars above or working the fields with the golden sunbathing them in its warm embrace, he felt an undeniable pull towards Natal. Her kindness, her compassion, and her unyielding faith in him tugged at the very essence of his being.

One evening, under a moonlit sky, with the scent of rice fields surrounding them, Yang finally found the words he had been struggling to express. He turned to Natal, his eyes filled with a deep longing, and said, "Natal, I may not know who I am, but I know one thing for sure. I know who you are. You are the girl that I am falling in love with."

Natal's heart skipped a beat as she looked into Yang's eyes, searching for any sign of hesitation or doubt. But what she found was an earnest sincerity that left her breathless. With the moon as their witness and the stars as their silent audience, their lips met in a soft, tender kiss.

It was a kiss that spoke of longing, of shared moments, and of a love that had blossomed in the most unexpected of places. In that stolen moment beneath the celestial expanse, they knew that their connection was not bound by the constraints of memory or time. Their love was a testament to the resilience of the human spirit and the enduring power of the heart.

As Yang's love for Natal continued to flourish, he found himself awakening to a life he never thought possible. The joy of love had breathed new life into him, and he was determined to cherish every moment by her side. Natal, with her radiant smile, long black hair, and enchanting eyes, had become the center of his world.

Their days were filled with laughter, shared dreams, and the warmth of their growing affection. But it was under the veil of night that their connection truly deepened. The moon and stars bore witness to their secret rendezvous, where stolen kisses and whispered promises painted the canvas of their love story.

On that fateful evening, as Bill and Natal found solace in each other's arms, their world was enveloped in a cocoon of quietude and tenderness. The moon cast a gentle glow over their embrace, painting their love with the ethereal hues of the night. It was a moment of deep connection, where words were unnecessary, and their hearts spoke a language of their own.

However, the tranquility of their reverie was disrupted by a voice that pierced through the night's serenity. It was Natal's grandmother, a figure revered for her wisdom and a custodian of age-old traditions. She called for Yang, whose name carried with it a sense of love and devotion. Reluctantly, Yang tore himself away from Natal's arms, leaving her with a lingering promise in his gaze, and followed the elderly woman to a secluded corner of their small home.

In the dim light, Natal's grandmother wore a somber expression as she began to explain the customs and norms of their village. She spoke of the deeply ingrained traditions that governed their lives, particularly the one concerning young, unmarried couples. To engage in relations that could lead to pregnancy before marriage was considered a grave transgression, one that would bring unimaginable shame and disgrace upon their family.

Her words weighed heavily upon Yang's heart. He listened intently, understanding the significance of tradition and the honor of their family. But he was resolute in his love for Natal, and he knew what he had to do. With a voice that trembled with determination, he addressed Natal's grandmother, asking for her blessing to marry Natal.

In that solemn moment, Yang vowed to uphold the traditions of their village and protect their family's honor at all costs. He declared his unwavering commitment to Natal and his determination to ensure that she would never be subjected to disgrace. His words were a testament to the depth of his love and the strength of his conviction.

The elderly woman, moved by Yang's sincerity and the love he held for her granddaughter, gave her consent. With her blessing, the path toward their marriage was paved, and their love story became forever entwined with the rich tapestry of their village's traditions.

After the night spent watching the moonlight together, Yang retreated to his room, the memory of their shared moments etched in his heart. The tranquility of the night had brought them closer, but Natal was left with a question that weighed heavily on her mind. She couldn't bear the uncertainty any longer, and so, with a sense of trepidation, she made her way to his door. Standing there, her heart racing, she asked him the question that had been haunting her thoughts. "Yang," she began, her voice trembling with a mixture of fear and hope, "did you decide to marry me because you have no place else to go, or did it come from your heart?"

Yang, with tenderness in his voice, approached the door and gently pulled her into an embrace. They stood there, wrapped in each other's arms, as if seeking refuge in the warmth of their connection. Then, he guided her to the edge of the bed, and they sat down, their eyes locked in a profound gaze.

With unwavering sincerity, Yang spoke from the depths of his soul. "Natal," he began, his voice a gentle caress of reassurance, "what I feel for you is vaster than the galaxies that adorn the night sky. It's a love that transcends time and circumstance." His words were a testament to the profound depth of his emotions.

He continued, his voice filled with unwavering certainty, "If I were given a thousand lifetimes and a thousand choices, I would choose you over and over again. Marrying you is not a decision born out of necessity, but a celebration of the love that has blossomed in my heart, a love that I cherish with every fiber of my being."

In that intimate moment, as they sat on the edge of the bed, their hearts intertwined, Natal felt a profound sense of reassurance and love. Yang's words were a balm for her fears, a declaration of a love that was as boundless as the universe itself. Their connection, born under the moon's gentle gaze, had deepened into a love that would endure, no matter the challenges that lay ahead.

Mr. & Mrs. Yang

Yang wanted to embrace the culture, he visited few of old men to teach him the traditional way of preparing to marry a Laotian woman. He wanted to give Natal to enjoy everything that she dreamed and knew about wedding ceremony.

The sunbathed the lush countryside of Laos in a warm, golden hue as the day of Yang and Natal's wedding arrived. It was a day that had been long-awaited, a celebration of love that would resonate through generations. Yang, standing tall in his resplendent traditional Laotian attire, felt a mix of excitement and deep contentment. Beside him, Natal radiated joy, and grace in her elegant burgundy attire. Their eyes locked, silently promising each other a lifetime of love and devotion.

As family and friends celebrate festivities commenced with the Baci ceremony, a time-honored Laotian tradition that symbolized the union of the couple. Elders and family members gathered around, each holding a white cotton string, or "sai sin," representing blessings and good luck. The strings were meticulously tied around the wrists of Yang and Natal, as well as their loved ones. With every knot, wishes for a prosperous and harmonious marriage filled the air. The couple was overwhelmed by the love and warmth of their family and community.

Amidst the joy and revelry, the couple received wisdom and blessings from the elders. Respected community members shared stories of enduring love and emphasized the importance of respect, understanding, and unity in marriage. Natal and Yang absorbed these lessons, knowing that their journey would be enriched by the wisdom of those who had walked this path before them.

As the Baci ceremony concluded, the rhythmic sounds of traditional Laotian music filled the air. Dancers, adorned in vibrant costumes, gracefully moved to the enchanting tunes of the khene and drums. The dance narrated the story of Yang and Natal's journey, from the day they met to this moment of union. The fluid movements and intricate steps conveyed the depth of their love. As the dancers swayed and spun, the couple couldn't help but feel that their love was woven into the very fabric of their culture.

As the night sky adorned itself with a tapestry of stars, family and friends gone home. Natal and Yang found themselves alone for a moment by the bonfire. The crackling flames cast a warm glow upon their faces as they held each other's hands. It was under this starry canopy that Yang finally spoke, his voice trembling with emotion. "Natal," he began, "I may not remember who I once was, but I know who you are. You are not just the girl who rescued me from the rice farm, you are my wife, my love, my friend, and future" with eyes shaded tears he continues to express his feeling to his newly wife. "I am falling in love with, more deeply with each passing day." With those heartfelt words, he leaned in and kissed her gently, sealing their love beneath the vast expanse of the night sky.

Their love, now reaffirmed with unwavering devotion, became a guiding light in the days that followed. The village embraced their union with warmth and acceptance, celebrated the marriage of Natal and Yang with a traditional ceremony that brought the entire community together. It was a joyous occasion that marked the fusion of two worlds, two souls, and two hearts that had found their home in each other.

As husband and wife, Yang and Natal embarked on a new chapter of their lives together. They worked side by side in the rice fields, planting the seeds of their future as they nurtured the crops that sustained their village. Their love story became an inspiration, a testament to the power of love to transcend boundaries and bring people together.

With each passing day, Yang's memory remained elusive, but he found solace in the love and companionship he shared with Natal. Their home, once a place of refuge for Yang, had now become a sanctuary of love, laughter, and shared dreams. They embraced the traditions of the village while forging a path of their own, and their love story continued to unfold with each sunrise and sunset.

The bond between Yang and Natal deepened, and their connection remained unbreakable, even as they faced the challenges and uncertainties of life. Together, they discovered the beauty of a love that was built on trust, resilience, and the belief that destiny had brought them together for a reason.

In the heart of the rice farm village, their love story became a cherished legend, a testament to the enduring power of love that transcends time and circumstance. Bill may have arrived as a man with no name, but Yang had found his identity in the love he shared with Natal, and in her, he had found his forever home.

As each dawn broke over the tranquil Laotian countryside, the world seemed to hold its breath in reverence for the love that had blossomed to the newlywed. The Sunday morning the air was crisp and pure, carrying with it the scent of fresh rice fields and blooming flowers. A soft, gentle breeze rustled through the leaves, as if whispering secrets to the newlyweds.

In the cozy bamboo-walled room, Yang stirred, his heart overflowing with a joy he couldn't quite explain. His eyes wandered to the sleeping figure beside him, and a tender smile played on his lips. Natal lay there, bathed in the soft, golden embrace of morning light. Her long, ebony hair seemed to capture the very essence of night's darkness transitioning into the radiant day.

The world outside came alive with the chorus of birds, celebrating the union that had taken place. Their melodic songs filled the air, creating a harmonious symphony of nature's blessings. Yang couldn't help but feel that the birds themselves were congratulating him on his choice.

As he continued to gaze at Natal, he marveled at the delicate curve of her eyelashes, the rise and fall of her peaceful breath, and the warmth of her presence beside him. The sunbeams caressed her cheeks, casting a gentle glow, and highlighting the subtle contours of her face. It was a portrait of serenity and grace.

In this moment, Yang knew that there was a special place in his heart, a place reserved exclusively for Natal. It was a place where the deepest, most profound love resided. He felt a profound sense of contentment, as if all the uncertainties that had clouded his past had evaporated, leaving only clarity and purpose.

The world outside continued its dance of awakening, but Yang and Natal remained cocooned in their private haven, where time seemed to stand still. He gently brushed a strand of hair from her face, leaning in to place a soft kiss on her forehead.

Yang carefully slipped out of the bed, leaving Natal to continue her peaceful slumber. With a smile that seemed to radiate warmth, he moved quietly through the room, his heart dancing with love and devotion.

In the corner of the room stood a tall vase filled with freshly picked wildflowers, a delicate reminder of the beauty that surrounded them. Yang couldn't resist plucking a few vibrant blooms, their colors mirroring Natal's grace.

Stepping out into the gentle morning light, he made his way to a cluster of coconut palms nearby. With practiced ease, he climbed one of the slender trees, his bare feet gripping the rough bark effortlessly. In no time, he had coaxed several young coconuts from the swaying branches.

Descending gracefully, Yang carefully cracked open the coconuts with a well-practiced skill. He poured their refreshing, slightly sweet water into a bamboo vessel, ensuring it remained pure and untouched by the outside world.

With the coconuts in hand, he returned to the room, where Natal was beginning to stir. The soft morning breeze seemed to follow him, bringing with it the gentle rustling of leaves and the sweet scent of the flowers that adorned the room.

Natal slowly opened her eyes, her gaze meeting Yang's as he approached the bed. The sight of him, holding the coconut water and flowers, seemed like a dream, a vision of love and devotion brought to life.

Yang tenderly helped Natal sit up, propping her with an assortment of cushions. He presented her with a fresh, young coconut, the water still glistening with droplets of morning dew. Natal's eyes sparkled with appreciation as she accepted the cool, refreshing gift. The water was a testament to the purity of their love, untouched by any impurities.

As Natal enjoyed her coconut water, Yang prepared a simple yet nourishing breakfast, all the while stealing glances at her with eyes full of admiration. He fed her with gentle care, each bite a silent declaration of his love and commitment.

Their morning was a delicate dance of intimacy and affection, as they shared tender words and stolen kisses. The world outside continued to wake, but within their private sanctuary, time seemed to linger, allowing their love to flourish and deepen.

In this sacred space, surrounded by the beauty of nature and the purity of their love, Yang and Natal found themselves wrapped in the morning's embrace, knowing that each day together would be a new beginning, filled with love and devotion.

Dreaming Of The Past

Dorothy sat by the window, her gaze fixed on the horizon as the sun dipped below the skyline, casting a warm, melancholic glow into the room. It had been three long, agonizing years since Bill disappeared in Vietnam, and the pain was still etched deep within her heart.

She had tried to move forward, as others had suggested. Friends and family had offered well-meaning advice, encouraging her to find new love and happiness. But Dorothy's heart remained steadfastly anchored in the past, a place where Bill's memory lived on in every corner of her life.

One evening, as the shadows lengthened and the room darkened, Sarah joined her by the window. The sisters shared a deep and unbreakable bond, born not only from their friendship ties but also from the shared love they had for Bill.

Sarah had seen her family's struggle, watched as Dorothy clung to the memories of their beloved brother. And as they sat there together, Sarah gently placed a hand on Dorothy's shoulder, her voice filled with love and understanding.

"Dorothy," she began softly, "I know how much you love Bill. We all do. He's forever a part of us, and nothing will ever replace him in our hearts. But I also know that Bill would want to see you happy, to see you living your life to the fullest."

Dorothy turned to look at Sarah, her eyes glistening with unshed tears. Sarah's words were a balm to her wounded soul, a reminder of the deep connection they shared not only with Bill but also with each other.

"I understand that you may never find anyone who could take Bill's place," Sarah continued, her voice filled with empathy. "But I believe that there's room in your heart for new love, for someone who can walk beside you on this journey of life."

Dorothy nodded with her heart heavy with emotions. She knew that Sarah was right, that Bill would want her to find happiness again. Yet, the path forward still felt uncertain, and she couldn't help but wonder if it was even possible to open her heart to someone new.

As the sisters sat there, their connection stronger than ever, they understood that the love they had for Bill would forever bind them together. In that moment, they found solace in each other's presence, knowing that, regardless of the challenges they faced, their love and sisterhood would always endure.

Sarah was determined to help her sister-in law embark on this new journey of finding love. She knew it wouldn't be easy, but she was willing to do whatever it took to see Dorothy happy again.

With every arranged date that had come and gone, Dorothy's hopes had faded like distant memories. Her friends and family had been well-meaning, eager to see her happy again, but the reality was that no one could ever replace Bill. She had decided to put an end to these futile attempts at love, to spare herself the disappointment that had become all too familiar.

Sarah knew Dorothy had always been a woman of strong conviction. Her heart had once been whole, filled with the boundless love she had shared with her late husband, Bill. But since his passing, her world had grown dimmer, and the prospect of finding another love that could even begin to compare seemed impossible.

One evening, as the sun dipped below the horizon, casting a warm, orange glow over the town, Dorothy sat down with her dear friend Sarah. She could see the concern in Sarah's eyes, knowing how much she had suffered. Taking a deep breath, she spoke with quiet determination.

"Sarah," she began, her voice steady, "I've decided that I can't keep chasing a love that mirrors what I had with Bill. It's not fair to these men, and it's certainly not fair to my heart. From now on, I'll be content with the love that Bill left behind in my heart. I won't actively seek love anymore."

Sarah, who had been supportive through all of Dorothy's trials, nodded solemnly. "I understand, Dorothy. I've seen how much you've struggled. But before we close this chapter, promise me you'll go on one last date, the one I've arranged for you. If it doesn't work out, I'll stand by your decision to stop searching for love. You deserve happiness, and I want to see you find it, even if it's in the love you hold for Bill."

Dorothy hesitated for a moment, then nodded in agreement. "Alright, Sarah, one last date. I'll go, but if it doesn't work out, I hope you'll understand that it's time for me to cherish the love I had and move forward in my own way."

As the two friends shared this heartfelt moment, they knew that whatever the future held, they would face it together. The sun dipped below the horizon, and a new chapter in Dorothy's journey toward healing and self-discovery was about to begin.

The last date was quickly arranged, and Sarah took charge of helping Dorothy get ready. They spent hours together, selecting the perfect outfit, doing her hair and makeup, and ensuring that she felt confident and beautiful. Sarah's unwavering presence was a source of comfort for Dorothy, who was stepping into the unknown.

"You look stunning," Sarah said with a warm smile as she put the finishing touches on Dorothy's makeup. "He's going to be blown away when he sees you. Dorothy offered a nervous but appreciative smile. "Thanks, Sarah. I couldn't do this without you." "You've got this," Sarah reassured her. "And remember, I'm just a phone call away if you need anything."

As Dorothy prepared to leave for her date, Sarah hugged her tightly. "Go out there and enjoy yourself," she said. "I'll be here looking after Bella, and when you come back, we can talk about how it went."

Dorothy took a deep breath, mustering her courage. With Sarah's support and encouragement, she felt a glimmer of hope that this new chapter in her life might hold the promise of love and happiness once more.

As Sarah sat in the living room, anxiously waiting for Dorothy to return from her date with Jackson, she couldn't help but reflect on her brother, Bill, and how he had always been the protective and caring older sibling. She wished he could have been there to meet Jackson, to give his approval, and to offer guidance to Dorothy in this new phase of her life.

When she heard the car pull into the driveway, Sarah's heart skipped a beat. She knew how important this evening was for her sister-in-law and best friend. She got up and looked out the window, seeing Jackson exit the car and walk Dorothy to the door. He displayed respect and kindness, and Sarah couldn't help but feel relieved that her first matchmaking attempt had gone well.

As Dorothy entered the house, she found Sarah waiting in the living room, a look of curiosity and anticipation on her face. Without wasting any time, Dorothy began to share her thoughts about Jackson.

"Sarah, he's a really nice guy," Dorothy said, her eyes lighting up with excitement. "He's respectful, attentive, and we had a great conversation. I actually enjoyed myself."

Sarah couldn't hide her relief and happiness at hearing her best friend's positive feedback. "I'm so glad to hear that. I knew Jackson was a good match for you. If you want, we can plan another date with him or explore other possibilities. It's entirely up to you."

Dorothy nodded appreciatively. "Thank you, Sarah. I think I'd like to see him again. He's different from anyone I've met before." With a smile on her face, she added, "I mean after Bill".

With a warm smile, Sarah knew that she had taken a small but important step in helping her sister find happiness once more. She couldn't help but look back at Bella's peaceful sleeping form, feeling a sense of hope for the future and a deep love for her family.

Dorothy & Jackson Blossom Love

As the weeks turned into months, Dorothy and Jackson's relationship blossomed. They enjoyed each other's company, shared their dreams and aspirations, and found solace in each other's arms. Dorothy had finally found a deep connection she thought she might never experience again, and Jackson was equally smitten with her.

One evening, after a particularly lovely date, Dorothy gathered the courage to broach a significant topic with Sarah. They were sitting in the living room, sipping on tea, when Dorothy carefully brought up the idea.

"Sarah," Dorothy began, her voice filled with both hope and trepidation, "I've been thinking. Jackson has become such an important part of my life, and I believe he's here to stay. Would you be okay if I introduced him to Bella?"

Sarah looked at Dorothy, her eyes filled with understanding and support. She had seen the happiness in Dorothy's eyes and knew that this was a step she wanted to take.

"Of course, Dorothy," Sarah replied with a warm smile. "I think it's a wonderful idea. Bella deserves to have someone like Jackson in her life. Just let me know when you want to arrange it, and I'll be there to help."

Dorothy felt a wave of relief wash over her. With her sister in law's blessing, she knew she was taking a significant step toward building a future with Jackson, a future that included Bella.

And so, the dinner was arranged, and the special evening arrived when Bella would meet Jackson, the man who had brought love and warmth back into her mother's life. It might have seemed fast to some, but when genuine love and connection are involved, time seems to stand still, allowing two souls to come together as if they were meant to be.

The evening for Bella's meeting with Jackson arrived, and Dorothy couldn't help but feel a mixture of excitement and nervousness. She had taken great care to prepare Bella for this special moment. She had explained that Jackson was a kind and loving person who cared for them both, just like a father would. Bella, although almost turning four years old, had a sense of her mother's emotions and could tell that something important was happening.

As Jackson walked through the front door, he greeted Bella with a warm smile and a gentle "Hi there, sweetie." Bella, who had been playing with her toys, looked up and met his eyes. There was an instant connection between them, something that Dorothy had hoped for and more. Bella's eyes lit up, and she responded with a delighted, "Hi!"

Dorothy watched from the side, her heart swelling with emotion as she witnessed the bond forming between Jackson and her daughter. They began to play together, building a tower with colorful blocks. Bella's giggles filled the room, and Jackson's laughter joined in. It was as if they had known each other forever.

Throughout the evening, Jackson showed genuine interest in Bella's world. He listened to her stories, admired her drawings, and even played her favorite games. It was clear that he wasn't just trying to win over Dorothy; he genuinely cared about Bella and was eager to be a part of her life.

Dorothy couldn't help but smile as she watched them. She felt immense gratitude for the connection that was growing between her daughter and the man she had come to love. Jackson was filling the void that had been left in Bella's life since Bill's disappearance. The sense of happiness and contentment that had eluded them for so long was beginning to return, and Dorothy knew in her heart that she had made the right choice in introducing Jackson to her family.

As the evening came to an end, Bella gave Jackson a big hug, and Dorothy saw the love and trust in her daughter's eyes. It was a beautiful sight, a moment of healing, and a step toward building a new family. In that connection between Bella and Jackson, Dorothy found hope, knowing that their future together was bright and full of possibilities.

Dorothy couldn't help but smile as she watched Jackson and Bella interact. It was as if a spark had ignited between them, a connection that transcended mere introductions. She had been apprehensive about introducing Bella to a new man, fearing that it would never measure up to the bond she had shared with Bill. But watching Jackson with her daughter, she felt a sense of hope she hadn't felt in years.

As they laughed and chatted, Bella's eyes lit up with genuine happiness. Dorothy prayed silently that Jackson would continue to be a source of care and tender support for her daughter. It had been a painful reality that Bella had lost her father, Bill, before she had the chance to meet him. Dorothy often blamed the Vietnam War for taking away one of the most beautiful gifts she could have given to her daughter: the chance to know and love the man she had chosen as her father.

Now, in Jackson, Dorothy saw a second chance. She knew he could never replace Bill, but he had the potential to fill the void in Bella's life. He could be the man who walked beside her, offering guidance, love, and support as she grew into the remarkable young woman Dorothy knew she was destined to become.

With a sense of gratitude and newfound hope, Dorothy realized that perhaps, just perhaps, love could find its way back into her heart as well. She would always cherish the love she had shared with Bill, but in Jackson, she saw the possibility of a new chapter, a new kind of love that would honor Bill's memory while allowing her heart to heal.

As the days turned into weeks and then into months, Bella's connection with Jackson deepened. He wasn't just a stepfather; he had become a steadfast presence in her life, a pillar of strength, and someone she could truly confide in. The bond that formed between them was nothing short of magical.

As Bella's fourth birthday approached, there was a palpable excitement in the air. The house was adorned with colorful balloons and decorations, a testament to the joy that had returned to their lives. The anticipation of the celebration filled every corner of the home.

On that special day, both sets of grandparents gathered around, their smiles reflecting the love they had for their precious Bella. Dorothy's parents, who had always been a constant source of support, held Bella close and whispered their love into her ear. And on Bill's side, his parents were equally thrilled to be a part of this celebration.

As the birthday cake with four candles was brought to the table, a mixture of emotions swirled within the room. Bella was seated between her two grandmothers. While Bill's mother was genuinely happy for Bella and Dorothy, her heart ached with the realization that her son, Bill, should have been there to witness this milestone. Tears welled up in her eyes, and she discreetly wiped them away, her emotions a blend of sorrow and happiness.

Sarah, standing beside her mother, gently placed a reassuring hand on her shoulder. "I know, Mom," she whispered softly. "It's bittersweet, isn't it? But remember, no one can ever replace Bill in Bella's heart. He'll always be her father, even if he's not with us."

With a nod, Bill's mother found solace in her daughter's words. She knew they were true, and she took comfort in the fact that Bella would grow up knowing the love of both her fathers – the one who had left too soon and the one who had entered her life to fill it with love and care.

As the room filled with laughter, singing, and the sweet scent of birthday cake, Dorothy stood at the kitchen window, looking out at the scene before her. She watched as Bella blew out the candles with Jackson by her side, the man who had brought newfound happiness into their lives.

Dorothy's eyes met Sarah's, and they shared a silent, knowing smile. It was a smile that spoke of the gratitude they both felt for the decisions they had made, for the love that had blossomed beyond their wildest dreams. It was a smile that said, "Look at the beautiful family we've become."

In that moment, Dorothy knew she had made the right choice in introducing Jackson into their lives. It was a decision that had brought joy, love, and a sense of wholeness back to their family, and as she watched Bella's joyful face, she couldn't help but feel that Bill was smiling down on them from above, proud of the love that continued to flourish in his absence.

Dorothy stood in her cap and gown, the graduation ceremony of the University of Washington about to begin. She looked out at the sea of graduates, feeling a mix of emotions. Five years had passed since she had walked these same halls as a young bride with dreams in her heart, and so much had changed.

In those four years, she had experienced the joy of becoming a mother, the deep sorrow of losing her beloved Bill, and the determination to pursue her dream of becoming a marine engineer. Life had taken her on a rollercoaster ride of emotions, but today was a day of triumph and celebration.

Her baby girl, Bella, was now a vibrant girl who constantly reminded Dorothy of Bill with her infectious laughter and curious nature. Though Bill was no longer there to witness their daughter's growth, Dorothy felt his presence in every smile and every word Bella spoke.

As the ceremony began, Dorothy couldn't help but remember her first graduation day when she had walked across the stage with

Bill's eyes on her. They had hope and plans for their future together, and she could still hear Bill's voice cheering her on.

But now, as she walked the stage again, it was Jackson who sat in the audience, clapping proudly as she received her degree in marine engineering. Jackson had been her rock, her source of strength during the darkest days of her life. He had stepped into the role of a loving father to Bella, and together, they had created a loving and supportive family.

As she accepted her diploma, Dorothy felt a sense of accomplishment and fulfillment. Her dreams of becoming an engineer had come true, and she knew that Bill would be proud of her. She also knew that he would want her to be happy, to move forward with her life, and to embrace the love that Jackson had to offer.

After the ceremony, Dorothy found herself surrounded by friends and family, including Sarah, who had also graduated that day. They congratulated her on her achievements, and as she looked at the people who had stood by her through thick and thin, she felt a deep sense of gratitude.

Yes, there were still moments of sadness when she missed Bill with all her heart, but she had learned to cherish the memories and keep his spirit alive in their home. Life had taken unexpected turns, but Dorothy had found the strength to keep moving forward, to pursue her dreams, and to love again.

As she looked at Bella playing with her friends, laughter echoing in the air, Dorothy knew that her journey was far from over. She had faced challenges and overcome them, and she was ready to embrace whatever the future had in store for her and her precious daughter, all while keeping Bill's memory alive in their hearts.

The sun had dipped below the horizon, casting a warm, golden glow over the graduation party hall. Dorothy and Jackson drove home from her graduation ceremony. The car's interior was filled with a sense of accomplishment and anticipation. The soft hum of the engine and the gentle rhythm of the tires on the road created a comforting backdrop to their thoughts.

As they approached a red traffic light, Jackson turned to Dorothy, his eyes filled with emotion, and he reached out to gently touches her face with his hand. The world outside seemed to fade away, leaving only the two of them in that tender moment. His voice quivered with sincerity as he spoke, "Dorothy, I love you more than words can express. Today, seeing you graduate and achieve your dream, my heart swells with pride and love. I want to spend the rest of my life with you, to cherish every moment together."

Dorothy's heart skipped a beat as she looked into his eyes, her own eyes glistening with tears of happiness. She knew that she had found a love that was deep and true, a love that had supported her through the darkest days and celebrated with her during the brightest moments. She whispered, "I love you too, Jackson, with all my heart."

Finally, they arrived home, and Jackson had prepared a special dinner for the three of them. The dining room was softly lit by candles, casting a warm and intimate atmosphere. The table was adorned with fresh flowers, and the aroma of a delicious home-cooked meal filled the air.

As they sat down to eat, Jackson's nerves became apparent, and he felt a lump in his throat. He excused himself from the table for a moment, and Dorothy exchanged a curious glance with Bella. When he returned, he knelt beside Bella's chair, his eyes filled with love and devotion.

He looked at Bella and said, "Bella, you mean the world to me. You've brought so much joy into our lives, and I want to be the best father I can be to you. But I also want to be there for your mother in every way possible. So, Bella, would you be okay if I asked your mother to marry me?"

Bella's eyes widened with innocent curiosity, and she looked from Jackson to her mother. Dorothy's heart swelled with emotion as she nodded with tears in her eyes. "Yes, Bella, Jackson has brought so much love into our lives, and I would be honored to marry him."

With those words, Jackson's face lit up with a radiant smile. He took Dorothy's hand, the diamond ring he had chosen glimmering in the candlelight. He looked into her eyes and asked, "Dorothy, will you make me the happiest man in the world and marry me?"

Overwhelmed with love and joy, Dorothy leaned in and kissed him tenderly before replying, "Yes, Jackson, a thousand times yes."

As they sealed their commitment with a kiss, Bella clapped her little hands with delight, her laughter filling the room. It was a moment of pure love and happiness, a new chapter in their lives filled with promises and dreams.

Two Separate Worlds

In two separate corners of the world, where fates had charted distinct courses, the love stories of Dorothy and Jackson in the tranquil embrace of Redmond, Washington, and Yang and Natal amidst the exotic landscapes of Laos, were unfurling in parallel, their lives intricately connected by an ethereal thread of love that defied the boundaries of time and distance.

Yang and Natal, Dorothy, and Jackson the couples made in heaven, though their stories were shaped by different forces. Dorothy, bearing the weight of the past in her heart, had learned that the present and future held promises of their own. She had come to understand that love wasn't just a story of teenage infatuation, but a journey that evolved and deepened with time.

Yang, on the other hand, had embraced the present fully, carving his own identity in the tapestry of life. He believed in living for today and letting the future take care of itself. In Laos, amidst the breathtaking landscapes, Yang and Natal's love was like the untamed rivers, flowing freely, unhindered by the obstacles of time.

Natal and Jackson were the fortunate ones, beneficiaries of the gifts of circumstance. A different world could have been their reality. What if the Vietnam War had unfolded differently? What if Bill's plane had not crumbled, depriving Natal of the best gift of her life? What if Jackson had never entered the picture? Dorothy might never have experienced the profound depths of mature love.

Bill and Dorothy's love story had been written in the ink of teenage infatuation, a sweet but fleeting chapter in their lives. Jackson, however, brought with him more than just love. He carried with him the weight of experience, the wisdom of maturity, and the sensibility of true, enduring love.

The new love that emerged from the tears and losses stood as firm as the ancient buildings that marked the history of the Roman Empire. Just as those historical structures held the imprints of a glorious past, the love stories of Yang and Natal, Dorothy, and Jackson, would be etched in the annals of time for years to come.

What if…just what if…they had taken different paths? The tapestry of life is woven with countless threads of possibility, but in this moment, in these lives, love had found its place, like the great figures of Rome who held the story of power and love, even when taken by the knife.

Now, with these two couples, the fruits of love and the endless potential of life would continue to be cherished. Their stories, like the history of Rome, would leave their marks on the world, a testament to the enduring power of love, connecting hearts across time and distance.

In the quiet moments of their lives, both couples contemplated the twists of fate that had led them to each other, and the resounding question of "why." Did Bill have to get lost in the tumultuous sea of war to be found by Natal? Did Dorothy have to endure countless nights of tears, her pillow soaking up her heartache, before her wounded heart found solace in Jackson's gentle hands? These questions hung in the air, like the ethereal threads of destiny weaving their stories together.

Natal often wondered if the war had been a necessary crucible, testing their strength and resolve. It had scattered her family across foreign lands, but it had also led her to Yang, whose kindness and unwavering support had been a beacon of hope in the darkest times. She couldn't help but think that perhaps, without the war, their paths might never have been crossed.

Dorothy, too, had her share of "what ifs." What if Bill had returned safely from Vietnam? What if they had continued their teenage love story into adulthood? But as she traced the lines on Jackson's hand, she found herself grateful for the twists of fate that had brought them together. The pain and loss had been their past, but the love they shared was the present and the future.

The couples chose to live in the moment, to embrace the beautiful future they were building together. They had discovered that love, like the ink that dripped onto the pages of their lives, had the power to rewrite their stories, to redefine their destinies. The "what ifs" no longer held them captive; instead, they propelled them forward.

As they walked hand in hand, their love stories intertwined, they understood that everything truly happened for a reason. The pain, the loss, and the uncertainty had led them to this point, where they had found each other and built a love that was unbreakable. They treasured the present and held hope for the future, knowing that their love was the most powerful force, capable of transforming even the most tragic of circumstances into something beautiful and profound.

With each day, their love deepened, their connection grew stronger, and the ink of their love stories continued to flow, creating a narrative filled with hope, resilience, and the unwavering belief that love had the power to overcome all odds.

Fading Past Vivid Present

Love between Dorothy and Jackson flourished with each sunrise, a testament to the profound and healing nature of their affection. Their connection grew not through mere words, but through shared dreams, unspoken fears, and the symphony of their laughter. Together, they wove a tapestry of love that enveloped them in a world entirely their own, a world crafted with tender care, an unwavering trust, and an unspoken promise of boundless support.

Dorothy hadn't consigned Bill to oblivion; instead, she enshrined his memory within the depths of her heart, an enduring treasure from her past. Bill's presence was woven into the fabric of her very being, an intimate guardian of her love that she carried with grace, knowing that he would forever occupy a sacred space within her soul.

Meanwhile, on the far side of the world, Yang and Natal's union blossomed, marked by Yang's obliviousness to the fragments of his past. The crucible of the Vietnam War had gifted Natal the enigmatic package of Yang a lost soul, found. Yet, in the heart-wrenching course of events, Yang's memory was ruthlessly erased by the war's unforgiving hand, leaving behind an enigmatic void where the vivid contours of his love for Dorothy had once flourished.

In his world, the memory of Dorothy was but a whisper in the wind, a poignant melody that had faded into the recesses of his consciousness. He cherished Natal's love as a lifeline, clinging to her unwavering support as he navigated the labyrinth of his memory loss.

Despite the chasm separating their worlds, the love that tethered Dorothy and Bill in spirit, though hidden within the depths of their hearts, endured as an unwavering testament to the enduring potency of love. It was a love that transcended the boundaries of time and geography, etching its presence onto the lives of those who bore its weight. In their own unique ways, Dorothy and Bill found solace and love in the embrace of different lovers, and their narratives continued to unfold—a poignant symphony of love, each chapter imbued with the timeless beauty of the love they had once known.

In the intricate tapestry of their lives, where threads of love connected past, present, and future, a profound and unbreakable bond held Dorothy and Jackson in a timeless embrace. With each passing day in the serene haven of Redmond, Washington, their love deepened, transcending earthly constraints to become a love story for the ages. It was a love that defied the ordinary, an exquisite dance of hearts entwined, their souls merging as if they were celestial bodies drawn together by an irresistible force.

Across the vast expanse of the ocean, in the lush landscapes of Laos, Natal and Yang, navigated the boundless ocean of their love.

Bill's memories, casualties of the relentless Vietnam War, had been swept away like footprints in the sand. Yet Natal had found him, a fragment of her heart from another time. They lived solely in the present, a realm where love knew no boundaries, where the past was an enigma and the future an unwritten love letter.

Despite the brightness of the present and the deepening connection between Dorothy and Jackson, there was a part of Dorothy's heart that remained devoted to the memories of Bill. She believed that cherishing those memories was a way to honor the love they had shared in their youth, and the sacrifices he had made as a soldier.

In the quiet corners of her mind, Dorothy would sometimes retreat to the past, where she would remember the tender moments, the laughter, and the dreams she had once shared with Bill. She would leaf through old letters and photographs, allowing herself to be transported back to a time when their love had been young and innocent.

Dorothy shared these moments with Jackson, who understood the importance of Bill's place in her heart. He never felt threatened by the past, for he knew that it had played a crucial role in shaping the woman he loved. He encouraged her to reminisce, to talk about Bill, and to keep his memory alive.

Dorothy's choice to keep Bill's memories alive wasn't a hindrance to her present with Jackson. Instead, it added depth to their relationship, highlighting the importance of acknowledging and respecting the past that had shaped them. In doing so, Dorothy demonstrated the strength of her love for Jackson, assuring him that their love was unique and irreplaceable, just as the love she had shared with Bill had been in its own way.

The past, while fading, remained an integral part of Dorothy's story, a testament to the enduring nature of love and memory. In the present, as she walked hand in hand with Jackson, she held the past close to her heart, a tribute to the love that had once been, and a celebration of the love that was now.

Together with Jackson, they would enter Bella's room, a sanctuary of memories, and read old letters to her. Each word was imbued with the warmth of Bill's love, and they wanted Bella to understand that even as the future beckoned with its brilliance, she should never forget the man she had never met Bill, the father she had been gifted.

As they read those letters aloud, their voices trembled with emotion, and their eyes glistened with unspoken tears. Each story painted vivid portraits of Bill's love, his laughter, and the profound legacy he had left behind. They wanted Bella to know the man who had been taken from them by the Vietnam War, the man whose love still resonated in the deepest recesses of their hearts.

In the depths of their love, deeper than the ocean's unfathomable expanse, Bella's radiant smile would bloom like a precious, sun-kissed flower every time Dorothy began to read. Her eyes, pools of pure adoration, would cast an affectionate glance at Jackson, a silent plea for him to take her hand and carry her into the tender world of her father's words.

One day, as Bella nestled into the warmth of her mother's embrace, she turned to Jackson, her heart brimming with childlike innocence and love, and she asked him to read the letter, the treasured gift from her father when she had turned one year old.

With a tenderness that mirrored the father she longed to know, Jackson began to read aloud the letter, the delicate paper cradled in his hands. The words flowed like a heartfelt lullaby, and Bella's eyes sparkled with the enchantment of hearing her father's voice through Jackson's gentle cadence.

"My darling first daughter, the newfound love of my life," the letter began, and Bella's heart swelled with emotion as she heard her father's words for the first time. "I don't know what to tell you, but I want you to know Daddy is fighting for freedom for our country and for the most important thing your freedom, my lovely Bella."

Jackson's voice carried the weight of Bill's love and longing, his eyes glistening as he continued reading, "I got your picture, don't tell your mother, but it makes me feel like I am very lucky to look like you, or rather, let me say, for you to look like me. We are beautifully loved."

Bella listened with rapt attention, her tiny hand reaching out to touch the photograph of her father that rested by her bedside. The letter continued, promising her a reunion on her second birthday, igniting a glimmer of hope in her young heart.

As Jackson finished reading the letter, Bella's eyes grew heavy with the warmth of her father's words, and she fell into a peaceful slumber. Jackson tenderly covered her with a soft blanket, and together, he and Dorothy walked to their room, the silence between them filled with unspoken emotions.

No words were needed, for their love, like a river that flowed deep and strong, connected their hearts in a profound way. In that quiet moment, their intertwined fingers spoke of shared dreams and aspirations, of love that transcended time and distance, and of the family they had become a testament to the enduring power of love, even when woven through the threads of memory and letters from the past.

Diana

The sun hung low in the sky, casting a warm, golden hue over the expansive rice fields that stretched out as far as the eye could see. Yang rode a simple motorbike with Natal nestled close behind him, her arms wrapped securely around his waist. They glided effortlessly through the narrow dirt paths that meandered between the lush green paddies.

As they rode through the rice farm, the gentle breeze rustled the tall, emerald stalks, creating a soothing, rhythmic symphony that seemed to harmonize with the beating of their hearts. The scent of the earth, rich and fertile, filled the air, mingling with the sweet fragrance of wildflowers that bloomed along the edges of the fields.

After their joyous wedding and affectionate marriage life had settled into a peaceful routine. Natal, however, had been feeling a bit under the weather lately, and together they decided to visit the local hospital to find out what might be the cause.

Their world changed in an instant when the doctor confirmed the reason for Natal's fatigue and discomfort, she was pregnant.

Yang's eyes welled up with tears of joy as the news sank in. He couldn't contain his emotions, and he cried tears of happiness right there in the doctor's office.

On the way back home, as they rode through the picturesque rice farm once more, Yang couldn't help but express his profound gratitude to Natal. He repeatedly thanked her for bringing such immense joy into their lives, for giving him the gift of family, and for filling their world with love and hope. Every curve of the winding dirt path seemed to hold a promise of a brighter future, a future they would now embark on together, hand in hand, with hearts full of love and anticipation.

As the days turned into weeks and the weeks into months, Yang's devotion to Natal and their unborn child knew no bounds. He refused to let her lift a finger around the house, insisting that her only job was to nurture their baby. He cooked hearty meals, fetched water from the nearby well, and tended to their home with meticulous care. Natal's love for Yang grew deeper with each passing day, as she witnessed his unwavering commitment and profound love.

Yang had not only found love in Natal but also in the tight-knit community of Laos. He immersed himself in the local culture, embracing the traditions, and participating in the daily life of the village. He no longer questioned who he was or where he came from, for home had become the place where his heart felt most at ease. He was no longer a stranger but a member of the community, and Laos was where he belonged.

The bond between Yang and Natal had grown stronger, and their love had brought them not only the gift of family but also the joy of belonging. Together, they had created a new home and a life filled with love, laughter, and the promise of a beautiful future in the heart of Laos.

As Natal's pregnancy progressed, Yang's love and devotion to her deepened even further. He attended every prenatal appointment with her, holding her hand and smiling as they listened to their baby's heartbeat together. He marveled at how Natal's body was changing, and he cherished every moment of this miraculous journey they were on.

In the evenings, Yang would sit with Natal by the bonfire, just as they had done in the early days of their relationship. They gazed at the stars above, and Natal would point out constellations and share stories from her childhood. Yang listened intently, his love for her growing with each word she spoke.

The day Natal went into labor was a moment suspended between anticipation and trepidation. Yang, his heart pounding in rhythm with hers, whisked her to the nearest clinic, his hand intertwined with hers, a silent promise of unwavering support. With each step, he whispered words of reassurance, his voice a balm against the backdrop of nerves.

As they crossed the threshold into parenthood, the air hummed with palpable anticipation. When the first cries of their newborn baby pierced the room, Yang's heart swelled with a torrent of emotions, a cascade of joy and wonderment. Cradling their baby girl in his trembling arms, he marveled at the miracle of life, her features a reflection of his own, a testament to their union.

In that tender moment, as father and daughter locked eyes for the first time, Yang felt the roots of his identity deepen within the soil of Laos. His journey from a man without a name to a Yang, and now a father, unfolded like a delicate tapestry woven by fate's gentle hand.

Beside him, Natal radiated with the glow of new motherhood, her eyes alight with boundless love and gratitude. As Yang enveloped her in a tender embrace, his voice a whisper against the canvas of their shared dreams, he found solace in the warmth of her embrace.

"Can we name our baby girl Diana?" he murmured, his words a prayer woven into the fabric of their love. Natal's smile, radiant as the morning sun, affirmed their shared vision, a testament to the unbreakable bond that bound them together.

In that moment, amidst the hushed whispers of the clinic and the fragrance of newborn innocence, they found solace in the promise of tomorrow. With Diana cradled in their arms, they embarked on a journey of endless possibility, their hearts intertwined in a dance of eternal devotion.

In the months that followed, Yang continued to care for Natal and their baby with unwavering dedication. He was there for every sleepless night, every diaper change, and every precious moment they shared as a family. His love for Natal and their child was boundless, and he couldn't imagine his life without them.

As their baby girl, Diana, blossomed, her laughter became the melody that filled the air, echoing through the halls of their home like a symphony of joy. Her infectious smiles illuminated the darkest corners of their hearts, casting aside any shadows of doubt or fear. For Yang and Natal, every coo, every giggle, became a testament to the miracle of parenthood, a gentle reminder of the boundless love that flowed between them.

In the quiet moments of the night, as Diana slumbered in peaceful repose, Yang and Natal found themselves marveling at the beauty of their creation. She was more than just a child; she was the embodiment of their hopes and dreams, a living testament to the depth of their love.

With each passing day, Diana's presence became the heartbeat of their home, infusing every corner with a sense of wonder and possibility. Her curious eyes, wide with innocence, bore witness to the world unfolding around her, a canvas waiting to be painted with the colors of her imagination.

In the gentle embrace of parenthood, Yang and Natal discovered a newfound strength, a bond that transcended the trials and tribulations of everyday life. Together, they navigated the ups and downs of parenthood, their love growing stronger with each passing moment.

As Diana took her first tentative steps, her laughter ringing like bells in the crisp morning air, Yang and Natal found themselves reflecting on their journey. They had weathered storms and scaled mountains, their love a beacon of light guiding them through the darkest of nights.

They had overcome challenges, forged a deep connection, and built a life together in a place they now called home. Laos, once a distant land filled with uncertainty, had become the cradle of their dreams, the backdrop against which their love story unfolded.

For Yang, each smile that graced Diana's lips was a reminder of the beauty of life itself, a gentle nudge from the universe urging him to cherish every moment. In her laughter, he found solace, a beacon of hope illuminating the path ahead.

Their love had not only changed their lives but had also transformed the heart of a man who had once been lost. Yang had found his purpose and his family, and he was grateful for every moment they shared in the embrace of Laos.

In the warmth of their home, surrounded by the laughter of their daughter, Yang and Natal discovered the true meaning of happiness.

Their journey was far from over, but as long as they had each other, they knew they could weather any storm that came their way.

Natal

Just six months after cradling their first child, Diana, in their arms, Natal and Yang were blessed with the delightful news of another addition to their growing family. The announcement filled their hearts with a symphony of emotions - an exhilarating blend of joy, anticipation, and profound gratitude.

As Natal's belly blossomed with the promise of new life, Yang found himself entranced by the miracle unfolding within her. Each morning, as he gently traced the curve of her belly, he felt the fluttering movements of their unborn child, a tender reminder of the miracle of creation. Their shared anticipation painted the air with a palpable sense of excitement and wonder.

In the soft glow of twilight, with the world bathed in the gentle hues of dusk, Yang would serenade Natal and their unborn child with soft melodies, his voice a soothing lullaby that reverberated through the walls of their home. Together, they would dance under the stars, their bodies swaying in rhythm to the melody of love that echoed in their hearts.

With each passing day, as Natal's pregnancy progressed, Yang's love for her deepened, rooted in the fertile soil of their shared dreams and aspirations. He cherished every moment, from the gentle flutter of their baby's kicks to the tender caress of Natal's hand against his own.

As they attended prenatal check-ups hand in hand, their hearts beat in synchrony, each thud a testament to the boundless love that bound them together. In those quiet moments of reflection, amidst the hustle and bustle of their daily lives, they found solace in the knowledge that their love was the anchor that steadied them through life's tempestuous seas.

In the midst of their shared anticipation, they reveled in the simple joys of parenthood - painting the nursery walls with hues of pastel, choosing names that whispered of dreams yet to be realized, and weaving dreams of a future filled with love and laughter.

As they awaited the arrival of their newest addition, surrounded by the verdant beauty of Laos, Natal and Yang found themselves awash in a sea of pure romance and boundless love. Their journey was far from over, but as long as they had each other, they knew that their love would endure, rooted deep within the fertile soil of their shared dreams.

The news of Natal's pregnancy was met with celebration and support from their close-knit community. Friends and family rejoiced with them, offering their best wishes and assistance as they prepared for the arrival of their second child. The memory of Natal's strength and the love she had brought into their lives continued to inspire and guide them as they embarked on this new chapter together.

Yang and Natal were filled with hope and a renewed sense of purpose. They were determined to create a beautiful life for their growing family and to honor the culture and tradition.

One serene evening, beneath the canopy of a star-strewn sky, Bill cradled Diana in his arms, her laughter ringing out like chimes in the cool night air. Natal, her radiant smile illuminated by the moon's soft glow, sipped hot tea, its warmth a comforting embrace against the evening chill. They sat together, a tableau of familial love, nestled in the embrace of their home.

As the night wore on, the laughter of their shared moments mingled with the gentle rustle of leaves, weaving a tapestry of joy and anticipation. It was in the midst of this tranquil scene that Natal's voice, tinged with excitement and a hint of urgency, shattered the peaceful silence.

"Yang, I think my water broke," she said, her words soft yet filled with the weight of impending change.

In that moment, time seemed to stand still. With a tender yet decisive gesture, Bill gathered Diana into his arms, her laughter trailing behind them like a cascade of stars, while Natal's grandmother stood watchful next door, ready to offer her wisdom and support.

With hearts racing and hands entwined, Natal and Yang embarked on a journey fraught with anticipation and hope. As they made their way to the hospital beneath the luminous night sky, their love illuminated the darkness, a beacon of light guiding them through the unknown.

In the quiet hum of the night, amidst the soft murmur of cicadas and the gentle whisper of the wind, they found solace in the knowledge that their love would be their compass, guiding them through the trials and triumphs of parenthood.

And so, beneath the watchful gaze of the stars, Natal and Yang ventured forth, their hearts intertwined in a dance of anticipation and love, ready to welcome their second daughter into the world.

As the moments of childbirth unfolded, joy and hope swiftly turned to despair. Natal, amidst the flurry of medical intervention, succumbed to unforeseen complications. Despite the valiant efforts of the medical team, her life slipped away, leaving behind a shattered realm of unfulfilled dreams and broken promises.

The room, once suffused with the radiant glow of anticipation, now became a somber tableau of grief and heartache. The air, thick with the weight of loss, hung heavy around Yang, enveloping him in a suffocating embrace of sorrow.

In the wake of Natal's passing, Yang's heart shattered into a million fractured pieces. He stood, a solitary figure amidst the sea of despair, unable to fathom the magnitude of the void left in her absence. The love of his life, the beacon of light that had illuminated his darkest days, had slipped beyond the veil of mortality, leaving behind a chasm of unspoken words and shattered dreams.

Beside him, their newborn daughter lay cradled in his arms, her innocent eyes oblivious to the anguish that enveloped her world. Yang's heart clenched with the weight of grief, knowing that she would never feel the warmth of Natal's embrace or hear the gentle cadence of her voice.

As he gazed upon their daughter, tears blurred his vision, each drop a silent testament to the agony that consumed him. He held the baby closer, her features mirroring Natal's in a hauntingly beautiful echo. Tears fell onto the infant's face, mingling with the traces of Natal's essence that lingered.

In that heart-wrenching moment, Yang's resolve crystallized. He whispered through choked sobs, "Natal is your name, baby girl.

Natal is the warmth in your laughter, the tenderness in your smile. Natal is the mother you'll never meet, but who will forever be a part of you."

He cradled Natal, the living embodiment of their shared love, closer to his heart, as if trying to bridge the gap between the realms of the living and the departed. In that quiet room, filled with the echoes of grief and the fragile breaths of new life, Yang vowed to carry Natal's legacy, to ensure that her love would continue to shape the destinies of the daughters she would never hold.

As the sun dipped low on the horizon, casting its golden hues upon the world, Yang and Natal's grandmother stood amidst a sea of mourners, their hearts heavy with the weight of grief. The air hung heavy with the scent of incense, its fragrant tendrils rising skyward in silent homage to the woman they had loved and lost.

The funeral procession wound its way through the narrow streets of the village, a somber symphony of mourning and remembrance. The rhythmic beat of drums echoed through the air, a solemn cadence that spoke of reverence and sorrow.

At the heart of the procession, Yang stood, his daughters cradled in his arms, their innocent faces a stark contrast to the somber tableau that surrounded them. With each step, the weight of their loss pressed heavy upon his shoulders, a burden too heavy to bear alone.

As they approached the graveyard, the scene unfolded before them like a haunting tableau. Rows upon rows of weathered headstones dotted the landscape, their silent sentinels bearing witness to the passage of time and the ebb and flow of life.

The earth, freshly turned and waiting, lay open before them, a stark reminder of the impermanence of existence. In the distance, the mournful strains of traditional Laotian melodies filled the air, their haunting melodies weaving a tapestry of grief and longing.

With trembling hands and tear-stained cheeks, Yang approached the graveside, his heart heavy with the weight of sorrow. Beside him, Natal's grandmother stood, her weathered face a mask of silent anguish, her grief a silent testament to the depth of their loss.

Together, they lowered Natal's coffin into the waiting earth, their hearts heavy with the weight of grief and the memories of a love that had transcended the boundaries of time and space. As the earth embraced her in its tender embrace, Yang whispered a silent goodbye, his voice choked with emotion.

In that sacred moment, amidst the echoes of grief and the whispers of farewell, he vowed to carry her memory in his heart, a beacon of light to guide him through the darkest of nights. And so, as the sun dipped beneath the horizon and the world faded into shadow, Yang stood, his soul heavy with the weight of sorrow, yet buoyed by the enduring legacy of love that had bound him to Natal.

Widower

In the days that followed, Yang was consumed by grief. He struggled to care for their newborn daughter, trying to fill the void left by Natal's absence. He held the tiny baby in his arms, tears streaming down his face, and whispered words of love and loss to her.

The community rallied around Yang and offered their support, knowing that he was now a single father facing an unimaginable tragedy. They helped him with the funeral arrangements, and they shared their stories of Natal's kindness, strength, and the love she had brought into their lives.

As Yang looked at his daughters, he saw traces of Natal in her eyes, her smile, and her spirit. He knew that he had to be strong for their child, to carry on Natal's legacy of love and resilience he had to name her after her mother. Despite the profound grief that weighed on his heart, he would do his best to be the father she deserved and to honor Natal's memory in every way possible.

Natal, a sweet little baby who bore a striking resemblance to her mother, was a challenging bundle of joy. She seemed to cry day and night, with each tear drop serving as a poignant reminder of her beautiful mother, whom she was named after. Natal's cries echoed through their home, a melody of longing and loss.

Despite Yang's strength and resilience, Natal's relentless crying often brought tears to his own eyes. He was a man who had faced the harsh realities of life in the midst of war, but Natal's cries touched a place in his heart that he never knew existed. He found himself overwhelmed with emotions and at a loss for how to comfort his daughter.

But Yang was determined to be there for this lost, young soul who had never had the chance to be held by her mother. He would cradle Natal in his arms, singing soft lullabies and whispering words of comfort into her tiny ear. His touch was warm and reassuring, a connection that was forged through love and shared grief.

Yang realized that, in caring for Natal, he was not only giving her the love she needed but also finding a way to heal his own heart. The bond between them grew stronger with each passing day, a testament to the enduring power of love and the ability to find solace amid loss. Natal, the beautiful reminder of her mother, became a beacon of hope and a source of healing for her father, as they navigated the challenges of life together.

Yes I will

Dorothy and Jackson had weathered the storms of life together. Their love had grown stronger, and they had decided to take the next step in their journey together and marriage. They will opt for an intimate ceremony in the comfort of their own backyard, surrounded by the memories they have created in their lakeside home.

Sarah, ever the supportive sister-law, was thrilled to step into the role of maid of honor once again. She knew how much this wedding meant to Dorothy, and she was determined to make it a day to remember. As the wedding preparations began, the sisters found themselves swept up in the excitement of planning a celebration of love.

But before the wedding would be the bridal shower, a special event organized by Sarah as a token of her love for her sister. She wanted to create beautiful memories for Dorothy to cherish, much like the memories Dorothy and Jackson had built together over the years. The plan was set, and the date was marked on the calendar.

In the weeks leading up to the bridal shower, Sarah tirelessly prepared for the occasion. She wanted every detail to be perfect, from the decorations to the menu. Dorothy deserved nothing less. It was a labor of love, and Sarah poured her heart and soul into making it an unforgettable day.

As the day of the bridal shower approached, there was a palpable sense of anticipation in the air. Dorothy, in her role as the bride-to-be, was both excited and touched by her sister's efforts. She could feel the love and support that surrounded her, and it filled her heart with warmth.

As the bridal shower day dawned, Sarah and her team of helpers were up early, putting the final touches on the preparations. Dorothy, unaware of the details, felt a sense of gratitude and anticipation. She knew that this celebration was a testament to the bonds of family and the enduring power of love.

The bridal shower would be a day of laughter, tears, and heartfelt speeches, a day to honor Dorothy and celebrate the love she had found in Jackson. It would be a reminder that even in the face of life's challenges and uncertainties, love could bloom, grow, and thrive.

And so, with the bridal shower just hours away, the two sisters Dorothy, and Sarah, stood together, united by their love for each other. They were ready to embark on this new chapter in Dorothy's life, a chapter that would be filled with joy, love, and the promise of a bright future with Jackson by her side.

Preparing For Forever

Dorothy and Jackson's decided to get married in their own backyard. This decision reflected the intimacy and deep connection that they shared. Their home by Lake Sammamish held countless memories, and they wanted to pledge their love and commitment surrounded by the very place that had witnessed their journey together.

As the wedding day inched closer, their home transformed into a hub of wedding preparations. Dorothy was radiant with excitement, her heart filled with anticipation. She had always dreamt of this day, and now it was finally coming to fruition.

The first order of business was selecting the perfect wedding date. After careful consideration, they chose a warm summer evening, when the sun would dip below the horizon, casting a warm, golden glow over the lake. It was a moment they hoped to savor forever.

Sarah, her faithful and dedicated sister, once again stepped into the role of maid of honor with enthusiasm. She knew that this wedding held immense significance for Dorothy, and she was determined to ensure every detail was meticulously planned.

Together, the sisters embarked on a whirlwind of wedding preparations. Invitations were sent out with a touch of personalization that reflected the couple's love story. Sarah took charge of coordinating the seating arrangements, making sure that family and friends would have the best view of the serene lake backdrop.

Their backyard underwent a stunning transformation. A pristine white aisle was laid out, lined with petals of their favorite flowers' white lilies and vibrant blue forget-me-nots, symbolizing the deep love they shared. A rustic wooden arch adorned with delicate garlands of greenery framed the spot where they would exchange their vows.

Dorothy's wedding gown was a masterpiece. It was a simple yet elegant design, adorned with lace that cascaded gracefully to the ground. She looked breathtakingly beautiful in it, and as she stood before the mirror during her fittings, her heart swelled with joy at the thought of walking down the aisle toward Jackson.

The floral arrangements were carefully selected to complement the natural beauty of the lakeside setting. White and blue flowers were woven together with verdant foliage to create centerpieces that exuded an air of rustic elegance. Their fragrance filled the air with a sweet, gentle perfume.

Dorothy and Jackson collaborated on writing their own vows, heartfelt promises that captured the essence of their love and the dreams they held for their future together. These vows were penned in a special notebook that would become a cherished keepsake of their wedding day.

As the day of the wedding drew nearer, friends and family rallied to help with last-minute tasks. Bella, an adorable six year old who had grown to love Jackson, was their little helper, eagerly taking on any task assigned to her. Together, they crafted handmade decorations that added a personal touch to the celebration.

In the days leading up to the wedding, Dorothy and Jackson took moments to steal away together by the lake, hand in hand. They reflected on their journey, reminiscing about the challenges they had overcome and the love that had grown stronger with each passing day. These moments deepened their connection and reaffirmed their decision to spend their lives together.

Yang Sleepless Night

As the days turned into weeks and the house felt emptier than ever before, Yang found himself engulfed in the overwhelming loneliness that accompanied grief. His nights were filled with the haunting cries of his infant daughter, a poignant reminder of the void Natal had left behind.

Night after night, as the infant's cries pierced the stillness, Yang would rise from his bed to tend to her. He would cradle her in his arms, rocking her gently while tears welled up in his eyes. The baby's cries seemed to echo the sadness in his heart, and he felt utterly helpless in comforting her.

Diana, the older sister, would often wake up from the sounds of her sister's cries and her father's attempts to soothe her. It was a chorus of sorrow that played out in the dead of night, a heartrending symphony of shared pain.

Yang's grief was a heavy burden, and the exhaustion of sleepless nights began to wear him down. One fateful night, as he was cradling his infant daughter as she slept Yang too succumbed to slumber. His dreams were vivid, filled with fragmented memories of a life he had once known. He saw flashes of Bella's picture, a snapshot of her innocence frozen in time. Suddenly, it was as if a doorway to his past had been cracked open, allowing him a glimpse into the life he had lost.

In his dream, he found himself transported to a time just before his ill-fated flight in Vietnam. He stood there, staring at the memories of Bella, his heart heavy with love and longing.

Suddenly, Yang jolted awake. The room was quiet, and his infant daughter slumbered peacefully in his arms. He looked around, disoriented, his heart racing. The realization washed over him like a tidal wave: he remembered who he was, the life he had lived, and the family he had left behind.

With his two daughters cradled in his arms, Yang made his way to Natal's grandmother, the wise woman who had guided them through their darkest days. Tears streamed down his cheeks as he embraced her tightly, his voice quivering with a mix of gratitude and sorrow. He explained that he had recovered his memories and felt an intense desire to return home and be reunited with his long-lost family.

Natal's grandmother, her eyes glistening with tears, held him close. She shared in the bittersweet joy of the moment, knowing that this journey would lead him back to a life he had once left behind but had never truly forgotten.

In the span of nearly five years, Yang had evolved into a man who carried the weight of both memory and resilience. The name Bill echoed in his mind, a reminder of a life that was now a vivid picture of a plane crash and the tumultuous journey that followed.

On this poignant day, Yang found himself embracing Natal's grandmother, the matriarch whose presence held a comforting warmth. Tears streamed down his face, and in that embrace, he surrendered to vulnerability, letting emotions flow freely like a river finding its course. He cried, not with the stoicism of a soldier, but with the rawness of a soul laid bare.

Natal's grandmother, a pillar of strength, gently consoled him. Her voice, a soothing melody, whispered assurances that resonated in the caverns of his heart. "Do not worry, my dear Yang," she said, her words a balm to his wounded spirit. In that moment, she became the harbinger of solace, a maternal figure offering sanctuary in a world still reeling from the echoes of tragedy.

Amidst the tears and embraces, she unveiled a glimmer of hope. "The mayor of the city is your cousin," she revealed, a revelation that danced between the lines of fate and familial ties. In this revelation, a lifeline emerged, connecting Yang to a network of support he hadn't anticipated. The mayor, a blood relative, held the key to unlocking the next chapter of Yang's journey.

With a knowing smile, Natal's grandmother continued, "And let me remind you, Yang, that the mayor's son is Kim your best friend." In this acknowledgment, the tendrils of friendship intertwined with the threads of family, creating a tapestry of connections that promised assistance and camaraderie.

The mayor's son, Kim, stood as a bridge between Yang and the vast unknown that lay ahead. He was not just a friend; he was a beacon of familiarity and support in a foreign land. Together, they would embark on a journey to the capital city of Laos, where the American embassy awaited. There, amidst the bureaucracy and paperwork, they would secure passports for Yang and his young daughters, a symbolic step toward a new beginning.

In the face of farewells and uncertainties, love and kinship emerged as guiding lights, illuminating the path ahead with the promise of a future where resilience would bloom, and the echoes of tragedy would be drowned in the melody of hope.

Road To Home

After years of wandering through the labyrinth of identity, with no homeland to claim as his own, Yang stood in a foreign land, clutching the embodiment of his renewed existence the passport. The arduous journey to prove his identity had taken a month, a testament to the complexities woven into the tapestry of his past.

In the quiet solitude of that pivotal moment, as the passports were handed to him, tears of joy welled up in Yang's eyes. The weight of his origin, a journey that began in Redmond as Bill and unfolded tragically in the shadows of Laos during the Vietnam War, now found solace in the tangible proof cradled within his hands.

The crisp pages of the passport held a narrative of resilience and redemption, a testament to the battles fought and overcome. As he flipped through the document, each page became a chapter in the novel of his life, the story of a man who lost himself but dared to find a renewed sense of belonging.

The strains of the American national anthem echoed in Yang's ears, a symphony of freedom that resonated with the depth of his tumultuous journey. The emblem of his nation, imprinted on those sacred documents, became a symbol not only of his past but also of the unwritten chapters awaiting him in the future.

With a mixture of smiles and tears, Yang gazed at the passports, absorbing the gravity of the moment. It was more than a piece of official documentation; it was a declaration of identity, a proclamation of existence that rippled through the very core of his being.

In that moment, he thought about his children, born in Laos and now, like him, bound by the threads of a shared history. The passports became a legacy, a promise to his offspring of a life forged from the ashes of adversity.

With a deep sense of gratitude, Yang bid farewell to Natal's grandmother. Her wisdom had been a guiding light through the darkest corridors of his despair, and her love, a sanctuary amidst the chaos of his past. Promising to return with his children whenever possible, Yang carried the torch of her wishes. It was a torch that illuminated the enduring bonds forged in the crucible of shared struggles, a testament to the indomitable human spirit.

As he stepped into the world, passports in hand, Yang embraced the future with a heart laden with gratitude, hope, and the echoes of an anthem that had found its place in the story of his redemption.

Approaching the airport, the hustle and bustle of activity surrounded him. The sight of airplanes on the tarmac stirred memories of his life as a pilot, a chapter nearly forgotten but now resurrected as a bridge connecting two worlds.

The airport staff processed his documents, and he watched as they stamped his passport, granting him permission to return to the

United States. It had been long years since he had left, and he had no idea what awaited him on the other side of the world.

With his daughters securely in his arms, Yang boarded the plane, a mixture of anticipation and trepidation coursing through him. The flight would carry them across oceans and continents, back to the place he had once called home but was now a distant memory.

As Yang watched the plane depart, leaving behind the country that had become his refuge, he looked down at his daughters, holding them tight. In that moment, gratitude and sorrow intertwined. He thanked God for every twist and turn in his life, for the land that had saved him, and for Natal the mother of his children, who had recently passed. During departure, a silent vow echoed within him to honor the past, embrace the present, and navigate the future with the enduring strength of love.

Throughout the journey, he gazed out of the airplane window, watching as the landscapes below changed from lush greenery to sprawling cities. Thoughts of his family, of Dorothy, and of Bella filled his mind. What would they say when they see him again, a man they had believed lost to them forever?

As the plane touched down on American soil, Yang held his daughters even closer, their presence a reminder of the life he had found in Laos and the family he had lost in the past. He was now on a path to reunite these two worlds, to bring together the love and memories that had been scattered to the winds.

With a heart full of hope and determination, Yang walked out of the airport, ready to face the unknown, with his two precious daughters by his side.

Returning to the United States after years lost in the turmoil of war, Yang's journey was not merely a physical passage across borders but a profound quest to rediscover his own identity. Landing in

Washington, D.C., the vibrant heartbeat of the nation, Yang's flight from Laos brought him face-to-face with the stark contrast between the bustling capital and the serene rural landscapes he had called home for so long.

As he disembarked from the plane, the iconic landmarks and bustling airports created a disconcerting backdrop. The sensory overload of a city that never slept clashed with the quietude of the jungles and fields he had traversed during his time in Laos. A sense of disconnection lingered in the air, a palpable distance between the man who once answered to the name Bill and the chaotic present awaiting him.

Reconnecting with family became one of the most daunting tasks for Yang. The years of separation had erased phone numbers and blurred the memory of even their exact address. Washington state held the promise of family, but the specifics were shrouded in the fog of forgotten memories. The anticipation and anxiety simmered within him as he embarked on the intricate process of tracing his roots.

Navigating the complexities of a modern American airport became a surreal experience for Yang and his daughters. The terminals, customs procedures, and security checks felt like alien rituals after the simplicity of rural Laos. The hum of technology and the orderly chaos of the airport were a stark contrast to the natural rhythms of life he had grown accustomed to.

However, the airport was not the final destination. Yang's journey continued in Washington, D.C., where bureaucratic intricacies awaited him. Clearing paperwork with the Pentagon added another layer of challenge and delay. Days were spent in the city, not only adjusting to the bureaucratic procedures but also allowing Yang to acclimate to the idea of being back in the United States.

In those days of paperwork and planning, Yang grappled with the surreal reality of his return. The familiar and the unfamiliar danced a delicate tango, and amidst the administrative hurdles, he found moments to reflect on the weight of his newfound identity. The pentagon became a symbolic bridge between his past and his future, a place where the echoes of war met the bureaucratic machinery of a nation.

With paperwork cleared and a plan in place, Yang stood at the threshold of Washington, D.C., ready to embark on the next leg of his journey a return to Washington state. Each step carried the weight of rediscovery, and the road ahead held the promise of rekindling familial ties and rewriting the chapters of a life interrupted by the chaos of war.

Homecoming Of Heart

The Seattle airport greeted Yang with a familiar sight the sound of raindrops tapping against the windows and the cool, misty breeze of Washington state. For the first time after long years, he had returned to a place that felt like home, even if he couldn't remember the details.

As he stepped out of the airport, the lush greenery and the scent of damp earth and pine trees embraced him like an old friend. There was a sense of calmness and belonging in the air, as if the very essence of the place whispered to himself, "You're back where you belong."

Hailing a taxi to Redmond, the wheels of Yang's journey turned with a mixture of excitement and trepidation. Through the window, he watched the cityscape unfold before him, each familiar landmark a thread weaving through the tapestry of his past. As he sat beside his daughters, a smile danced on his lips, his gaze drifting between the passing scenery and the faces of his children, their presence a beacon of hope and belonging.

Redmond greeted him with open arms, its streets teeming with memories waiting to be rekindled. The bustling neighborhoods and quaint corners whispered tales of bygone days, reminding Yang of the fragments of his childhood buried deep within his heart. Despite the veil of amnesia shrouding his past, the city resonated with a sense of familiarity, a silent reassurance that he was returning to a place that held the key to his identity.

Arriving at his mother's house, emotions surged within Yang like a tempest unleashed. The quaint facade of the familiar abode stood as a sentinel against the passage of time, a silent witness to the moments that shaped his existence. As he stepped out of the taxi, his pulse quickened with anticipation, the threshold of his childhood home beckoning him with the promise of reunion.

The air hummed with anticipation as Yang approached the door, each footfall echoing the cadence of his heartbeat. Would they recognize him? Would the echoes of his past find resonance in the hearts of his family? Questions lingered like ghosts in the corridors of his mind, their answers hidden behind the veil of uncertainty.

With trembling hands, Yang reached out to knock, the sound reverberating through the stillness of the neighborhood. Seconds stretched into eternity as he waited, his breath caught in the throes of anticipation. And then, as if guided by the hand of fate, the door swung open, revealing the threshold of a home long yearned for.

In that moment, time stood still. Tears welled in Yang's eyes as he beheld the faces of his family, their eyes alight with recognition and love. Embraces exchanged; words spoken in whispers that echoed through the chambers of his soul. In the embrace of his loved ones,

Yang found solace, a sanctuary in the arms of those who had never ceased to believe in his return.

As he crossed the threshold into the warmth of his childhood home, Yang knew that he had come full circle. Amidst the laughter and tears, amidst the echoes of a past reclaimed, he found himself anew a son, a father, a man whose journey had led him home.

With his children nestled in his arms, Yang stood before the door of his childhood home, his heart brimming with a kaleidoscope of emotions. Tears of joy mingled with the gentle smile gracing his lips as he reached out to touch the doorbell. His gaze softened as he met Diana's eyes, his daughter's innocence mirrored in her unwavering trust. "Darling, in this house is where your father is from," he whispered, planting a tender kiss on Natal's forehead before sharing a smile.

As the door swung open, Yang's father stood before him, his eyes a whirlwind of disbelief and overwhelming joy. Without a word, they embraced, their souls entwined in a deep, heartfelt hug. It was a reunion that transcended the limitations of language, a connection forged in the crucible of time and memory.

Minutes later, Yang's mother appeared, her eyes glistening with tears of happiness as she rushed into her son's embrace. Through tears and laughter, they shared a moment of sheer, unadulterated love. It took a few precious minutes before his mother's arms enveloped him fully, a silent acknowledgment of the son she thought she had lost.

With his parents by his side, Yang recounted his extraordinary journey the amnesia, the years spent in Laos, and the two beautiful children who now stood beside him. They spoke of his daily struggle to remember who he was, his heart tethered to the memories of Dorothy and Bella, the faces that had kept him anchored to his past.

His parents listened with rapt attention, their hearts swelling with pride and joy as they absorbed every detail. And then, as if guided by an unspoken understanding, his mother enveloped his children in her embrace, her eyes reflecting a wisdom born of years gone by. "Son, everything happens for a reason," she said with a sad smile, her words carrying the weight of a lifetime's worth of experiences.

The timing of Yang's return was serendipitous. Dorothy, the love he had left behind, was getting married later that day. It was an unexpected twist of fate, a thread of destiny woven into the fabric of his return. His mother's invitation to attend the wedding carried with it the promise of closure, of answers to questions that had haunted him for so long.

With a shared nod of agreement, Yang and his mother resolved to attend Dorothy and Jackson's wedding, their hearts brimming with hope and anticipation. For in the midst of celebration and newfound connections, there lies the possibility of healing, of reconciling the past with the present, and embracing the promise of a future yet unwritten.

Love Rediscovered

Yang, or Bill as he was known to Dorothy, wrestled with a torrent of emotions as they made their way to the wedding venue. With each passing mile, the weight of uncertainty bore down on him. Did Dorothy still harbor the same love he held for her, or had time erased their connection, leaving only memories in its wake? The questions clawed at his heart, but he remained resolute in his desire to face the truth, no matter the outcome.

As the car carrying Yang and his family neared the venue, anticipation crackled in the air like static electricity. The prospect of this reunion, this collision of past and present, filled the atmosphere with a tangible sense of destiny. Yang smoothed his suit, the fabric a metaphor for the hope pulsing within his heart. He envisioned the moment when Dorothy would lay eyes on him, hoping against hope that their shared history would flood back, washing away the barriers that time had erected.

The car came to a stop, and the scene unfolded before them like a scene from a dream. Sarah and Jane, Dorothy's bridesmaids, flitted about the entrance, their movements a blur of nervous excitement. And then, as if guided by some unseen hand, Sarah's cry pierced the air, a sharp intake of breath that reverberated through the gathering throng.

"Bill!"

The single word echoed like a bell tolling in the distance, drawing Dorothy's attention like a moth to a flame. Confusion furrowed her brow, her thoughts momentarily clouded by the unexpected interruption. But then, as her gaze followed Sarah's trembling finger, time seemed to stand still.

There, amidst the crowd, was Bill the man she had loved, the man who had vanished from her life without a trace, leaving behind a void that had never truly been filled. In that moment, the world around her blurred, the sounds and colors blending into a kaleidoscope of emotions. It felt as though she had been transported back in time, to a place where their love had flourished beneath the canopy of starlit skies.

Their eyes met through the window of the approaching car, and in that instant, a lifetime of memories crashed over her like a tidal wave. The laughter they had shared, the kisses stolen by the shores of Lake Sammamish, the dreams they had woven together, they flooded her senses, overwhelming her fragile composure.

Unable to bear the weight of it all, Dorothy's world tilted on its axis, and she crumpled to the ground, the tumult of emotions sending her spiraling into darkness. Her bridesmaids rushed to her side, their voices a chorus of concern as they sought to rouse her from the depths of unconsciousness.

For Yang, witnessing Dorothy's collapse was a visceral reminder of the power of their shared history, of the love that had once bound them together. As he rushed to her side, his heart heavy with a cocktail of emotions, he knew that this reunion was only the beginning of the prologue to a story that had yet to be written.

For Dorothy, the wedding day had transformed into something beyond her wildest imagination. The man she had mourned, the man she had never truly said goodbye to, was standing at the threshold of her life once again. As she drifted into unconsciousness, she couldn't help but wonder if this was a dream or a miraculous twist of fate, a chance to rewrite the story of a love that had been lost but never forgotten.

A Startling Reunion

Jackson stood amidst the whirlwind of emotions, his heart pounding in his chest as he tried to make sense of the surreal scene unfolding before him. His bride, Dorothy, lay unconscious on the ground, surrounded by a flurry of worry and confusion. His mind raced, grappling with the sudden turn of events and the flood of uncertainty that engulfed him.

Bill, the enigmatic figure who had mysteriously reappeared after years of silence, stood nearby, his children by his side. Bella, a daughter he had never known, and his own daughters nestled in his arms. The shock rippled through Jackson, but he maintained a facade of composure, understanding that this moment was as overwhelming for him as it was for Jackson.

Amidst the chaos, young Bella, oblivious to the complexities that hung heavy in the air, bounded towards Jackson with an innocent smile on her face. "Daddy!" she exclaimed, her voice ringing with pure affection. In that fleeting moment, love and confusion danced in the air, as Bella embraced the man who had been a father figure to her for most of her life.

For Jackson, the encounter was a whirlwind of emotions. He looked into Bella's eyes, seeing traces of her resemblance to Dorothy, and felt a surge of tenderness mixed with bewilderment. The lines between reality and surrealism blurred as he tried to comprehend the implications of Bill's return and the implications for his relationship with Dorothy.

In that poignant moment, as Bella clung to Jackson, a sense of connection pulsed through the air. It was a testament to the complexities of love and family, where bonds formed in unexpected ways and hearts intertwined across the boundaries of time and circumstance.

As the commotion continued to swirl around them, Jackson's gaze flickered between Dorothy's unconscious form and the enigmatic figure of Bill. Emotions surged within him, a tumultuous sea of love, uncertainty, and hope. In that startling reunion, amidst tears and heartache, Jackson found himself grappling with the profound truths of love's resilience and the unforeseen twists of fate that shaped their lives.

Bill watched this unfold, a mix of emotions churning inside him. For the first time, he heard his daughter's voice, and she is calling another man "daddy." It was both heartwarming and heartbreaking, a poignant reminder of the years he had missed and the gap he needed to bridge.

With the crowd abuzz with whispers and gasps, Dorothy's father, a steady and composed presence amid the turmoil, stepped forward. He looked at Jackson and Bill, his voice commanding attention.

"Ladies and gentlemen," he began, his words resonating with gravitas, "it appears that today, on this momentous occasion, fate has given us a unique twist of destiny. We must put the celebrations on hold for a while and seek clarity."

His words hung in the air, and the onlookers fell into an uneasy silence, eager to understand the unfolding drama.

Jackson and Bill, both standing at the epicenter of this emotional storm, locked their eyes. Without uttering a word, they extended their hands toward each other and shook hands a silent understanding that they needed to come together to navigate this complex web of relationships.

Jackson then turned to Bella, the little girl who had captured his heart. He gently knelt and introduced her to Bill with warmth and sincerity. "Bella, sweetheart, say hello to your father," he said.

Bill, holding his Diana and Natal, gazed at Bella, and for the first time in years, he felt the warmth of fatherhood that had eluded him for so long. It was a moment of reconciliation, of acknowledging the bonds that connected them all.

Dorothy, her senses slowly returning, found herself in a surreal situation. She listened intently as Bill began to explain his harrowing journey, from the plane crash in Vietnam to the chance encounter with Natal and her grandmother, the passing of Natal, and his eventual decision to return to the USA with their children.

Bill's words carried the weight of the years they had spent apart, and they hung in the air like an unspoken question. He offered her an unexpected choice, a choice that held their shared history in the balance. With an open heart and a sincere desire to see her happy, he said, "Dorothy, if you've moved on, if your heart belongs to Jackson now,

Tears welled up in Dorothy's eyes as she tried to process the tumultuous turn her wedding day had taken. Her heart was a tumultuous sea of emotions the years of longing and unanswered questions, the joy of seeing Bill again, and the commitment she had made to Jackson.

She looked at Bill, the man she had once vowed to spend her life with and realized that she needed time to understand her own feelings. The connection they had shared in the past was undeniable, and she couldn't simply dismiss it. But she had also built a new life with Jackson, a life that had brought her joy and love.

Bill watched her, his own heart heavy with uncertainty. He knew that the path forward was uncertain and fraught with challenges, but he was willing to explore it, if only for the sake of their children and the love that had once bound them together.

In their room, as the gravity of the situation settled, Dorothy made a difficult decision. She called Jackson inside, her heart heavy with the truth she was about to reveal. With a heavy sigh, she handed him his ring, the symbol of their love, and told him, "Jackson, I'm still in love with the man who has just walked into our wedding." Tears welled up in her eyes as she leaned on his shoulder, seeking comfort, and understanding.

Jackson held her close, his heart filled with a mix of emotions. He knew that Dorothy's past had come rushing back in an unexpected and profound way. He embraced her, assuring her that he would stand by her side, no matter the challenges they faced.

With Jackson's support, Dorothy walked out of the room and into the presence of Bill, Bella, Diana, and Natal. Her eyes met Bill's, and she knew that she needed to be honest with him, just as she had been with Jackson. With tears streaming down her cheeks, she confessed, "Bill, I still belong to you, but we have a lot to rebuild in our relationship."

Bill looked at her, his eyes filled with a complex mix of emotions hope, uncertainty, and a profound sense of longing. He knew that their journey would not be easy, that they carried the weight of years of separation and change. Yet, in that moment, he felt a glimmer of hope, a spark of possibility that he had never imagined when he first arrived at the wedding.

The presence of their children, Bella, Diana, and Natal, was a testament to the love they had once shared and the challenges they had faced. As they looked at each other, the path ahead remained uncertain, but the promise of a second chance at love and family bound them together in a new beginning.

Dorothy, still wearing her wedding dress, approached Natal and took her gently from Bill's arms. With a voice filled with tenderness, she asked, "What's your name?" Bill, standing beside her, answered proudly, "Natal Yang, and this is Diana Yang."

Dorothy looked deep into their eyes, a mixture of emotions swirling within her. She felt a sense of wonder and disbelief at the family she never thought she would see again. With tears welling up in her eyes and a warm smile on her face, she spoke from the heart, "Welcome home."

Together, they walked into the living room, where their extended family was waiting. The room was filled with an atmosphere of both excitement and trepidation.

The Lost Chapter Unfolds

In the hush of those early days since Bill's return, every moment was a testament to the depth of their love. It had been weeks, but it felt like a lifetime since they had been reunited, and yet, as their eyes locked and their hearts intertwined, the connection between them remained as unbreakable as ever. It was as if the years apart had merely been a pause in the symphony of their love.

They found themselves finishing each other's sentences, their thoughts, and hearts so in sync that words seemed almost unnecessary. The war had stolen their love and connection were now a distant memory, replaced by the warmth of their embrace.

Love, it seemed, had more surprises in store. Bill had returned not only with his own history but with two young souls in tow. Natal and Diana, the children of the woman who had saved him in Laos. In their innocent eyes, he discovered a new well of affection, a connection that tugged at his heartstrings.

Yet, amidst this newfound love, there was a missing piece of the puzzle Bella. While Dorothy easily felt for what it used to be. Bella doesn't understand the reality. She couldn't stop asking when Jackson would come back home. As hard as Bill tried to win Bella heart, was not easy to wipe the Jackson picture from Bella's mind.

So many times, the situation brought Bill to tears, the thought of images of her, captured in a photograph, brought a rush of emotions back to reality. It was her face that seemed to trigger his memory, reminding him of who he once was after long years of absence.

Bill couldn't help but think back to the timing of Bella's conception, a sweet and tender memory. It was the first day he had made love to Dorothy, his new wife, the woman who had remained pure and untouched until she found her forever in him. A few days after that cherished moment, he had been sent to Vietnam, and his life had taken an unexpected turn.

But Bill wasn't the only one grappling with the complexities of this new chapter. Dorothy now found herself a mother to three beautiful daughters. She carried the weight of knowing that Natal had been there for Bill during his absence, while she had cried and longed for him. The thought tugged at her heart, but she was determined to be the mother of Bills daughters.

She believed in the serendipity of life, the chain of events that had led to this moment. With unwavering determination, she promised herself to create a happy home, a place where her three daughters, born from love and connection, would flourish. Their love and connection, forged by her and Bill, would be the foundation upon which their new life would thrive.

Indeed, as the days unfolded, Dorothy faced the challenge of connecting with Natal and Diana, who clung closely to their father,

Bill. It was a tender dance, a journey of trust and understanding, as she worked to build a bridge of love between them. Their love was undeniable, but the path to becoming a family would take time and patience.

Natal and Diana were little echoes of Bill, a testament to the bond they shared during his absence. Their eyes would light up when they saw him, and their laughter would ring out in his presence. Dorothy admired their connection and found solace in the fact that her beloved Bill had never truly been alone during those long years away from her.

Yet, amidst this tender web of relationships, Bill's heart longed to find a connection with Bella, the daughter he had never seen when she was born. Bella, however, had formed a deep attachment to Jackson, her almost stepfather. Her laughter filled the house, and her smiles were reserved for the man who had been there during her formative years.

Meanwhile, Dorothy found strength in the love that surrounded her. She held steadfast to her promise, determined to be the mother these children had missed. Every day was a new opportunity to create a happy, loving home where the bonds of family grew stronger with each passing moment.

Together, they navigated the complexities of love, connection, and family. Theirs was a story of resilience, where hearts that had been separated by time and distance now beat as one, creating a symphony of love that would carry them forward into the uncertain yet promising future.

Longing of Motherhood

One major point of contention emerged when Dorothy expressed her desire to have a second child. It was a dream she had held close to her heart, envisioning a larger family that included children of their own. But Bill, haunted by the tragic loss of Natal, the mother of his two children, was gripped by the fear of history repeating itself.

Dorothy's heart ached, misinterpreting Bill's reluctance as a lack of desire for more children with her. The misunderstanding marked their first significant challenge as a couple. Bill desperately wanted to reassure her, not wanting her to think he didn't want to share this experience with her. After deep conversations, they finally reached an agreement they would try for one more child, and that would be all.

Their journey towards expanding their family began with hope and optimism. Dorothy was ready to become a mother once more, her heart full of anticipation. However, her body wasn't quite prepared, and months passed with no success.

Then, one day, the joyous news arrived Dorothy was pregnant. Both were overjoyed, but Bill's elation was tinged with fear, his past nightmare haunting him. He resolved to protect her with unwavering love, taking on the responsibilities of caring for their children and the household, all while maintaining his job at Boeing's Ranton main office.

Five months into Dorothy's pregnancy, she reveled in the sensation of their baby growing inside her. Her dream of a bigger family, of having three children of her own, seemed to be within reach. She had shared this dream with Bill before they got married, and he had embraced it.

Then, one fateful night, the nightmare Bill had feared became a reality. Dorothy awoke him in distress, and their bed was stained with blood. Panic set in as Dorothy cried, knowing that they had lost the baby she had longed for. It was a devastating blow, especially considering her desire for a larger family.

Bill, his heart heavy with sorrow, took their children to his sister Sarah's home while he awaited news on Dorothy's condition at the hospital. The clock ticked past 3 am, and his mind couldn't help but revisit the painful memories of the day he lost Natal.

Tears welled in his eyes as the fear of facing the prospect of raising three children without their mother gripped him. He couldn't bear to think of losing Dorothy, too. The doctor finally emerged and delivered a mixture of relief and sadness, confirming that Dorothy was stable but had lost their baby boy.

Bill couldn't help but picture the son he had dreamed of holding in his arms. His eyes glistened as he thanked the doctor, a mix of gratitude and grief overwhelming him. The doctor reassured him that Dorothy would be okay and suggested they could try again in a few months.

Bill didn't like the idea of trying again, but he kept his thoughts to himself, not wanting to upset Dorothy further. He entered her room, gently taking her hand in his. Tears welled in his eyes as he spoke softly, "I hate seeing you like this. I can't bear the thought of anything happening to you. I need you to be healthy, Dorothy. I can't imagine my life without you."

Dorothy smiled weakly, assuring him that she was okay and that in a few months, they could try once more. Bill's heart was heavy with the weight of their shared dreams and the fear of losing the love of his life, but he held onto the hope that the future would bring them happiness and healing.

In the days following their heartbreaking hospital visit, an emotional storm raged within Dorothy. Her feelings were a tempest, a tumultuous sea of sorrow and frustration. Tears fell like rain, each one carrying the weight of her despair. She couldn't help but feel that her body had betrayed her, letting her down when she yearned to give Bill the son, they both longed for. The ache in her soul was a relentless reminder of her perceived failure.

Meanwhile, Bill struggled in his own way. He found himself avoiding intimacy with Dorothy, in a desperate attempt to prevent another pregnancy. Each time they made love, he held onto those moments as if he could freeze time. The fear of going through the agony of loss again weighed heavily on his mind.

Dorothy, however, didn't understand Bill's actions. The misunderstanding created a rift in their marriage, sowing seeds of unease and doubt. It was as though they were dancing around a painful truth neither of them could fully grasp.

As the days wore on, the shadows of Bill's past began to creep into his present. Post-traumatic memories from the war resurfaced, casting a dark cloud over his thoughts. He started having nightmares, reliving the harrowing experiences, and mourning the friends he had lost.

These heavy burdens weighed Bill down, causing him to withdraw from Dorothy. The once warm and passionate connection they shared seemed to have dimmed. It was as if their love, once an unbreakable bond, was now being tested in ways they could never have imagined.

In the midst of their pain and isolation, they yearned for a way back to the love that had once defined their marriage, a love that had endured trials and tribulations before. But as they navigated this new chapter, the road ahead seemed uncertain and filled with the shadows of their shared sorrow.

Is Love Enough?

Amidst the turmoil in their marriage, Sarah found herself torn between her loyalty to her best friend Dorothy and her love for her brother Bill. She had always been the neutral ground, a bridge of understanding between them, but now she was faced with a difficult choice. Her heart ached for both.

One evening, as the rain softly pattered against the windowpanes in Redmond, Dorothy and Sarah managed to steal some precious moments for themselves. It had been a while since they had just been two friends sharing a cup of coffee, a rare respite from their busy lives as mothers.

Dorothy, with her three young children, and Sarah, a new mother herself, sat down to talk about the crossroads they found themselves at. Amidst the warm ambiance of the coffee shop, they delved into the depths of their lives.

Dorothy confided in Sarah, sharing the pain of her husband pulling away from her. She described the heart-wrenching nightmares that haunted Bill, the screams that echoed through the night as he relived the horrors of his time in Vietnam. Her voice trembled as she revealed her plea for him to see a therapist, a plea that had fallen on deaf ears.

"Sarah, my dear friend," Dorothy began, her eyes welling up with tears, "there have been nights when I couldn't sleep, listening to your brother's torment, knowing I can't help him, and he won't let me in."

Sarah listened intently, tears streaming down her cheeks. She had never fully realized the depth of her brother's inner struggles, the scars he carried from the war.

As Dorothy continued, she dropped another bombshell, revealing Bill's intention to undergo a procedure to prevent having more children. "Your brother believes a second child is a curse, and he doesn't want to take the risk," Dorothy confessed, her voice tinged with sadness.

Sarah felt as though she were walking on eggshells, caught between her brother's fears and Dorothy's longing. She understood both perspectives and empathized with their emotional turmoil. She spoke softly, her love for them evident in her words. "You both mean the world to me. I can see why Bill feels the way he does, given his history, but I also understand your desire for more children. No matter what, I love you both."

After a few more cups of coffee, their conversation was a blend of smiles and tears. Sarah droves back to Seattle, where she lived, while Dorothy returned to her beautiful house in Redmond. Standing by the window, she gazed at her children playing and her husband swimming in Lake Sammamish. The reflection of their lives danced in the water, a mosaic of love, longing, and uncertainty.

Amidst the tranquil beauty of Lake Sammamish, the world seemed to slow down, allowing the emotions and sensations of the moment to linger. The soft, earthy scent of the lake filled the air, mingling with the occasional whiff of pine from the surrounding trees. A gentle breeze rustled the leaves, and the late afternoon sun cast a warm, golden glow across the water's surface.

Dorothy stood by the window, taking in the picturesque scene. Her heart swelled as she watched her children playing by the water, their laughter a symphony of joy. Bill, immersed in the shimmering lake, was a silhouette of strength and resilience, a man who had weathered storms both within and beyond.

As Dorothy joined her husband and children, her laughter echoed across the water, and she plunged into the lake, embracing the playful chaos of family. The children, sensing their mother's arrival, greeted her with joyful splashes and shouts of excitement. The love among them was palpable, a bond that transcended blood ties.

Dorothy, touched by the warmth of the moment, made a decision that had been brewing in her heart. She approached Bill, the water lapping at their feet, and looked into his eyes with unwavering determination.

"Bill," she began, her voice steady yet filled with emotion, "I want to make it official. I want to adopt Diana and Natal as my own children, legally and forever. They mean the world to me, and I want them to know that they are truly a part of me."

Bill, taken aback by the depth of Dorothy's love and commitment, felt a rush of emotions welling up inside him. He knew that this was a moment that went beyond words, beyond the depths of their shared history.

As the water of Lake Sammamish gently lapped at their ankles, Bill's heart swelled with relief and gratitude. Without hesitation, he pulled Dorothy into a tight embrace, holding her close as if trying to convey the depth of his love through the strength of his arms.

A smile graced his lips as he gazed at the children playing in the water, their innocent laughter echoing in the stillness of the evening. Bill couldn't help but feel a profound sense of contentment, knowing that his wife, the most beautiful woman in his world, had just extended her love to embrace their family even further.

Turning to the children, Bill's eyes sparkled with pride and affection. He asked them, "Do you know who the most beautiful woman in the world is?"

With gleeful smiles and a chorus of voices, the children replied, "mommy!"

In that moment, amidst the peacefulness of Lake Sammamish, with the sun gently sinking below the horizon, they were a family united by love, by adoption, and by the profound beauty of their shared journey.

The paperwork to officially adopt Natal and Diana was a significant step in their journey. Dorothy, with unwavering determination, signed her name with a sense of profound commitment and love. She understood that these children, with their shared last name of Yang, were not just joining her family but becoming a part of her heart.

Bill, deeply moved by Dorothy's gesture, had another request. He wanted Bella, his first-born daughter with Dorothy, to carry the name Yang as well. His eyes held a mixture of hope and longing as he made this request, the smile on his face tinged with emotion.

With a loving smile of her own, Dorothy agreed wholeheartedly. She leaned in to kiss him, their love sealing this newfound bond. "My love," she whispered, "I am a Yang too. I believe that the name Yang not only kept you alive but also brought you to me. We will all honor Natal, the mother of your children and now my children, by adding Yang to all our names."

Leaving the lawyer's office, they walked hand in hand, a family united not only by blood but by love and shared dreams. As they ventured into this new chapter together, they understood that challenges lay ahead. But they were determined to face them with unwavering love and commitment.

The Yang's

Years had flowed like a gentle river, and the challenges of life had only served to strengthen the bond within the family. Dorothy and her children had made it a tradition to spend their summer vacations in Laos, a land that had become their second home. Here, amidst the lush landscapes and the warm embrace of family, Natal and Diana had the chance to connect with their mother's side of the family.

Over the years, the girls had formed deep connections with their great-grandmother, aunties, and uncle in Laos. The summers were a time of renewal, a journey back to their roots, and a chance to reconnect with the land that held so many memories.

Thirteen years later Bella 19, Diana 15 and Natal 14 were on the cusp of new adventures. For the first time, they embarked on their journey to Laos without their parents by their side. Bill and Dorothy had lovingly seen them off at the airport, knowing that they were leaving their girls in capable hands.

The green mountains house in Laos awaited them, a haven of comfort and familiarity. It was a place where laughter echoed through the rooms, and the smell of traditional Laotian dishes wafted through the air. Here, the girls felt a deep sense of belonging, a connection to their mother's heritage that had been nurtured year after year.

As a father, Bill couldn't help but be anxious about his teenage daughters being so far away. His worries were like gusts of wind, sweeping through his heart. He kissed them goodbye with tears in his eyes and reminded them to be careful, to make wise choices, and not to be swayed by the allure of summer flings.

As they left, Bill couldn't help but hold onto them a little longer, his heart full of love and concern. In his fatherly wisdom, he knew the world was full of temptations and distractions for young hearts. He whispered words of advice and caution, his voice filled with the weight of his love and the depth of his wishes for their safety and happiness.

Bella, Natal and Diana, with their youthful exuberance, reassured their father that they would be responsible and make him proud. They knew the trust he had placed in them was a precious gift, one they would cherish and honor.

And so, under the bright moon of the summer months in Laos, amidst the laughter of family and the scent of home-cooked meals, the girls began to experience the sweet innocence of first kisses and the joys of teenage summers. Their hearts danced to the rhythm of life, a testament to the enduring human spirit and the deep connections that transcended time and distance.

The summer was a tapestry of vibrant colors and cherished moments. The top of the mountain house stood as a beacon, welcoming Bella, Natal, and Diana, who had grown to love this place as their second home.

Days were spent with the rice farms as their playground. The girls, their laughter echoing through the warm air, would swim in the river waters, their youthful spirits embracing the freedom of the river. The sun kissed their skin as they built sandcastles and collected seashells, the river's rhythm serenading their hearts.

Amidst the backdrop of lush greenery and the scent of tropical blooms, Bella, Natal, and Diana took on a special role in their summer haven. They volunteered to teach English to local kindergarteners, the exchange of language bridging cultures and creating bonds that transcended borders. The children's eager faces and bright eyes were a testament to the power of learning and connection.

The joy the girls experienced extended beyond the classroom. They formed bonds with local children, boys, and girls alike. Together, they ran through rice farms, their laughter ringing out like music in the tranquil countryside. The rich, earthy scent of the fields filled their noses, a reminder of the land's bounty and the hard work that sustained it.

Diana and Natal were not just visitors to this land; they were a part of it. They felt the roots of their mother's heritage deeply, their souls resonating with the rhythm of Laos. The smiles of the locals, the kindness of their great-grandmother, and the wisdom of their aunts and uncle all painted a vivid picture of love and connection.

As the summer days dwindled, there was a bittersweet longing in the air. The last few days brought the anticipation of their parents' arrival. Bill and Dorothy, the pillars of their family, joined them, and the beach house brimmed with warmth and love.

Together, they reveled in the beauty of the land and its people. They shared meals that held the essence of Laos, flavors that spoke of tradition and love. They listened to stories that spanned generations, tales that wove the past into the present.

Underneath the expansive sky, as the sun dipped below the horizon, the family savored their time together. Their laughter and shared experiences were a testament to the deep connection between the land and its people, a connection that had touched their hearts and would forever remain etched in their memories.

As the summer drew to a close, they knew they would soon be saying goodbye to this enchanting land. Yet, the bonds they had formed, the lessons they had learned, and the love they had shared would stay with them, a cherished treasure that would guide their hearts back home to Washington, where the spirit of Laos would forever be a part of their family's story.

Empty Nest

In a chapter brimming with joy, a profound sense of belonging, and a deep connection to the past and the present, the family found themselves at a significant juncture they hadn't seen coming. Time had flown by, and all the girls had not only graduated from high school but had chosen educational paths that took them far from their childhood home.

Bella, the beacon of ambition and determination, had chosen the bustling streets of New York. where she is in her last year of law school at Columbia University. Her dreams were as grand as the city itself, and she radiated a sense of purpose that inspired everyone around her.

Diana, the quiet and gentle soul, had found her place at Rice University in Houston, Texas. Her love for the stars and the cosmos had led her on a journey of discovery, and she embraced her studies with humility and grace. Her words were few but carried depth, and it took time to truly understand the beauty of her spirit.

The latest addition to this academic adventure was Natal, who had been dropped off at the hallowed halls of Harvard University. Her path led her toward medicine, and her brilliance shone as she embarked on her pre-med studies. Natal's intellect was a testament to her mother's legacy, and it filled Bill with a complex mix of joy and grief.

As Bill looked at Natal, he couldn't help but think of her mother, the woman who had touched his life so profoundly. He wondered what Natal's mother might have achieved if she had been given the opportunities that Natal now had. Natal bore a striking resemblance to her mother, both in looks and intelligence, and it was a constant reminder of the life he had lost.

Yet, in the midst of these emotions, Bill found solace in the fact that Natal was a gift from above, a living legacy of his past and a beacon of hope for the future. She was proof that life could bring unexpected joys even in the face of heartache.

Bill often reflected on his journey, on the twists of fate that had brought Bella into his life. Her presence was a guiding light, a reminder that love could lead him back home. In Bella, he saw the strength to face the challenges of the present and the promise of a brighter tomorrow.

As the family navigated this new chapter, with each girl following her own unique path, they couldn't escape the profound sense of belonging and connection that held them together. They were a family defined by love, resilience, and the unbreakable bonds that transcended time and distance. In the tapestry of their lives, woven with threads of joy and grief, they found the beauty of their shared journey, a journey that had led them to this moment of hope and possibility.

In the tranquil embrace of an empty nest, Dorothy and Bill discovered a love that had evolved and deepened over the years. Their connection was not just rooted in romance but in the shared journey of raising their daughters and the profound love they had for each other and their family.

With their daughters now pursuing their own dreams across the country, Dorothy and Bill found themselves with newfound time and freedom. It was a chance to rediscover the love that had first brought them together, a love that had been tested and strengthened through the joys and challenges of parenthood.

Every evening, rain, or shine, they would walk along the shores of Lake Sammamish, hand in hand. The lake had been witnessing their love story, and it held a special place in their hearts. The water sparkled under the setting sun, and the gentle waves whispered tales of their journey together.

They would bring a bottle of wine, a canvas, and a set of paints with them. As they strolled along the shore, they would pause to savor the beauty of the moment, the soft caress of the breeze, the distant call of birds, and the vibrant colors of the setting sun painting the sky.

Sitting side by side, they would sip wine, share stories, and sometimes simply bask in the comfortable silence of their shared companionship. The years had woven a tapestry of memories, and each day added new threads, painting a portrait of a love that had only grown stronger with time.

Their evenings by the lake were not just about reminiscing but also about looking forward. They eagerly awaited telegrams and calls from their daughters, the threads that kept their family tapestry connected across the miles. They would read letters, telegrams from their girls, their hearts swelling with pride at the women their daughters had become.

With the lake as their witness and the setting sun as their canvas, Dorothy and Bill rekindled their love, not as parents but as partners, as lovers, and as friends. Theirs was a love story that had come full circle, a story of enduring love, shared dreams, and the beauty of finding love anew in the golden years of life.

The Soul Thief

Dorothy's life had taken an unexpected turn as the signs of memory loss began to surface in for Bill in his mid-70's. It was a gradual descent into the depths of confusion, a journey that had started with simple forgetfulness. Keys misplaced, names muddled, and small things mixed up, these were the early indicators of the storm that was brewing within her beloved husband.

Bill, once regarded as one of the smartest and most capable individuals, now found himself grappling with an elusive fog that clouded his once-sharp mind. Dorothy couldn't quite put her finger on what was happening to the man she had loved for so many years. He was not just her beloved husband; he was the father of their three precious daughters.

As the days passed, Dorothy watched with a heavy heart as Bill's condition worsened. The man who had once been the pillar of strength for their family was now the one in need of care and support. Simple tasks became arduous challenges, and the memories of their life together began to slip through his grasp like sand through open fingers.

Dorothy's love for Bill remained unwavering, and she stood by his side as the storm of memory loss raged on. She became his memory, the keeper of their shared past. She patiently reminded him of their daughters' names and the moments they had cherished as a family. She held onto the memories, the laughter, and the love they had built together.

In the face of this heart-wrenching journey, Dorothy's love shone even brighter. She knew that the man she loved was still there, somewhere deep within, and she was determined to find him. She faced the challenges with courage, determination, and unwavering love, embracing the present while honoring the past. In their journey through memory loss, they discovered the enduring power of love to navigate the most difficult chapter in their journey.

Alzheimer's, a merciless thief, had stolen Bill's memories one by one, as though erasing the very essence of his being. Dorothy sat at the dining table of the assisted living facility, her heart heavy with the weight of witnessing her husband's slow descent into the abyss of this cruel disease.

Bill, at the age of 90, had indeed lived a good and meaningful life. He had shared adventures with Dorothy, traveled the world, and devoted himself to his family and community. Yet, now, his days were spent grappling with the relentless monster that was Alzheimer's.

As Dorothy gazed at Bill, she couldn't help but wonder how they had arrived at this painful juncture in their lives. The man before her was no longer the vibrant soul she had known for decades. His once-sharp mind, filled with the memories of their life together, had become a fragmented mosaic of confusion and uncertainty.

Simple things, like the names of their own grandchildren, eluded him. The faces of his daughters Bella, Diana, and Natal were like fleeting shadows, appearing, and disappearing in the fog of his deteriorating mind. It was a heartbreaking paradox that he could still recall their names but often failed to recognize them when they stood before him.

Today was meant to be a day of celebration, a milestone birthday for Bill. His daughters, now adults with families of their own, had come to honor their father. They brought with them the next generation, eager to share in the love and joy that had always been a cornerstone of their family.

Bill, in his moments of clarity, would embrace his daughters with a love that transcended the bounds of memory. He would hold them close, his heart recognizing the profound connection they shared. In those fleeting instances, the man they knew and loved would briefly resurface, and his daughters would treasure those precious moments.

Yet, the cruel reality of Alzheimer's would soon steal those moments away. Bill's grasp on the present and the past was like sand slipping through his fingers. The disease, relentless and unforgiving, had robbed him of his memories and, in many ways, his soul.

As Dorothy watched her husband's battle with Alzheimer's, she couldn't help but mourn the loss of the man she had loved so deeply. It was a sorrow that went beyond words, a pain that cut to the core of her being. She yearned for the days when Bill's mind had been a treasure trove of shared experiences, of laughter, and of the life they had built together.

Alzheimer's was not just a disease of the mind; it was a thief of the soul, a heart-wrenching journey of gradual loss and fading memories. And as Dorothy sat by Bill's side, she held onto the fragments of the man she loved, cherishing each moment of connection and love that remained, even as the disease sought to steal them away.

Bella, Diana, and Natal, along with their own children, had gathered to spend a precious day with their father, Bill. They took him to Lake Sammamish, the place that held countless memories and remained their family home. Bill stood there, a flicker of recognition in his eyes, as though a fragment of his past had briefly returned.

Natal, his beloved daughter, approached him with tears in her eyes, her heart heavy with the weight of the disease that had stolen her father's essence. She embraced him tightly, her sobs echoing the grief and frustration of watching her father slip away into the depths of Alzheimer's. She couldn't comprehend why such a cruel fate had befallen the man who had been her rock and her hero.

Throughout the day, they shared moments of laughter and connection with Bill, reliving cherished memories and creating new ones. Their children reveled in the presence of their grandfather, even if it was a version of him that had become increasingly elusive.

As the day drew to a close, a bittersweet sorrow settled over them. They knew they had to return their parents to the assisted living facility, their new home. It was a place that had become a necessity, a place where Bill could receive the care he needed in the face of this relentless disease.

Leaving their parents behind was never easy. Each goodbye was a poignant reminder of the miles that separated them, the physical and emotional distance that Alzheimer's had imposed on their family. They yearned to hold onto the moments they had shared, even as they braced themselves for the challenges that lay ahead.

With heavy hearts, they kissed their parents and promised to return soon, their love serving as a lifeline that stretched across the miles. As they departed, the bitter taste of separation mingled with the sweetness of the love that bound them together, a love that transcended the boundaries of time and distance.

In the quiet solitude of their shared room at the assisted living facility, Dorothy grappled with a profound sense of loneliness and sadness. She had watched her daughters and grandchildren leave, their departure leaving an emptiness that seemed to echo through the room. Yet, despite the overwhelming emotions that threatened to consume her, she knew that she had made a solemn vow, one that echoed in the depths of her heart: "Till death do us part, in sickness and in health."

Bill, the love of her life, stood before her a man who had once stood six feet tall, his mind a shining beacon of brilliance, and his soul a testament to his beautiful character. But now, Alzheimer's had cast its relentless shadow, and Dorothy could hardly recognize the man who had been her partner in life's grand journey.

Dorothy often found herself lost in reverie, sitting beside her husband, and reflecting on the life they had shared. She would close her eyes and recall the miles they had walked along the shores of Lake Sammamish, their laughter and shared dreams buoyed by the tranquil waters. The smile that had always graced Bill's face remained etched in her memory, a testament to the joy they had found in each other's company.

But now, as she looked at him, she couldn't help but mourn the loss of the man he once was, the man she had fallen in love with and built a life alongside. Alzheimer's had stolen his memories, his clarity, and, in some ways, his very soul. It was cruelty that seemed to lack all mercy, a relentless thief that showed no remorse.

Despite the tears that often welled in her eyes, Dorothy remained steadfast in her commitment to be there for Bill. She knew that their love story was not defined by the trials they faced but by the unwavering bond they shared. In her quiet moments, she would hold onto their memories and the love that had weathered countless storms.

As she gazed at Bill, she saw not just the man he had become but also the man he had always been a man whose smile had illuminated their journey, a man whose love had been the foundation of their life together. And though Alzheimer's had cast a shadow, she remained resolute in her love and devotion, a beacon of unwavering support in the midst of a relentless storm.

As she sat there, her mind would often drift back to a haunting question: How had they arrived at this point? The journey they had undertaken together, filled with love and shared experiences, had now led them to a place where memory and clarity were fleeting, and the once-familiar terrain of their lives had become a labyrinth of uncertainty.

It was during these moments of contemplation that a voice would echo in her mind, a voice that belonged to one of the caregivers who had become a constant presence in their lives. The voice would say, "Knock knock, Miss Dorothy, I came to give a shower to our Handsome feller. Is he ready?" Amina asked with a beautiful smile on her face. It was a simple request, but it carried the weight of reminder, a reminder of the relentless battle they were waging against the monsters of disease and age.

Dorothy would respond with a smile, though it was often a smile that masked the pain that lingered just beneath the surface. "He is all yours," she would say, her voice carrying a gentle yet painful acceptance. "Please handle him with care." It was a plea that held a lifetime of love and protection, a plea that acknowledged the fragility of the man she had adored for so many years.

The caregiver would always respond with a respectful "Yes, ma'am," and set about the task at hand, providing the care and assistance that Bill needed. It was a ritual that had become a part of their daily existence, a reminder of the role reversal that had occurred, where once Bill had been the strong and capable protector, and now he relied on the care and support of others.

Dorothy, at the age of 86, was not a spring chicken anymore, as she often quipped with a touch of humor. Yet, her body had remained resilient, defying the years that had passed. She was one of the fortunate ones to still possess her health and vitality, a stark contrast to the challenges that Bill faced each day.

In these moments, Dorothy couldn't escape the complex emotions that swirled within her a mix of love, loss, gratitude, and sorrow. She had become a caretaker, a role she had never anticipated, and it was a role that tested her strength and resilience with each passing day.

As she sat there, her thoughts wandering through the labyrinth of their shared journey, she found solace in the knowledge that their love remained steadfast. It was a love that transcended the boundaries of time and circumstance, a love that had carried them through a lifetime of joys and challenges, and a love that would endure as they faced the trials of aging and Alzheimer's together.

In the assisted living facility that had become their new home, Dorothy and Bill experienced a unique blend of joy and sadness. It was a place where the rhythm of life had slowed, where calendars were no longer filled with bustling events and plans that they once relished. Instead, they had become residents of the facility, reliant on caregivers for their daily needs, and unable to enjoy the freedoms they once took for granted.

Each morning, Dorothy would rise from her bed, her walker by her side a faithful companion on her journey. With slow and deliberate steps, she would make her way to the window to greet the day. She would retrieve the morning newspaper, a small ritual that connected her to the outside world and offered a glimpse of the events beyond the walls of their home.

Once she had the news in hand, Dorothy would turn her attention to the daily events calendar. It was a schedule that had replaced the full calendars of their past, a calendar that outlined the activities and opportunities for engagement that the facility provided. It was a lifeline to a sense of purpose and community.

Most mornings, Bill found himself lost in the fog of Alzheimer's, his interest in the events of the day waning. Yet, each morning, Dorothy would sit by his side, her voice strong and unwavering, reading the news aloud to him, sharing the stories of the world, and offering a sense of continuity in a life that had become increasingly fragmented.

As she finished with the news, she would turn to the calendar, her voice filled with a gentle enthusiasm. She would ask Bill if he would like to attend any of the day's events, her hope for his participation shining through. But, more often than not, the answer would be a resigned "no."

Dorothy, undeterred, would proceed with her own routine. She would attend a power class, where chair exercises allowed her to maintain her physical strength and resilience. Afterward, she and Bill would reunite for breakfast, a simple but cherished moment of togetherness.

According to the schedule, their day often led them to join the other residents for a game of bingo. It was a communal activity, a chance to connect with fellow residents and share in the joys of friendly competition.

Home Is Where Heart Is

The assisted living facility had become a new chapter in their lives, a place where the roles and routines they once knew had shifted. It was a place where the symphony of life played a different tune, but the melody of love and companionship continued to resonate, weaving a tapestry of togetherness and resilience.

Amidst the challenges of aging and illness, they found moments of joy and connection. In shared conversations, laughter, and the comfort of companionship, they discovered that life's most precious moments could still be experienced. The passage of time had altered their physical abilities, but it couldn't diminish the depth of their emotions or the beauty of the human spirit.

The residents of the facility came to understand that the rhythm of life had indeed changed, but it hadn't silenced the music of love and belonging. It was a place where they supported each other, sharing the stories of their lives, their dreams, and their hopes.

In this sanctuary of understanding, they navigated the complexities of aging and the uncertainty of health. They found comfort in knowing they were not alone, that they had companions who walked alongside them on this journey.

Life had presented formidable challenges, but they had come to realize that together, they were stronger. They cherished the moments of happiness and contentment, finding solace in the bonds they had forged.

As Dorothy sat in her chair, her gaze fell upon the other residents who, like her husband, were engaged in a relentless battle against this monstrous affliction. Each face in the room told a story, a story of a life once vibrant, now overshadowed by the unforgiving grip of Alzheimer's.

Among these residents, there were individuals who had achieved remarkable feats in their lives. Doctors who had saved countless lives, lawyers who had championed justice, and parents who had nurtured and guided their children with boundless love, all of them now faced the relentless march of this disease.

In this assisted living facility, the diversity of backgrounds and experiences was evident. Some of the residents were in their 70s, once vibrant and full of life, their spirits now encaged by the merciless progression of Alzheimer's. It was a cruel paradox, watching these individuals lose pieces of themselves each day, their memories slipping through their fingers like grains of sand.

The disease knew no bounds, showing no mercy to the brilliant minds it had once illuminated. It was a thief of memories, an eraser of identities, and a destroyer of the very essence of what made each person unique.

For some families, the assisted living facility became a place where the pain of separation was profound. It was a place to forget their loved ones, a heart-wrenching decision that was often driven by the harsh reality of Alzheimer's disease. For the families and loved ones of these residents, the agony ran deep.

They had borne witness to the slow and relentless unraveling of the individuals they cherished. Alzheimer's had been a merciless thief, robbing them of their memories, their abilities, their independence, and ultimately their very sense of self. It was a cruel and relentless journey that could feel like watching a loved one slip away, bit by bit, day by day.

Alzheimer's disease, often described as "the devil," had the power to create a profound sense of separation within families. It wasn't just a separation of physical presence; it was the separation from the memories, the shared experiences, and the essence of the person they had known and loved for so long.

For families and loved ones, the emotional toll was immense. They grappled with the anguish of seeing their dear ones become strangers within their own bodies. They faced the heartbreak of trying to connect with individuals who could no longer recognize them, the pain of answering questions that would be forgotten moments later, and the challenge of providing care to those who could no longer express their gratitude.

In the face of such a relentless adversary, Alzheimer's disease, families, and loved ones held on to the moments of clarity and connection, however fleeting they might be. They were united by a profound love and the desire to provide comfort and support, even in the face of this relentless devil that had taken hold of their cherished family members.

Despite the anguish and separation, they sought solace in the knowledge that love transcended memory and that their bonds were stronger than the cruel grip of Alzheimer's. Their journey was a testament to the strength of the human spirit, the power of love, and the enduring hope that one day, a cure would be found to reunite those who had been separated by this devastating disease.

Breath In Breath Out

Breath in, breath out, take one day at a time, these words had become Dorothy's mantra, a lifeline she clung to as she navigated the heart-wrenching labyrinth of Alzheimer's disease with her beloved Bill. Each morning, she would rise from her bed and open the curtains, revealing a world that seemed to move on without them. Bill lay beside her, his face peaceful in slumber, a stark contrast to the turmoil within his mind.

As she settled into her favorite window seat, her gaze would drift to the garden outside. Vibrant flowers and the morning dance of bees and butterflies painted a picture of life in its purest form. Dorothy counted the butterflies, their kaleidoscope of colors a fleeting respite from the heavy reality that surrounded her. In these moments, joy touched her heart, if only briefly, before the cruel truth of their circumstances crept back in.

The Alzheimer's assistants living facility was a realm of both despair and connection, where the disease stole not only memories but the essence of those it ensnared. Dorothy's heart ached not just for Bill but for every soul battling the same monstrous adversary. It was a shared struggle, transcending individual stories, a collective fight against an adversary that showed no mercy.

Seated among fellow residents, Dorothy couldn't help but marvel at the profound injustice of it all. How could a single disease dare to rob so many of their essence, their memories, their very selves? It was a question without answers, a challenge without a clear path forward. Yet, amid the darkness, a glimmer of hope persisted a hope that, together, they could find moments of connection, compassion, and shared humanity, even as Alzheimer's sought to extinguish their individual lights.

Dorothy's attention often gravitated to one particular resident; a woman named Kimberley. She had a penchant for weaving conversations that seemed to defy logic, thoughts and ideas intertwined in a bewildering tapestry. Dorothy, with a heart full of empathy, gave her undivided attention.

Kimberley poked in riddles, her words a dance between realms unknown. But Dorothy, with kindness and patience, listened intently, her laughter punctuating the inexplicable exchanges. In those moments, Dorothy's soul resonated with empathy. It was a bittersweet connection, a link to another soul grappling with the same relentless disease that had touched her husband's life. It was a reminder that Alzheimer's did not discriminate, affecting individuals in unique and mystifying ways.

Dorothy's laughter, shared with Resident Number 215 Kimberley, was a testament to her compassion. It acknowledged that beneath the shroud of Alzheimer's, there remained a person with thoughts, feelings, and a need for connection. It reflected Dorothy's steadfast belief in the worth of every individual, no matter how Alzheimer's had reshaped their reality.

As they conversed, Dorothy's soul swayed between hope and sorrow. Hope that one day, a cure for this unyielding disease will be found, and those like Kimberley will rediscover clarity of thought and memory. Sorrow for the present moment, where Alzheimer's wove its intricate tapestry of confusion and disarray.

In the face of such profound challenges, Dorothy's enduring empathy and faith in the power of human connection shone brightly. She knew that, even amid the chaos Alzheimer's wrought, moments of genuine connection and shared humanity transcended the boundaries of the disease. And as she continued to laugh and engage with Kimberley, she clung to the hope that, one day, that laughter would ring freely without the shadow of Alzheimer's.

In the quiet moments that followed, Dorothy often found herself outside her room, her body aching, her thoughts returning to Bill. There was a tender ache in her heart, a yearning to be by his side, even though she had just left him in their room. She knew that he would be sitting there alone, his mind a labyrinth of memories and confusion.

With determination, Dorothy would rise from her chair, her trusty walker in hand, and make her way back to their room, heavy-hearted but resolute. She knew that love was a journey filled with unexpected twists, and Alzheimer's was the most formidable of adversaries.

Yet, along her path, she frequently encountered Resident Number 240 John, a man who had once been a news reporter. He would engage Dorothy in conversations about the weather and regale her with tales of his time during the war. It was a narrative that had become a daily fixture in their lives, each day a repetition of the last.

The caregivers, familiar with the well-rehearsed story, had memorized every word. Yet, for Dorothy, every encounter was an opportunity to listen anew, to lend an ear to the stories of a man who had once made a living by sharing the world's news. She would stand there for a few moments, nodding and pretending as though it was the first time, she was hearing familiar tales.

With politeness and grace, she would eventually excuse herself from the conversation and continue her journey back to her husband, the weight of their shared history a solemn anchor in her heart.

As she slowly approached the elevator, she noticed Jane, a woman who had recently lost her husband, standing there, lost, and uncertain. Jane's eyes were filled with sorrow, her gaze distant as if searching for something that had vanished. Janes smiled warmly and stepped closer, "I'm heading to the 9th floor. Where are you going?"

Jane's voice trembled as she responded, her vulnerability laid bare, "I'm going there too." It was a place that didn't exist, but Dorothy understood the need to play along, to create connections in a world where reality often slipped through their fingers.

Jane often initiated conversations, pouring out her heart about the pain of being left behind by her children. "I don't know what I did to them," she would say, tears welling in her eyes. "They know I love them, but I guess they don't care about me anymore."

Dorothy would gently squeeze Jane's hand and meet her gaze, her eyes reflecting understanding and compassion. "They love you," she'd reassure her. "Remember, you are safe here, and we are all friends." Jane's tears would subside, and the conversation would shift to brighter topics, like the morning's breakfast.

In these moments, Dorothy exemplified the extraordinary capacity of the human heart to find solace and connection even in the midst of profound loss and confusion. As the elevator door slowly opened, she offered Jane a warm smile, a lifeline in their shared journey through the labyrinth of Alzheimer's, where love and compassion were the guiding stars in their darkest hours.

As Jane headed back to the dining room, her footsteps echoing down the hallway, Dorothy made her way towards her room. As she approached her door, she noticed Mary standing there, patiently waiting. Dorothy smiled warmly and greeted her friend. "Mary, what brings you here? Is everything alright?" Mary nodded, her eyes reflecting a mix of emotions. "I just wanted to talk to you, Dorothy. You always listen, and I need someone to talk to right now."

Dorothy nodded, understanding the importance of these moments of connection. She gently placed a hand on Mary's shoulder and guided her into the room. They took their seats by the window, the familiar tableau of their card games now transformed into a sanctuary of trust and companionship.

With a sigh, Mary began to speak, her voice tinged with vulnerability. She shared her thoughts, her fears, and the memories of her late husband. Dorothy listened with the same compassion and empathy she had always offered.

As the, their conversation flowed freely, the room bathed in the soft glow of the setting sun. For Dorothy and Mary, these moments were more than just words exchanged; they were a lifeline in a world that often seemed confusing and distant.

In that room, Alzheimer's was momentarily forgotten, and their friendship, solidified through shared stories and heartfelt confessions, continued to flourish. Dorothy ayes gazed at the movie poster.

Dorothy chuckled softly at Mary's candid response. Mary had always been refreshingly direct, never mincing words. "Alright, no cartoons, I promise," Dorothy replied with a playful twinkle in her eye. "To my room, it is then."

They made their way to Dorothy's room, their shared laughter filling the hallway. Dorothy's room was adorned with pictures and mementos of a life well-lived, a visual timeline of her journey with Bill. As they settled in, Dorothy retrieved a deck of cards from a drawer, their familiar faces worn from countless games played.

Seated at a small table by the window, they shuffled the cards with practiced ease. The room was filled with the soft rustling of cards and the gentle hum of conversation. The world outside carried on, oblivious to the simple joy unfolding within those walls.

As the game progressed, Dorothy couldn't help but feel a sense of gratitude for this unexpected friendship. In the midst of Alzheimer's, where memories slipped away like sand through fingers, she had found a kindred spirit in Mary. They shared stories, whispered secrets, and reveled in the simple pleasure of each other's company.

Mary's sharp wit and unfiltered honesty added a delightful twist to their games. "You know, Dorothy," Mary said with a mischievous grin, "I once read that playing cards keeps the mind sharp. Maybe that's why I'm so good at it!" She winked, her eyes sparkling with humor.

Dorothy laughed heartily. "Well, you're not wrong, Mary. And your big mouth certainly keeps the conversation lively."

Their laughter echoed down the hallway, drawing smiles from passing caregivers and residents. In that room, Alzheimer's seemed to recede, if only for a while, leaving behind two friends who refused to let the shadows of the past define their present.

As they played cards, the sun dipped below the horizon, casting a warm glow into the room. Mary glanced out the window, her gaze fixed on the fading light. "You know, Dorothy," she began, her tone softer, "I used to watch sunsets with my husband. It was our thing, you know? We'd sit on the porch, hold hands, and just watch as the sky turned all those beautiful shades of orange and pink."

Dorothy's heart ached with empathy. She knew that behind Mary's frank demeanor lay a well of emotions, of memories and love that refused to be forgotten. "That sounds absolutely beautiful, Mary," she replied, her voice gentle. "Tell me more about those moments."

And so, in the waning light of day, they shared stories of love and loss, of cherished memories and the bittersweet beauty of life. Alzheimer's may have threatened to steal Mary's past, but in that room, their friendship blossomed anew, creating moments that were all the more precious for being shared.

As the evening deepened, their card game continued, each play and conversation a testament to the resilience of the human spirit. Together, they forged a bond that defied the confines of Alzheimer's, proving that, even in the face of life's greatest challenges, there was room for laughter, friendship, and the enduring magic of the present moment.

To keep her mind alive and her heart full, Dorothy joined the "Golden Girls" at the facility, a group of spirited residents who shared her love for vibrant, meaningful activities. Most days, she eagerly ventured out to meet her fellow "Golden Girls." Together, they would embark on a kaleidoscope of experiences that painted their days with laughter, joy, and cherished memories.

The group reveled in arranging bouquets of fresh flowers, their fingers deftly weaving a tapestry of colors and scents that brought life to their shared space. Bingo nights were filled with spirited competition and contagious enthusiasm, as they marked their cards in unison, hoping for that elusive call of "Bingo!" to ring through the room.

Card games became a delightful daily ritual, the familiar sound of shuffled decks and the camaraderie of friendly competition bonding them ever closer. Sometimes, they'd gather to listen to nostalgic melodies, the tunes of their youth flooding their hearts with bittersweet nostalgia. And on special occasions, they'd gather in the facility's quaint theater to watch old movies, their laughter and commentary filling the room like echoes of a bygone era.

Yet, as much as Dorothy cherished these moments with her Golden Girls, her heart always led her back to her beloved Bill. Returning to their room, she'd find him sitting there, his eyes a kaleidoscope of emotions, searching for a glimmer of recognition amid the fog of Alzheimer's.

In those sacred moments, the depth of their love shone brightly. Dorothy would bend down and plant a gentle kiss on Bill's forehead, a ritual that never failed to ignite a spark of recognition. His face would light up, and he'd whisper, "Is this my Dorothy?" in a voice filled with tenderness, a voice that melted her heart.

With a voice brimming with love and reassurance, she'd reply, "Yes, love, it's your Dorothy." In those simple words, their connection remained unbroken, a testament to the enduring power of their love.

Their love was a force that transcended the barriers of time and memory, a love that Alzheimer's could never erase. In the midst of the chaos and confusion that clouded their days, Dorothy and Bill's love remained steadfast, a beacon of light that guided them through the darkest moments.

Dorothy would open the fridge and retrieve cold chocolate milk for him. As he savored each sip, Dorothy would take a newspaper and read it aloud to him. Sometimes, he would grasp the essence of her words, a flicker of understanding in his eyes, but there were times when the world remained a puzzle he couldn't unravel.

Dorothy's heart ached with the desire to do more, to engage in a multitude of activities offered by the facility's daily schedule. Yet the thought of leaving Bill alone in their room, adrift in a sea of fragmented memories, weighed heavily on her. So, on rare occasions, she'd invite some friends from the Golden Girls to join her in their room for a lively card game.

Those evenings, laughter and camaraderie filled the air as they played cards and shared stories. It was a small oasis of joy amidst the challenges they faced. Dorothy's friends, aware of her unwavering devotion to Bill, had become her support system, a source of strength that allowed her to navigate the complex journey of love, loss, and the enduring spirit of togetherness in the face of Alzheimer's.

Goodbye Is Not An Easy Word

As the months rolled on, the passing of residents became an almost haunting routine, casting a shadow over the facility and making it increasingly challenging to form new connections. Dorothy had known her share of farewells, but today's news was particularly heartbreaking.

Heading to the dining room for dinner, Dorothy's footsteps felt heavier than usual. Her heart sank as she caught sight of a framed photo of Mary with the most familiar yet painfully poignant words beneath it: "In memory of Mary." Tears welled up in Dorothy's eyes, and she couldn't help but walk closer to the picture, as if seeking answers in the somber tribute.

She remembered Mary vividly, for it was just last night that they sat in her room, playing cards, and sharing stories. Dorothy's emotions overcame her, and she turned to Bill, his eyes searching for understanding. "Dorothy! My love, are you crying?" he asked with genuine concern.

With a forced smile, she replied, "Not at all, my love." But the facade was paper-thin, and Bill sensed the sorrow beneath the surface.

Together, they walked to the dining room, but Dorothy's heart was deeply affected by Mary's passing. Mary had been a woman who understood her, a friend in this complex world of fading memories. What made this loss even more profound was the fact that Mary's mind had remained remarkably intact. Alzheimer's hadn't yet fully claimed her, and yet, death had come knocking.

As they sat down at their table, their usual routine disrupted by the absence of their friend, the waiter approached with a compassionate glance. "Hey, Miss Dorothy, what do you want for dinner? Special, or something specific?"

Dorothy's eyes were filled with tears as she looked directly at the waiter. "What happened to my friend? I was playing cards with her last night." Her voice quivered with emotion.

The waiter, equally touched by the loss, gently held Dorothy's hand. "The caregivers found her gone this morning. We are all waiting to know what happened to her."

Dorothy was deeply affected by Mary's sudden departure. Mary had been a lovely lady who didn't know how to control her mouth. She had been diagnosed just last year, and the speed of her decline was a cruel reminder of Alzheimer's unpredictable nature. Tears streamed down Dorothy's cheeks as she looked at the waiter.

"I think I'll pass on dinner, just apple juice will do," Dorothy said, her voice filled with sadness. The waiter bent down, meeting Dorothy's gaze directly. "Miss Dorothy, I know how hard this is for all of us, especially for you, but please, pretty please, can you at least have a cup of soup?"

Dorothy managed a painful smile. "Alright, a cup of soup it is."

Around the dining room, many residents remained oblivious to the recent loss, not out of indifference, but because their memories were like overloaded computers, with no space to store new information. They moved through life, each day a reset button, forgetting even the simplest of details, like what they had for lunch or whether they'd visited the restroom.

As they sat at the table, Bill beside her, Dorothy couldn't shake the weight of Mary's absence. Her mind wandered, wondering who might be next, and whether it was wise to forge new friendships when the pain of losing them was inevitable.

The waiter returned with plates of food for the table, and as usual, Mary's empty chair served as a painful reminder of their loss. "Here you go, Bill. I hope you'll like it," the waiter said, offering a kind smile.

Dorothy gazed at her bowl of soup, her eyes welling up as she looked at Mary's vacant seat. Tears fell, and she quickly wiped them away. The waiter, noticing her distress, approached and offered a comforting hug. With a tearful smile, Dorothy joked, "Don't get old, my friend. If you can fight aging, please start now."

The waiter chuckled and replied, "I consider it a privilege to reach where you are, Dorothy. Not many people live to see their 80s."

Dorothy playfully pulled the waiter closer. "Yet it doesn't guarantee you'll reach 80 with all your brain cells intact."

They shared a genuine laugh, and Bill, with tender care, wiped away a lingering crumb of food from his lips, silently cherishing the moments of joy and connection amidst the backdrop of Alzheimer's relentless advance.

As the night settled in, Dorothy and Bill retired to their room. Bill, weary from the day's events, soon succumbed to sleep, his breathing steady and peaceful. Dorothy, however, found herself lying awake, the weight of memories and emotions pressing upon her heart.

She lay there, bathed in the soft glow of the room's dimmed light, contemplating the journey of her life. She had traveled through the vibrant tapestry of existence, from her childhood friend Sara, Bill's beloved sister, and now to Mary. Each person had woven their unique threads into the fabric of her life, leaving an indelible mark on her heart.

As Dorothy gazed at the ceiling, a question nagged at her: Was she lucky to have lived a life so full of connections and friendships, or was it a cruel twist of fate that these bonds were often cut short by time and circumstance?

She couldn't help but think of Sara, her childhood confidante, who had been her partner in mischief and shared dreams. Life had taken them on separate paths, and they had drifted apart, their friendship a memory now cherished in the corners of her mind. Her absence still left a void in Dorothy's heart, a void that could never truly be filled.

And now, Mary, the understanding companion in the world of Alzheimer's, had left her side, leaving behind a profound emptiness.

Dorothy's thoughts swirled like leaves caught in a gentle breeze. She wondered if she was cursed to be the one left behind, to watch those she cared about slip away, one by one. The pain of loss weighed heavily on her soul, and she couldn't help but question the purpose of these fleeting connections.

But then, as if drawn by an invisible force, her gaze shifted to Bill. He lay beside her, his face serene in slumber. The lines of age and memory loss were etched across his features, but he was here, breathing softly, his heart beating steadily.

Dorothy reached out and gently kissed his forehead. In that tender moment, she felt a profound sense of gratitude wash over her. She realized that life was indeed a ride, filled with highs and lows, with joy and sorrow, with love and loss.

Yes, she had seen friends come and go, and the pain of their departures had left scars in her heart. But she had also been given the gift of enduring love, a love that transcended the boundaries of time and memory. Bill had been her constant companion on this rollercoaster of life, and she couldn't imagine a journey without him.

As she looked at Bill, peacefully sleeping beside her, she knew that, despite the challenges they faced, they were still on this ride together. The ride of life, with all its twists and turns, was a gift to be treasured, and she was grateful for every moment she could share with the man lying beside her.

With a heart full of love and gratitude, Dorothy closed her eyes, finding solace in the warmth of the man she loved and the memories they continued to create together, one precious moment at a time.

Walk At The Lake

The morning after Mary's passing weighed heavily on Dorothy's heart. Mary had been a dear friend for the past six months, and her absence left a gaping hole in Dorothy's world. She couldn't hold back the tears, and the thought of leaving her room seemed unbearable.

Recognizing the depth of Dorothy's grief, Amina decided to act. She knew this was not a good day for Dorothy or Bill, and she wanted to bring some solace to their lives. After a conversation with her director of care Amina was given permission to call the family.

Natal knew it would be particularly difficult for her mother, and she asked the director to prepare her parents' bags for an extended weekend with her.

Natal had been living on the East Coast for years, having moved away after finishing school and getting married in Boston. However, after a bitter divorce and with her children now married and have home of their own, she decided to take a job at Swedish Hospital in Redmond to be closer to her parents.

Dorothy and Bill had chosen not to sell their beautiful family home, making it a logical choice for Natal to move in. Her sisters, Diana, and Bella, lived far away in Houston and New York, respectively, and it was Natal's deep love for her parents that led her back to Washington.

Once settled in her parents' home, Natal didn't make many changes. She wanted to feel at home, surrounded by familiar walls that held cherished memories. She kept the height markings on the wall, a testament to the years of growth and love that had filled the house.

Natal rose from the bed and glanced out the window, where the view of Lake Sammamish stretched before her. She smiled as she recalled her younger self, running and jumping into the lake, hearing her mother's voice cautioning her against the cold water. Those memories brought warmth to her heart.

After a long, hot shower, Natal made herself a cup of coffee and got ready to pick up her parents. As she drove to the facility, the picturesque view of Lake Sammamish served as a backdrop to her contemplative thoughts. She couldn't help but question whether it was the right decision to keep her parents in assisted living. The weight of the responsibility felt heavy on her shoulders, and she decided to call her sisters for their input.

With both her sisters on the phone, Natal shared her concerns about their parents' living situation. Bella, who lived in New York with her four children and nine grandchildren, mentioned the logistical challenges of distance and the painful memory of when their father nearly burned the house down. Diana, residing in Houston with her own family, agreed that assisted living wasn't the first choice.

Diana suggested that they all meet at their parents' home during Thanksgiving and discuss the possibility of bringing their parents back home. Natal agreed, recognizing that she would need help caring for their parents, especially since she would be working full time. They decided to hire two caregivers to assist them.

With a plan in place, Natal felt reassured. She knew it wouldn't be easy, but the thought of having her parents back in their home, where they belonged, brought her comfort.

When Natal arrived at the facility, she headed straight to the director's office to inform her of their plans. The director expressed gratitude for having Dorothy in their community, describing her as a light that brightened everyone's day. Natal explained that her mother had a deep attachment to their family home, which held sentimental value.

As Natal exited the director's office, she made her way to her parents' room. She knocked, but there was no answer. After a few tries, she used her key to enter. Amina, one of the caregivers, informed Natal that Dorothy was still in bed, her spirits were low due to Mary's passing.

Natal thanked Amina for her care and shared her plan to take her parents' home for the weekend in the hopes of uplifting Dorothy's spirits. As Natal entered the room, she found Bill sitting on the swing chair. His eyes lit up upon seeing her, and he greeted her with a heartfelt compliment.

Natal hugged her father tightly, and in that small touch, memories long held in her heart awakened. Tears filled her eyes as she remembered their last summer together in Laos, visiting her mother's grave. The headstone read, "Natal, you are not just a star, you are my galaxy." She kissed her father's forehead and whispered in his ear,

"You've been the sun in my dark days and the moon in my nights. I love you, Dad."

Natal then turned her attention to her mother, who was still in bed. She sat on the edge and gently touched her. "Mama, wake up, it's time to get up." Dorothy opened her eyes, her face lighting up with a smile. "I thought you were coming tomorrow to visit. Are you okay?" Dorothy asked, her motherly concern evident.

Natal explained that it was Thursday, and she was off for the weekend, so she had come to take them home. She wanted to spend quality time with them. "Mama, your baby girl needs you," she said with a smile, pulling Dorothy up to a sitting position.

Dorothy slowly got up, and they both headed to the bathroom to get ready for the long weekend at home. Before leaving, Dorothy requested a stop at her favorite donut place, a small indulgence that Natal was more than happy to grant.

As Natal drove to her parents' home, she couldn't contain her happiness. Her heart was filled with gratitude for the chance to spend time with them. She watched her father in the rearview mirror, a man who had once been strong, a war pilot, a Boeing engineer, and a loving husband and father. Now, he sat in the backseat like a child, unsure of where life was taking him.

The thought of losing him to the disease was a painful one. Natal reflected on the limits of human existence, realizing that no matter how hard one tried to outrun it, time remained undefeated. She made a silent vow to cherish every second with her parents and to keep them close as long as she could. She whispered to herself that nothing, but the end of time would ever separate them.

Arriving home, Bill's face lit up like a child entering a playground. Natal opened the car door and assisted her parents in. Dorothy's eyes sparkled at the sight of the box of donuts. "Now I know I'm home. Would you please make a cup of coffee and bring those donuts here?" Dorothy requested with a smile. Natal chuckled, knowing how much her mother loved those donuts. "Mama, just two for now. Remember, less sugar for you."

Dorothy laughed and playfully grabbed the box. "What do I have to lose? I'm too old to worry about my hourglass figure." They all laughed and settled down near the window, gazing at the beautiful view of Lake Sammamish, cherishing this precious moment of togetherness.

The morning sun cast its gentle light through the bedroom window, painting the room with a warm, golden glow. Outside, a symphony of birdsong filled the air, their melodious tunes weaving a soothing tapestry of sound. Dorothy awoke to this enchanting morning serenade and stood by the window, gazing out at the picturesque view of the lake. This view had been a silent witness to the many chapters of their lives, a constant companion through the years.

As she looked at the tranquil waters of the lake, Dorothy's thoughts wandered back to when they had brought Bella home. She remembered the anticipation and excitement, the nervousness that came with the responsibility of caring for their little girl. A tear of nostalgia escaped her eye as she pictured the first night when Bill had brought Diana and Natal home.

Time had passed in the blink of an eye, and her heart swelled with pride and love for her family. Has been a while since Bill and Dorothy slept in their house.

Seams as she closed her eyes and the morning arrived, Dorothy turned her gaze to Bill, who was sleeping by her side, Dorothy couldn't help but smile through her tears. She remembered the sleepless nights when Natal had cried inconsolably, while Bill seemed to sleep peacefully through it all. "Yet nothing changes," she mused, "Bill falls asleep just as soundly now as he did then."

Dorothy gently nudged Bill's feet to rouse him. "Bill, it's time for you to take your pills," she reminded him. As they both got ready for the day, Natal was busy preparing a picnic basket filled with their favorite treats.

By nearly ten in the morning, Dorothy and Bill found themselves at the dining table, where Natal had prepared a delicious breakfast. The atmosphere was light and joyful, a stark contrast to the weight of recent events. Natal shared the good news with her parents, revealing that she and her sisters had discussed their living arrangements.

"I think it would be a wonderful idea for both of you to come home and live with me," Natal proposed, her eyes filled with hope a anticipation. "After all, this is your house." Laughter filled the room as they embraced this new chapter in their lives.

Following breakfast, Natal led her parents to the picturesque lake where they had shared countless picnics and memories. She had prepared a bench adorned with fresh flowers and a basket filled with their favorite goodies. As Bill and Dorothy enjoyed their picnic, Natal decided to take a leisurely walk along the lakeshore. "Okay, kids, be nice to each other. I'm going for a walk," Natal playfully told her parents before setting off.

Dorothy gazed at the bench and couldn't help but smile. "Honey, we've been enjoying this view for the past seventy years. It's where we had our first kiss, where we fell in love." Bill gently held Dorothy's hand; his eyes locked onto hers. "I could never forget, my love. If I ever forget about you and our love, then I would truly be lost."

Dorothy kissed her husband, resting her head on his shoulder as they sat by the serene lake. Birds danced in the sky, and fish gracefully swam in the clear waters of Lake Sammamish. It was a moment of quiet contentment, a snapshot of their enduring love.

The weekend passed by in a blur of cherished memories. Dorothy and Bill walked along the familiar trails, reminiscing about the smiles, laughter, tears, and even a few arguments they had shared under the towering trees. These paths had been witnessing countless conversations, promises made, and love that had grown stronger with each passing year.

As the sun began to set on Sunday evening, Dorothy gently reminded Bill that they would be returning to the assisted living facility soon. Bill nodded in acknowledgment, taking slow, deliberate steps toward their home.

Natal stood at the main entrance, watching her parents' happy faces as they approached. She knew she had made the right decision to bring them back home, if only for a little while. As Bill drew closer to her, he couldn't help but smile.

"My galaxy," he said to Natal, "one thing I want you to know is that when my time comes, I want my ashes to be spread by this lake, under that tree, and some by the tree in our backyard. I want to be here, protecting you forever."

Tears welled up in Natal's eyes as she turned to Dorothy, eager to hear her mother's wishes for the next life. Without hesitation, Dorothy turned to look at Bill with unwavering love in her eyes. "Wherever this handsome man will be, I'll be happy to be with him."

Natal looked at her parents with gratitude and admiration. "Mama and Daddy, you've taught me to love beyond measure. Thank you so much for that."

Before they left to return to the facility, Natal made a quick stop at the donut shop. The joy in Dorothy's eyes as she saw the donuts was reminiscent of a child in a candy store. As they savored the sweet treats, they couldn't help but feel that roles had reversed over the years children had become parents, and parents had become children once more.

Home Sweet Home

For two months, Natal had worked tirelessly to transform her childhood home into a senior citizen-friendly haven. Every corner of the house was meticulously examined and altered to ensure her parents' safety and comfort. Bathrooms were equipped with sturdy rails, the toilet in their room resembled something you might find in a hospital, and every essential item they might need was within easy reach. Natal wanted her parents to feel like they were returning to a place that not only held cherished memories but also catered to their needs in this new phase of their lives.

As Thanksgiving approached, Natal's sisters, Diana, and Bella, arrived a week early to help with the preparations. The house that had once been filled with the laughter and youthful energy of the three girls was now host to a reunion of grandmothers, a reminder of the passage of time. They walked through the familiar rooms, reminiscing about their shared childhood and expressing gratitude to their parents for raising them in this loving home.

Together, the three sisters embarked on a mission to make this Thanksgiving a truly special one. They spent hours planning, from the decor to the dishes, ensuring that every detail would contribute to the warmth and joy of the occasion. They even made arrangements for their children, who had grown into a big, extended family.

The grandkids were eagerly anticipating this Thanksgiving celebration. They had heard stories of the house, its history, and the traditions that had been passed down through generations. To them, it was a place where family bonds were nurtured and cherished.

As the special day drew near, the excitement grew. Natal, Diana, and Bella coordinated with their children to ensure that everyone would be in Redmond for the grand Thanksgiving surprise. It was a reunion that would not only bring joy and laughter but also serve as a heartfelt expression of love and gratitude to their parents, who had given them a lifetime of cherished memories in that very house.

The plan was set on Wednesday, just before Thanksgiving, they would all gather to pick up their parents and bring them to the house filled with generations of love and memories. It was a reunion that promised to be a beautiful testament to the enduring bonds of family and the timeless traditions that had been passed down through the years.

On Wednesday night, the family's house in Redmond buzzed with excitement as guests began to arrive for the much-anticipated Thanksgiving celebration. Natal's son, a master chef, had taken it upon himself to orchestrate a culinary masterpiece that would leave everyone in awe. The guest list included cousins, Natal's, Bella's, and Diana's sons and daughters, along with their spouses and children. Even Sara's kids, who always cherished these family gatherings, joined in the festivities.

The evening was a tapestry of joy, as generations mingled in the cozy ambiance of the family home. Laughter echoed through the halls as cousins played games, siblings engaged in heartfelt conversations, and little ones ran around, their giggles adding to the symphony of happiness. The sound of music filled the air, beckoning guests to the dance floor, where young and old grooved to the rhythm, celebrating the bonds that bound them together.

Natal's son, the master chef, was the culinary maestro of the night, orchestrating a feast that promised to be a memorable one. The aroma of roasting turkey and the sizzle of savory sides wafted through the house, creating an enticing scent that drew everyone closer to the kitchen. With each dish he prepared, he poured his heart and soul into the culinary creations, knowing that the meal would be a testament to family, tradition, and love.

As the night wore on and the stars illuminated the sky, Natal, Bella, and Diana found themselves in their parents' room, just like the old days. They sat on the bed, a circle of love and nostalgia, sharing stories that transported them back to their childhood.

Dorothy's heart swelled with warmth as she listened to her daughters' voices, a sweet melody that echoed with memories. Bill, though his memory was fading, mixed in his own tales, and the room became a treasure trove of family history.

It was a night filled with anticipation, not just for the feast that awaited them the next day but for the precious moments of togetherness they were already sharing. In that room, surrounded by the love of their children, Bill and Dorothy felt like they had traveled back in time, reliving the moments that had defined their family. They all knew that the upcoming Thanksgiving would be a special one, a day to honor tradition, create new memories, and, most importantly, celebrate the enduring bonds of family.

Thanksgiving Day arrived in all its glory, and the family home in Redmond was a hive of activity from the crack of dawn. The aroma of roasted turkey, sage-infused stuffing, and buttery mashed potatoes filled every nook and cranny, promising a feast of epic proportions. The dining table, adorned with an assortment of gleaming silverware and elegant china, stood as the centerpiece of the day's festivities.

Natal, Bella, and Diana had been up since the early hours, orchestrating a culinary symphony. Their children, with eager hands and hearts, had joined in the kitchen festivities, slicing vegetables, whipping cream for pies, and basting the turkey with fragrant herbs. The tantalizing scent of the turkey's crispy skin and succulent meat wafted through the house, weaving a spell that beckoned everyone to the feast that awaited them.

As the sun cast a warm, golden hue over the backyard, the family gathered for a meal that was the culmination of hours of love, effort, and tradition. The table groaned under the weight of Thanksgiving classics: a perfectly bronzed turkey, a buttery sea of mashed potatoes, green bean casserole topped with crispy fried onions, cranberry sauce with a hint of orange zest, and steaming gravy that promised to marry all these flavors into one heavenly union.

The vibe was one of warmth, gratitude, and love. Glasses clinked as they were raised in toasts to family, togetherness, and the memories they were creating. The room echoed with laughter, stories from the past, and the joyful clamor of children. It was a tableau of tradition and change, as Diana and her family, now Texans, passionately cheered for the Cowboys, while the rest of the family remained staunch Seahawks supporters. Good-natured ribbing and playful banter filled the air as the football game played on the television in the background.

Dorothy, though she hadn't been feeling her best, reveled in the moment. She watched with a heart full of pride as her children and grandchildren laughed, shared stories, and savored the delicious feast before them. Her gaze lingered on Bill, the love of her life, sitting beside her. She marveled at the legacy they had created together a family tree that had grown strong and vibrant from the seed of their love.

She quietly left her seat and walked over to Bill, who was engrossed in the football game. She took his hand, and they sat together, watching the game unfold on the screen. The love and connection they shared, built over a lifetime, filled the room. Dorothy cherished this moment, knowing that their love had been the foundation upon which this beautiful family had been built.

Thanksgiving was more than just a meal; it was a celebration of love, tradition, and the bonds that held this family together. The scents, the sounds, and the smiles that filled the room painted a picture of warmth and togetherness that would be cherished for years to come.

As the night wore on and the family continued to enjoy their post-Thanksgiving festivities, Dorothy and Bill retired to their bedroom. Dorothy's earlier discomfort had not abated; in fact, it had grown more pronounced. She couldn't ignore the nagging pain in her chest any longer.

Dorothy decided to call Natal, her ever-reliable daughter who was not just a loving child but also a doctor. She knew that Natal's expertise would provide her with the best guidance.

Natal answered her mother's call with concern in her voice. Dorothy explained how she felt, likening it to a sensation of gas but one that was more persistent and unsettling. Natal, after asking a series of questions to gauge the situation, decided it was best to administer some medication to alleviate her mother's discomfort.

With Natal's soothing voice on the other end of the line, Dorothy followed her instructions and took the medication. Natal reassured her mother, reminding her that if the pain persisted or worsened, they wouldn't hesitate to rush her to the hospital.

Dorothy appreciated Natal's care and concern but insisted that she wasn't in dire straits just yet. She promised to keep a close eye on her condition and contact her daughter if things took a turn for the worse.

With that, they exchanged "I love you" and goodnight wishes. Dorothy settled into bed, hoping the discomfort would ease, and she could rest peacefully, knowing her family was just a call away if she needed them.

The night had settled into a profound stillness. The house, once filled with laughter and merriment, now rested in a serene calm. Outside, the moonlight cast a soft, silvery glow on the tranquil surface of Lake Sammamish. The very same lake that had witnessed the love story of Dorothy and Bill over the years, reflecting their joys, their memories, and their enduring bond.

Bill lay in peaceful slumber, unaware of the events unfolding around him. His steady breaths rose and fell in a rhythmic pattern, a soothing lullaby in the quiet of the night. He was a picture of contentment, blissfully lost in dreams, with a hint of a smile gracing his lips.

Dorothy, however, lay beside him, unable to find solace in the embrace of sleep. The pain that had nagged at her throughout the evening had not subsided; it had only grown more relentless. She had tried to be discreet, not wanting to disturb Bill's peaceful rest. Her love for him, even in her suffering, was boundless.

But as the hours passed, the pain became unbearable. She tried to move her hand, but it was as if her body had forsaken her. The agony intensified, and Dorothy's grasp on consciousness began to wane. She yearned to wake Bill, to tell him how much she loved him one last time, but her voice had abandoned her, and her strength was slipping away.

In her final moments, Dorothy turned to Bill, pulled herself as close to him as she could, and embraced him with all the love her frail body could muster. Bill, in the depths of sleep, instinctively responded, wrapping his arms around her. It was a tender, wordless farewell, a testament to a love that had spanned decades and was now bidding its poignant adieu.

As Dorothy's soul departed, a sense of serenity settled upon her, like the soft touch of a breeze on a warm summer day. In the peacefulness of that night, her journey came to an end.

Dorothy Farewell

The following morning, the sun rose, casting a warm and hopeful light upon the house. But the day brought with it a heavy heart, for Dorothy and Bill were missing from the family's midst. The clock struck 10 a.m., and still, their absence lingered like a shadow.

Natal, concerned by the prolonged silence, made her way to her parents' room. She found Bill still in his peaceful slumber, but her eyes were drawn to her mother. Dorothy's stillness was profound, her hand lifeless in Bill's embrace. She had passed away quietly in the night, leaving behind the love that had warmed the hearts of all who knew her.

Natal, with a heavy heart, held her mother's hand for the last time, tears welling in her eyes. She knew she had to be the bearer of this heartbreaking news to her sisters. Diana, upon hearing the devastating truth, broke into inconsolable sobs. Natal, her own eyes glistening with tears, tried to console her sister, urging her to be strong for Bill's sake.

Together, Bella, Natal and Diana gathered their family, their voices heavy with grief, to share the news of their beloved parents' passing. The joyous day that had shone so brightly the night before had been replaced by an overwhelming sorrow. The family held each other, their hearts heavy, feeling the immense void left by the loss of two souls who had illuminated their lives.

The transition from the happiest day of their lives to the profound sorrow of the next was a jarring one. Tears flowed freely as Bella, Natal, and Diana wept together, realizing that they had lost the most important person in their family. Their grief was heavy, like a relentless storm that refused to abate.

Amidst their tears, they turned to their father, Bill, who sat lost in deep pain. He clutched at the fragments of memory, and in a few moments, he would remember that Dorothy was gone. His brows furrowed, and with a bewildered expression, he would often ask where his beloved wife was, as if he could feel her absence but couldn't grasp the reality of her departure.

Diana, trying to find some solace in action, suggested that since the entire family was present, they should proceed with the funeral arrangements. Natal nodded in agreement, and they decided to hold the ceremony immediately.

The family gathered by the tranquil shores of Lake Sammamish, the same place where Bill and Dorothy's love story had begun. It was only fitting that it should be the setting for their final farewell. The plan was to spread Dorothy's ashes around the tree by the lake, allowing her to become a part of the serene landscape they had cherished together.

Some of her ashes would also find their resting place within the depths of the lake itself, symbolizing her connection to the waters that had witnessed their love. The remaining ashes would be interred at the base of the grand tree in the backyard, where their love had blossomed and endured.

As the ceremony concluded, the family members took turns to scatter the ashes, each with their own heartfelt words of farewell. It was a bittersweet moment, one filled with sorrow but also with a profound sense of closure.

Bill, in his moments of clarity, requested that he be the one to spread Dorothy's ashes in the lake when the time was right for him. The family nodded in agreement, understanding the depth of his love and his need to have that private moment with his beloved.

After a week of the family staying together, reminiscing about their cherished memories, and offering each other solace, they gradually began to return to their own lives. Natal, however, remained with her father in the house, determined to be a constant source of support during this difficult time.

Father & daughter Love

In the quiet moments they shared, Natal and Bill found solace in each other's presence. They mourned Dorothy's loss together, sharing stories, laughter, and tears as they navigated the complex landscape of grief. The house, once a bustling hub of family gatherings and joy, now held the weight of their sorrow and their memories.

The transition from the happiest day of their lives to the profound sorrow of the next was a jarring one. Tears flowed freely as Bella, Natal, and Diana wept together, realizing that they had lost the most important person in their family. Their grief was heavy, like a relentless storm that refused to abate.

Amidst their tears, they turned to their father, Bill, who sat lost in deep pain. He clutched at the fragments of memory, and in a few moments, he would remember that Dorothy was gone. His brows furrowed, and with a bewildered expression, he would often ask where his beloved wife was, as if he could feel her absence but couldn't grasp the reality of her departure.

Three months had passed since the day Dorothy left their world, leaving a void that could never be filled. Bill's once-vibrant memories were now like fragile wisps of smoke, slipping in and out of his consciousness. During this fog, Natal stood as a pillar of strength, a source of unwavering support for her father.

The environment around them mirrored the passage of time. The lake still shimmered under the sun's gentle caress, its waves whispering secrets to the wind. The same birds that Dorothy and Bill had so often admired still sang their melodious tunes, their songs a poignant reminder of moments long gone.

Natal had taken on the role of ensuring Bill's well-being, both physically and emotionally. She made sure he knew that he was loved, not just by her, but by her children and grandchildren as well. Through Zoom calls, they brought the whole family together, and Bill felt the warmth of their love, even if his memory could not retain all the details.

Their evening walks had become a sacred ritual, a time for both Natal and Bill to connect with each other and with their cherished memories. They would stroll along the familiar paths, feeling the crunch of leaves beneath their feet and inhaling the earthy scent of the forest. Together, they'd sit on the same bench that had witnessed countless conversations between Dorothy and Bill.

One day, as the sun dipped below the horizon, casting a warm, amber glow across the lake, Bill took Natal's hand in his own weathered one. He gazed at her with eyes that held a lifetime of love and wisdom and simply said, "Thank you."

Natal, touched by his words, asked why she was given her name, Natal. Bill chuckled softly, explaining that when he first held her as a newborn, he felt the spirit of her mother enter his soul. "Your mother is the reason I am standing here today. She saved my life," he whispered, his voice heavy with emotion.

Bill confessed the depth of his love for Natal's mother and his amazement at how it was possible to love two people so profoundly. As he spoke, he looked deep into Natal's eyes, his gaze a mixture of pride and tenderness. "I may forget many things now, but there are memories buried deep within my soul that remain," he confessed, his voice trembling. "I don't know how much longer I'll remember, but I want you to know how much I love you, Natal."

Natal, her own eyes glistening with tears, reached for her father's hand and pressed it gently to her lips. "I love you, old man. You are my world," she replied, her voice trembling with emotion. "And when your time comes, just go. Go be with your loved ones, Dad. We will be fine. Remember, you are loved."

Bill gave her a beautiful, albeit fragile, smile and made a heartfelt request. "When I am gone, spread my ashes on this tree, in the backyard, and mix my ashes with Dorothy's. Then, spread them together in the lake, and some take me back to Laos. I want to be closer to your mother and Dorothy. I can find a way to love these two women, even on the other side of the world."

Natal nodded, tears streaming down her face. In that tender moment, they both understood that love could transcend the boundaries of memory and time. Bill's love for Natal's mother, Dorothy, and Natal herself remained steadfast, a testament to the enduring power of the heart.

Their story was one of true love and loss, a testament to the deep emotions and feelings that bind humanity together. Bill and Natal sat in silence on the bench by lake Sammamish, the fading light of the setting sun casting long shadows around them. The world seemed to pause for a few precious minutes as they listened to the symphony of birdsong and the gentle lapping of the lake's waves.

Natal, her heart heavy with the weight of their shared grief and love, stood up and gently helped her father into his wheelchair. The years had taken their toll on Bill, but his spirit remained undimmed. As she began to push him back toward the house, Bill looked at her with a smile that held a world of memories. "You are like your mother, you know. A galaxy shining so bright."

Natal couldn't help but laugh at his choice of words. "Why do you always describe Mom as a galaxy?" she asked, genuinely curious.

Bill chuckled, the sound a mix of nostalgia and affection. "Your mother loved stars," he explained. "I remember back when I was in Laos, before Diana and you were born. We used to spend countless nights outside so she could count the stars. I loved that woman, her eyes, just like yours." He paused for a moment; his gaze distant as he reminisced. "And when I look at Bella, she's just like Dorothy. I'm so lucky to have been loved by two extraordinary women."

As they made their way back inside the house, Natal handed Bill his walker. He took it with a determined look in his eye. "Next time, I'll just walk. I don't like the wheelchair," he declared with a hint of stubbornness.

Natal couldn't help but laugh again. "Okay, old man, we'll see about that."

After dinner, Natal turned on the TV for Bill as he settled into his favorite chair to rest. This new life they were navigating was different, marked by loss and change, but it was also a testament to the enduring power of love and family. As Bill drifted off to sleep, Natal knew that their journey together was far from over, and she was determined to cherish every moment they had left.

Tears fell like raindrops from the sky, mingling with the steady downpour that had persisted throughout the night. The lake nearby sang a melancholy tune as its waters flowed relentlessly. Morning arrived, but there was no warmth in its embrace, only a somber acknowledgment of the world's sorrow.

The rain had finally ceased, and as if in response to nature's silence, the birds in the back yard began to sing, their voices piercing the air with both beauty and sadness.

It was unusual for Natal to sleep until 8 am, especially on a Sunday when there was typically no caregiver for Bill. She woke abruptly, glanced at the clock, and immediately leaped out of bed. Rushing to the restroom, she took a quick shower and then proceeded to the kitchen to make coffee. After brewing the morning necessity, she meticulously sorted her father's pills before making her way to his room.

As quiet as a whisper, Natal opened the door and tiptoed to the bedroom. Her heart sank as she approached the still form in the bed. She gently drew back the covers and discovered that Bill had passed away peacefully in his sleep. Overwhelmed by grief, she sat down beside her father's lifeless body and wept uncontrollably. The tears flowed freely, echoing the sorrow of her heart.

Natal knew what she had to do. She reached for her phone and, with trembling hands, dialed her sisters. Her voice choked with emotion as she delivered the devastating news. Bella and Diana, thousands of miles away, promised her they would make their way to the airport and catch the next available flight to Washington. In times like these, distance seemed an insurmountable barrier.

Natal needed to find solace, to make sense of the overwhelming loss that had shattered her world. She walked to the bench that had become a sacred space for her and her father, a place of quiet conversations and shared moments. As she sat there, memories washed over her like waves, and she realized that she had been her father's favorite not just because she was the youngest, but because her father's love for her was a reflection of his deep love for her mother.

In the quiet solitude by the lake shore, Natal pondered life's profound questions. What would life have been like if her mother hadn't passed away? Who would she be if Dorothy, the woman who had shaped her life, had not been a part of her story? These questions weighed heavily on her heart as she grappled with the magnitude of her father's passing.

After hours of tears and reflection by the lake, Natal finally rose from the bench and made her way home. With a heavy heart, she called the funeral home to begin the solemn arrangements for her father's final journey. The world had been enveloped in tears, and Natal could only hope that her father had found peace in the embrace of eternity, reunited at last with the love of his life, Dorothy, and his galaxy Natal.

The sun had set, casting long shadows across the tranquil waters of Lake Sammamish. The gentle ripples of the lake softly lapped at the shore, creating a soothing lullaby that accompanied the symphony of birdsong filling the air. It was a picturesque scene, bathed in the soft, fading hues of twilight, as if nature itself had paused to pay tribute to the moment.

Bill Yang The Man He Was

Natal's sisters had arrived, and their hugs were a lifeline of comfort amidst the sea of sorrow. Tears glistened in their eyes as they shared a deep and profound understanding of the loss, they all bore. As they took a long walk to the lake, a place that had become sacred in their family's lore, they allowed the memories to wash over them, like the gentle waves that kissed the shore.

The scent of the lake hung in the air, a delicate blend of earth, water, and the faint perfume of wildflowers that grew nearby. It was a fragrance that spoke of familiarity and nostalgia, a reminder of countless family gatherings, picnics, and quiet moments of reflection.

As they strolled along the shore, Diana opened her heart, sharing a cherished memory of her first kiss, a moment of youthful innocence and discovery that had unfolded under the watchful gaze of the lake's waters. Bella, with a nostalgic smile, recounted the day she had experienced the transition into womanhood, an event that marked her journey into adulthood. Natal, her eyes glistening with remembrance, spoke of the night she had lost her virginity, a moment of vulnerability and profound connection with another human soul.

Each story etched its mark on the very land they walked upon, intertwining their lives with the essence of the lake itself. If the shore could speak, it would whisper tales of their joys and sorrows, their laughter and tears, and the love that had woven the tapestry of their family together.

Arriving at the familiar bench that had become a place of solace, they sat down and clasped each other's hands, grounding themselves in the shared weight of their parents' passing. It was on this very spot that they had discussed the arrangements for their parents' final journey. Some of the ashes would find their resting place in Laos, where they would rest alongside Natal's grave. It was a poignant decision, a way of ensuring that their parents remained close, even in death.

In the hushed serenity of the moment, the rhythmic ebb and flow of the lake's waves seemed to offer a sense of reassurance, a reminder that life's eternal cycle continued unabated. The bond between the sisters grew stronger as they sat in contemplative silence, realizing that their parents had indeed lived a life rich in love and cherished moments.

Taking a deep breath, they looked out over the tranquil lake, its waters reflecting the soft glow of twilight. The beauty of the place struck them anew, a poignant reminder that life was not just about the memories of the past but also the beauty of the present. Each sunset marked the promise of a new dawn, and each day held the potential for new beginnings.

With a shared sense of acceptance and love, they squeezed each other's hands, drawing strength from their unity in grief. The lake, the towering trees, and the memories of their parents would remain, a testament to the enduring legacy of a family bound by love. The lake had been their silent witness, and their parents' love had been the guiding star, forever shining brightly in their hearts.

Bill Yang Smith's life was a testament to the enduring power of love, sacrifice, and unwavering commitment. He was more than just a father; he was a source of strength, wisdom, and boundless inspiration for his children, grandchildren, and the entire family. As they gathered to celebrate his remarkable journey, they couldn't help but be profoundly moved by the legacy he had left behind.

Bill's story began with a childhood fascination, an unquenchable passion for aviation that ignited in him a lifelong dream. He was the wide-eyed boy who gazed at the heavens, yearning to soar amidst the clouds. His dream was not destined to remain a mere fantasy; it was a dream he would tenaciously pursue.

Exceptional in his academic pursuits, Bill earned a place at the prestigious West Point Military Academy, a testament to his discipline, leadership, and unwavering commitment to duty. Graduating as a proud alumnus, he embarked on a journey in the United States Air Force, where he would serve his country with honor and bravery.

The call of duty led him to the tumultuous skies of the Vietnam War, where he displayed remarkable courage as a pilot. He faced the harrowing challenges of combat with unwavering resolve, earning the respect and admiration of his comrades. Bill wasn't just a soldier; he was a genuine hero who risked his life to defend the ideals he held dear.

During his service in Vietnam, a twist of fate led to the loss of his memory, erasing his past and leaving him adrift in a sea of uncertainty. It was during this trying time that destiny intervened once more. Bill found Natal, a compassionate and loving woman who would rescue him from oblivion. Their love story would evolve into a beautiful journey, resulting in a marriage and the blessing of two wonderful daughters, Diana and Natal.

But Bill's journey was far from over. His life took another momentous turn when he reunited with Dorothy, a woman whose heart resonated perfectly with his own. Together, they forged a love story that defied words, transcending into a realm of deep affection, and understanding. Their enduring love was etched in the letters they exchanged, each one a testament to the profound connection they shared.

As parents, Bill and Dorothy were extraordinary. They embraced the roles of nurturing and guiding their children with boundless love. Bill wasn't merely a father; he was a mentor, a confidant, and an exemplar of honor. His daughters admired him, seeing in him a guardian who protected and cherished their family.

To their daughters' husbands, Bill extended a warm and welcoming embrace, assuming the role of a second father. His laughter, his warm smile, and his guidance endeared him to them, making him not just a father-in-law but a cherished part of their lives.

As their family continued to expand, Bill became a beloved grandfather. His eyes would light up with joy whenever his grandchildren entered the room. He would regale them with tales of his own childhood adventures, imparting not just wisdom but also a deep sense of wonder.

Bill's life was a symphony of accomplishments and milestones, a testament to the extraordinary individual he was. As his daughters sat down to write his eulogy, they delved into the depths of their hearts, recalling the man who had shaped their lives. They discovered a trove of letters exchanged between their parents, each letter revealing the profound love that had grown stronger with every passing day.

With love and reverence, they began the eulogy, addressing their beloved father, a man they described as the most remarkable in the world. They spoke of his role as not just a father but as the best man to his daughters, sons-in-law, and cherished grandchildren. Their words painted a vivid portrait of the profound impact he had on their lives, emphasizing the love, guidance, and wisdom he had generously shared.

As they concluded the eulogy, they bid their beloved father farewell, knowing that he had lived a life that was truly well-deserved. There were no regrets, only cherished memories of a man who had embraced life with unwavering determination and grace. In their hearts, they held the certainty that Bill's Yang legacy would endure, shining as a beacon of love and inspiration for generations to come. With tears in their eyes and love overflowing in their hearts, they whispered their final farewell, "We love you, Dad." Bill Yang Smith's legacy would forever be etched in their hearts and in the annals of their family's history.

The sun had set, casting a warm, golden glow over Lake Sammamish, where the waves gently whispered their timeless secrets to the shore. The sisters, Diana, Bella, and Natal, sat together on the familiar bench, the very seat where their parents had shared so many quiet moments. As they looked out at the tranquil waters, their hearts felt heavy, yet strangely comforted by the love that enveloped them.

The memories of their parents, Bill and Dorothy, lingered in the air, like a sweet, melancholic melody that played softly in their minds. The legacy of their extraordinary father and the enduring love of their mother would forever be etched in the fabric of their lives.

The scent of the lake, the rustling of leaves, and the distant call of the birds seemed to harmonize with their thoughts, a gentle reminder that life flowed like the river they gazed upon. The stories of their childhood, the laughter, and the tears, were all woven into the very land they sat upon. If the shore could speak, it would reveal tales of their family history, written in the footprints left behind.

Their parents had found their first kiss at this very lake, marking the beginning of a love story that had spanned decades. Here, Diana had shared her first kiss with a boy, Bella had crossed the threshold into womanhood, and Natal had ventured into the realm of adulthood, each milestone etching their identities into the landscape.

With clasped hands and hearts full of gratitude, they looked at each other, realizing that their parents had lived a life well-lived. It was time to let them go, to release their spirits to the heavens, where they would find eternal peace together.

At the same bench, they had planned the funeral, and now, they would say their final goodbyes. Their parents' ashes would find their resting places, in Laos, where they would be reunited with Natal, and here, beneath the soil of their childhood home.

As they breathed in the crisp evening air, they acknowledged the pain of their loss, the tears that had fallen, and the laughter that had filled their lives. Their parents had given them a precious gift the understanding that life was meant to be cherished and that love, even in death, was a bond that could never be broken.

With a shared understanding of acceptance and love, they whispered their final words to their beloved parents, "Thank you for a lifetime of love, Dad and Mom. We carry your legacy in our hearts. Goodbye."

The last tear fell, not in sorrow, but in celebration of a life well-lived, a love that had endured, and a family forever bound by the threads of shared memories. As they rose from the bench and began their journey back home, they knew that their parents' spirits would forever dwell in the cherished corners of their hearts, guiding them with love and light.

And so, the sun dipped below the horizon, casting a final, warm embrace over Lake Sammamish, as if bidding its own farewell to a family who had found strength, love, and the profound beauty of life's most precious moments, even in the face of loss. The night unfolded, and the stars shone brightly above, a celestial tribute to a love that would forever illuminate their lives.

From My Heart to Yours

My Dearest Readers,

As I come to the close of "Remembering Us: When the Memory Fades, the Love Remains," my heart brims with emotions too vast to be contained within the confines of words. This journey, crafted with love and woven with the threads of our shared experiences, has been nothing short of profound.

To each of you who have embarked on this poignant odyssey with me, I extend my deepest gratitude and heartfelt appreciation. Your presence, your companionship, has been the guiding light that illuminated the darkest corners of memory's maze.

"Remembering Us" is not merely a story; it is a testament to the enduring power of love, even in the face of the soul thief that is Alzheimer's. It is a reminder that while memories may fade, the love that binds us remains steadfast, a beacon of hope in the tumultuous sea of uncertainty.

During life's trials and tribulations, you have journeyed alongside me, embracing the characters, their joys, their sorrows, and their unyielding resilience. Your unwavering support has been the fuel that ignited the flames of inspiration, propelling me forward with each turn of the page.

As the final chapter draws to a close, I want you to know that your presence has been more than just a fleeting moment in time; it has been a cherished gift, a reminder of the beauty and complexity of human experience.

To those who walk the path of Alzheimer's, to those who have witnessed its relentless grip on the ones they hold dear, I see you. I honor your strength, your courage, and your unwavering commitment to love, even in the face of unimaginable loss. As we bid farewell to the characters who have become dear to our hearts, let us carry their stories with us, a reminder of the fragility and resilience of the human spirit. And may we, too, find solace in the knowledge that while memories may fade, the love that binds us endures, an eternal flame that shines brightly in the darkness.

With deepest gratitude and boundless love,

Honeymoon Naima Mohammed Al-jabri

The end

Thank you so much

Honeymoon Naima Mohammed Al-Jabri, an accomplished Indie filmmaker, holds a degree in Radio Television and Film from Texas Southern University. "Remembering Us" marks her second novel, following the successful debut of "Leila - The Grin and Grief" in 2023. Beyond her literary achievements, Al-Jabri is also recognized as the creative mind behind the children's book, "Amani." This captivating tale follows the adventures of Amani, a curious African girl with a passion for exploring and discovering the rich history and beauty of the African continent.

In addition to her contributions to literature, Honeymoon has left an indelible mark on the world of cinema. With a keen eye for storytelling, she has produced and directed five compelling films, showcasing her versatility and dedication to the art of filmmaking. Al-Jabri's commitment to both literature and film underscores her multifaceted talent and unwavering passion for creative expression.

www.ingramcontent.com/pod-product-compliance
Lightning Source LLC
Chambersburg PA
CBHW050852160426
43194CB00011B/2124